Museum Store
Management

Museum Store Management

Mary Miley Theobald

American Association for State and Local History
Nashville, Tennessee

Published by the American Association for State and Local History, an international non-profit membership organization. For membership information, please contact Membership Services, 615-255-2971.

96 95 94 93 92 91   8 7 6 5 4 3 2 1

Library of Congress Cataloging-in-Publication Data

Theobald, Mary Miley, 1952–
    Museum store management / Mary Miley Theobald.
       p. cm.
    Includes bibliographical references.
    ISBN 0-942063-14-7
    1. Museum stores—Management. I. Title.
    HF5469.65.T44 1991
    658.8′7—dc20   91–16191
                                          CIP

Contents

APPENDIXES   *199*

Acknowledgments

Abook is not written by its author alone and this one is no exception. I would like to thank the people who helped by providing information, constructive criticism, ideas, and encouragement, especially:

Susan P. Stair and Gail K. Burger, who started me on the road to retail management and product development at Colonial Williamsburg too many years ago, and

Thomas H. Aageson, Sandra Mottner, Kristin Fischer, and Donna Sheppard, whose tireless review of early manuscripts significantly improved the end result.

Museum Store Management

Introduction

No one seems to know when the first museum shop opened its doors. Museum shops did not begin with a bang, they evolved over the years, growing imperceptibly from a postcard rack at the information desk into today's mini-department store with complex product lines, sophisticated promotional material, and eye-catching displays.

How nice it would be to say that this evolution has been proceeding along specified channels according to some overall master plan, or at least that museum shops have been working toward a generally-held concept of the ideal. Unfortunately the shop has always been positioned so far outside the realm of the museum's interests that little thought has been devoted to its existence, let alone its purposes, goals, or ideal state. An informal poll taken over the past few years by students in my museum studies class at Virginia Commonwealth University showed that less than one in ten shops had an articulated mission statement or defined goal. Most shop managers or museum directors indicated surprise at the question and responded carelessly, "To make money, of course."

Of course *not*. If dollars were the only purpose, or even the main one, we would be far better served by renting space in the nearest mall and cashing in on the latest fads. "Naturally it has to be educational too," many managers hasten to add. But does it *have* to be? Who says? Is non-educational merchandise illegal, as one manager told me? (Thoughts of a police raid on a museum store to seize the uneducational merchandise flickered through my mind.) "I use volunteers, so our products don't have to be educational," confided another manager. Is that so?

The lack of a consensus as to just what museum stores should be doing has led to different types of operations. Larger museums with larger stores seldom suffer from this identity crisis; most have wrestled with such issues on their way up and, while we may fault them for leaning too far in one direction or the other, it is an issue they have addressed and continue to address. It is usually at the smaller institutions where the Trustees or the Director, eyes glued to the bottom line, fail to look up and pose the larger question. Not knowing how the store fits into the museum's overall plan leads to no fit at all. The result has been plenty of criticism, both from

3

within the particular museum and from within the museum community at large. Unfortunately it is criticism too often expressed in the negative. "You shouldn't do that," or "This stuff is junk," rather than "You should be trying to achieve this."

The growth of the museum store has not been purposely managed, it has simply occurred. Small and medium size museums are only beginning to become aware of their shops and the perception that *Something Needs To Be Done* to improve them is starting to take hold. Few know where to turn. Some erroneously look to the giants in the museum store pantheon, the Smithsonian or the Metropolitan Museum of Fine Arts for instance, and blindly go about trying to copy their activities, merchandise, and methods without wondering whether such a formula is applicable or even desirable for their own museum. We sometimes forget that those big glamorous shops didn't leap directly to that status overnight, that there were many years, many stages, and many mistakes along the way that should be duly noted by a fledgling operation. Nor should we fail to ask ourselves, Is that sort of operation we honestly want for our own museum? Probably not. While there are undoubtedly good ideas to be gleaned from any museum store, what works for one may be inappropriate for another. I hasten to add that some of the sales programs in the nation's most prestigious museums make poor role models. Some have lost their way, ethically speaking, to the point where a product's educational aspect is a mere technicality, a nuisance in the way of improved sales.

Most of the impetus for the shop's growth has come from outside the museum world. As federal funding dwindles and new tax laws lessen the attractiveness of private donations, museums find themselves requiring more money than ever before. Increasingly they are turning to retail sales to provide the needed dollars. The rising demand for new programs (minority programs, school programs, community outreach programs) and the clamor for a greater number, variety, and quality of exhibits are not necessarily matched by rising revenue. Two notable new and expensive necessities, computerization and conservation, scarcely existed twenty years ago. Not to be ignored is public demand for more sophisticated lines of sales items and larger, more comprehensive shops. It is no wonder that starting a shop or expanding or upgrading an existing one are projects at the top of many museum agendas.

Museums, like it or not, have become trendy, the "in" place to shop, and the public's expectations are no longer met by a corner sales desk with postcards and guidebooks. The phrase "museum quality" has come to signify "top quality and good taste" to the public at large, although museum professionals, quite correctly, find the term meaningless. One reporter put it bluntly, "Museums are cornering the market on pretty powerful stuff: nothing short of Taste and Culture."[1] The museum is left to itself to struggle with the pros and cons of meeting these rising expectations.

It is not surprising that the same decades that witnessed this desk-to-store metamorphosis in the larger museums, the 60s and 70s, also saw the development of aggressive museum marketing (which is only now starting to filter down to the smaller establishments), the growth of so-called relevant exhibits, and the beginning of elaborate cultural events, all designed to entice the general public into the museum's hallowed halls for some enjoyable education. And it worked. Today's museum-going population comprises all social and economic classes. Museums have shaken away their elitist aura by laboring earnestly to eliminate the intimidating cultural snobbism associated with most since their inception. Museums have become "user friendly" and more sensitive to public wants and needs. The growth of the shop is but one manifestation of this trend.

There is no reason to conclude that we are looking at the end result of this slow development—in fact, there is every indication that the museum shop is only starting to come into its own. Art museums, fewer in number than their history counterparts and usually larger, have taken the lead in creating ethical, tasteful shops. Progressing from the postcard rack to notecards, posters, prints, children's coloring books, origami, and colorforms, they, more than any other museum group, are clear about relating the store to their educational mission and defining its parameters. As a group they generally practice what they preach.

Not so the history museum. Because their range of product possibilities is so much larger, they have been more easily led astray along the "gift shop" path. Art museum managers are not intrinsically more virtuous—the temptations have been fewer and less enticing. Art museum shops have been restricted by the two dimensionality of their museum collections. Their sales items, be they calendars, scarves, posters, or needlework, are largely two dimensional, like their collections. They do more in the way of pictorial reproductions and seldom enter the muddier waters of adaptations, interpretations, and the like. Indeed, some art museums, the National Gallery of Art in Washington is one, restrict their shops to two-dimensional merchandise. Explained Director J. Carter Brown at the Museum Store Association's 1990 annual meeting, "That does keep you out of the gee-gaws, and it does emphasize the educational aspect of books, [pictorial] reproductions, slides, and such."

It is the smaller history museum shops in particular that suffer from lack of focus and the absence of professional direction. They are usually managed by devoted, hard-working volunteers who have never had any guidance or exposure to the concept of a museum store versus a gift shop. And so they operate gift shops where the only measure of success is in dollars. Directors of small history museums, jacks-of-all-trades that they are, rarely involve themselves in their shops. Perhaps it is because they seldom have any experience or training in retail operations; perhaps it is simply overwork. While they may intuitively sense that their shops could do better, they are unable to put a finger on the problems and are overloaded anyway in areas where they *do* have expertise. "Lord knows," lamented a friend of mine who runs a historic house, "I have more than I can handle without tackling the shop."

Science museums have an easier time with their shops, theoretically at least, than do history museums. They seldom become involved in product development, thereby avoiding the reproductions/adaptations/interpretations dilemma. Vendors supplying science related games, toys, and projects are more plentiful than are vendors with ready-made products for history museums because the science merchandise has overlapping sales applicability to other science museum shops and to regular toy stores that history and art merchandise lacks. For instance, a manufacturer with a good magnet game or model kit can sell it to the town science museum, to most other science museum stores across the country, and to most commercial toy stores across the country. The manufacturer who develops a doll with a historically accurate costume is restricted to history museums that represent that particular period, region, and socio-economic class, and is not going to find much interest from the commercial toy stores due to the doll's relatively limited appeal and price.

Product relatedness is clearer in science museum shops. Magnets, kites, dinosaurs, balloons, bubbles, models, kaleidoscopes, and polished stones all teach children scientific facts or principles and are therefore indisputably educational. Children are the largest component of science museum visitors and are easier targets for educational merchandise than adults. These days when toy manufacturers are ostentatiously producing the so-called educational toy, it is often forgotten that virtually any toy can be educational. A ball can teach a child about gravity and improve hand-eye coordination; crayons teach colors, encourage creativity, and improve fine motor kills.

There is considerable controversy within the museum world on the topic of sales. Leading the anti-sales movement are museum professionals who feel that commercialism has no place within the scope of museum activities. This legitimate concern, albeit one I do not share, can usually be relieved by an understated shop that devotes itself entirely to books and other publications unquestionably related to the museum's educational mission. The anti-sales museum professionals are joined in their condemnation of stores by other more self-serving groups from outside the museum such as the Small Business Association lobby that perceives the tax-free status of the shops as unfair competition, and the antiques and fine arts dealers like the Art Dealers Association of America which, having described reproductions as lacking intrinsic aesthetic worth and resale value, called upon museums to stop making "pretentious" (translate: expensive) reproductions all together. Such rhetoric is easily dismissed, not because it is wrong per se but because it is so blatantly profit-motivated.[2] The moral indignation of such associations was not aroused until the shops were perceived as competitors; when museum sales operations were insignificant and threatened no one's pocketbook there was no outcry.

The standard apology for museum sales activities, "Because we need the money," may also be true but is equally irrelevant. If the shop's only reason for being is money, then the museum is operating a gift shop rather than a museum store and it has little justification for existence.

The legitimate concern for museums revolves around the issue of control and priority. Former art museum director Sherman E. Lee gave a speech at the Metropolitan Museum in 1978 expressing the fear that the marketing function was starting to dominate the sales process, overriding aesthetic and educational consideration. Will sales rule the museum or vice versa?

> A work is chosen for reproduction, not because of its place within an educational context, or because of its intrinsic aesthetic worth, but because of its marketability. Usually the choice is made not by a curator or educator but by persons on a sales staff. Arguments are piously made that the process aids the appreciation of art, and more pragmatically that the sales provide income for scholarly or educational uses when in reality the selection is made because the item is appealing to a large customer base and because modern manufacturing processes are capable of mass-producing it at a reasonable cost.[3]

This then is the museum's legitimate concern: not money *or* education but money *and* education; how to achieve the proper balance whereby the educational goals maintain their ascendancy and the profits grow. If museum shops were run ethically and educationally, criticism and opposition would almost disappear.

This short book is aimed at the small and medium size history museum—historic sites, historic houses, maritime museums, transportation museums, natural history museums, and historical societies—with little or no staff and even less money. The presence of these two resources permits different priorities but the fundamentals vary little. Other types of museums—art museums, science museums, zoos, aquariums, children's museums, planetariums, and botanic gardens—will find nearly every topic discussed equally applicable to their operations with the exception of some of the sub-chapters on product development.

This book is very basic, very introductory, and very economy-minded. It assumes nothing. In my travels to small museums across the country I have found them to be run by bright, capable, and dedicated people who, with the rudiments of the concept of a museum store and a few retailing basics, can coax miraculous improvements from their operations in both profits and educational contribution. I congratulate the reader who finds this book simplistic. For those in the more advanced stages looking for personal improvement, I recommend tracking down as many of the articles in the Published Resources section as applicable to your situation, studying a copy of Thomas Aagseon's *Financial Analysis for Museum Stores* (described in the Published Resources section), instituting your own plan for an annual business analysis, and volunteering to initiate and participate in seminars and workshops offered by the Museum Store Association, the American Association of Museums, and the American Association for State and Local History to share your abilities and experiences with others.

Notes

1. William L. Hamilton, "Culture for Sale: Museums Get Smart," *Metropolitan Home,* February 1988, p. 50.
2. While we may recognize their rhetoric for the smokescreen it is, museums dare not underestimate their power or determination. The SBA and other like-minded groups have launched a major effort within Congress to revoke the tax-exempt status of not-for-profit sales operations. They are a vocal and well-funded lobby. Chapter 9 spends more time on this subject.
3. Sherman E. Lee, "Life, Liberty, and the Pursuit of . . . What?" *Art Journal,* Summer 1978, p. 325.

1

A Museum Store—What Is It?

A Museum Store or a Gift Shop?

1. Does virtually *all* of your merchandise relate to your museum's collection, historical period, or purpose?
2. Do the shop's employees receive the same substantive museum training as your interpretive staff?
3. Do shop employees engage in active interpretation of the educational merit of the products?
4. Does your shop include written product information with most of its merchandise?
5. Is the shop manager an integral part of the museum's administrative process, participating in the planning of upcoming exhibits, activities, publications, and events that have an impact on the shop?
6. If your shop is currently claiming exemption from federal taxes, are you familiar with recent IRS rulings on museum stores and are you prepared for an audit?

If you answered *NO* to any of these questions, you are not alone. Precious few museum stores across the country can claim an affirmative response to all, or even most, of them. But if your museum wants to operate a *museum store,* as opposed to a gift shop, *YES* answers are obligatory.

A true museum store is a hybrid, a cross between a gift shop and a museum exhibit. It is *an integral part of the museum that contributes to the institution's stated purposes both financially and educationally.*

Museum Store Features

Several features distinguish a museum store from a gift shop but the most significant is the addition of educational obligations to the tenets of good retailing. In establishing the goals of a museum store, it is essential that the educational mission take precedence over income production. The goals might be listed in order of importance as follows:

1. To contribute to the *educational* purposes[1] of the museum.
2. To return to the museum the greatest possible *dollar* contribution.
3. To assist with the museum's *marketing* efforts by generating good publicity, attracting visitors, and treating customers in a courteous and hospitable manner.

Giving priority to education over dollars does not suggest that dollars are not important. We all know better. Money generated by museum shops is critical to the continued operation of many institutions, both large and small. Educational priority is simply the recognition that merchandise is not selected on the sole basis of anticipated sales. Even if the revenue from Mickey Mouse dolls would pay the annual light bill, they aren't added to the shop at a Civil War battle site.

It may in fact be appropriate for a museum store to carry some items *solely* for educational purposes. In Colonial Williamsburg's John Greenhow Store, opened to the public in 1983, manager Jean Ferguson carries bolts of fabric, two enormous grindstones, and bags of casting sand to indicate the range of goods stocked by that eighteenth-century merchant. The historical statement these products make by being visible on the shelves supersedes their poor sales potential. A gift shop would choose Mickey Mouse dolls and omit the grindstones because its frame of reference for such decisions is purely economic.

Most museum stores keep certain highly educational merchandise in their inventory in spite of its poor turnover. A definitive publication that sells only one copy a year may have a significant place on a museum store shelf. It wouldn't have a prayer at the local outlet of a national bookstore chain.

Education and Profit

Now to be educational *and* profitable is no easy thing. The trick is to identify or develop related products that will both educate and sell, and to manage these assets in such a manner as to maximize the store's dollar contribution to the museum. Or, more specifically—

1. Tie into your museum's goals. Limit the product line to related merchandise. More on this later.

   2. *Contribute income to the museum through good retail shop management.* This consists of sound purchasing of related products, good inventory control, effective personnel management, attractive visual merchandising, and the maintenance of a safe and pleasant work environment.

   3. *Contribute to the museum's positive community image.* Courteous interaction with the visitors and a hospitable, knowledgeable staff can answer visitors' questions and meet their needs. Pleasant customer service is critical.

   4. *Become an integral part of the museum.* A gift shop can function independently, a museum store cannot. Shop managers or sales directors should be included in all regular staff meetings and planning sessions so that they will know what is going on: what exhibits are planned, what artifacts have been recently moved, acquired, or deaccessioned, when school groups are expected and how many, what the focus of the tour guides' new interpretation is to be, what publicity is being sought, and so on. All of this information has direct bearing on the sales efforts. The amount of staff needed, the type of products developed, the direction of the product interpretation, and the inventory levels depend upon factors outside the shop itself. The sales manager should, in turn, enhance the team concept within the store by keeping the rest of the staff well-informed about museum and store activities.

   5. *Attract museum visitors to your shop.* Strive for 100% of the museum's visitation, although realistically the only way to achieve that is to route visitors through the shop as they exit, something done very effectively at Historic Savannah's Davenport House shop and at some of the houses on the Historic Newport, Rhode Island tour.
   Some museum stores attempt to reach beyond the obvious to the general public. The justification is based on the theory that people who frequent the shop will sooner or later be lured into the exhibit area. The shop is bringing people to the museum instead of vice versa. This seems flawed. While a visitor should never feel obligated to sign up for the tour every time he returns to buy a gift, the shop should draw its customers from the pool of museum visitors. Certainly we want to encourage visitors to return to the shop again and again, whether or not they choose to tour the exhibit areas each time, but actively recruiting the general public into the shop *alone,* by means of advertising or other promotional gimmicks, does not seem the best course to take. Many shops with unique, top quality

merchandise do develop a loyal customer base that drops in periodically for unusual gifts. For the most part, these are active museum-goers for whom purchases at the shop are simply another manifestation of their support for the institution.

6. *Identify your customers and address their needs.* A single shop can serve many groups of people. Ask, whom are we serving? If one answer is students, are they primary or secondary schoolchildren or college students? Are the adults young, single, parents, middle-aged, grandparents, senior citizens, male or female? Do you serve scholars, teachers, graduate students, or people pursuing private research projects? These categories are fairly self-evident. To categorize further you will need a questionnaire. It may be worth inquiring at a local college or university business school whether a student or class would be interested in taking on the development of a questionnaire as well as the actual survey as a class project or for a small fee. Larger cities have marketing firms that will do this for you but the cost may be prohibitive. A sample questionnaire is given in Appendix A to serve as the starting point for your own effort should you decide to tackle this in-house. For more information, consult the AAM's recent publication, *Visitor Survey's: A User's Manual* by R. Korn and L. Sowd (American Association of Museums: 1990). (Call 202-298-1818 to order.) With an accurate idea of your customer profile, you are better prepared to spot merchandising opportunities, measure the success of store promotions, set appropriate retail prices, and make good buying decisions.

7. *Structure your merchandise purchasing.* You should have a wide range of retails, from expensive to small change. Try to have something for every pocketbook that comes into your shop. If you know that during the fall the vast majority of your customers are vacationing senior citizens on their way south, gear your products to the mid- to high-price range. If springtime brings busload after busload of fourth graders, the bulk of your merchandise should have low price points. Never skew everything to the majority. One southern historic house, patronized almost exclusively by well-to-do senior citizens, still makes a point to carry a few baskets of low end merchandise for the occasional child who passes through. Ideally, we could calculate that if 6% of our visitation was comprised of schoolchildren, then 6% of the merchandise was targeted to that group, etc.

8. *Think of every product as an educational opportunity.* If your merchandise is related to the museum's collection or educational mission, it does indeed present a chance to contribute to your institution's pur-

poses. Phase out the sales items that offer no redeeming educational value. Use both verbal and written product information with your merchandise by training employees to interpret the products and by developing written information on each product or product category. The most interesting, educational item in your shop will remain mute without verbal or written product information. There is no point in wasting time buying or developing a good related product line if you cannot follow through with the educational message.

9. *Be realistic*. Significant changes seldom occur overnight. List your priorities and work out a schedule to accomplish them step by step. Formulate an overall goal and several intermediate ones to get there. Let others know what you are doing and congratulate yourself and your shop employees at the completion of every step. If others are involved, organize some group recognition for the staff at significant intervals—a picnic on the grounds, ice cream sundaes, or whatever. Chapter 10 deals more with formulating a plan and drawing up a realistic schedule for accomplishing it.

Note

1. Throughout this book, "educational goals" should be construed to include all of the museum's goals, whether predominantly educational or not. For instance, if one goal of an institution is to preserve textiles, the shop should sell acid-free tissue and storage boxes and hand out basic instructions on textile conservation to promote good conservation practice in the home.

2

Planning for a Store

The majority of museum stores are located where they are for no good reason. "We began our shop years ago and the basement was the only space we had," explained one museum director, clearly wishing something better had been available. Or "The new tool shed built last year left the stables empty, so we decided to start a store." Realistically, most shops must "make do" with whatever quarters they can scrounge up, and this is not necessarily bad. An atypical location can help make the shop unique, giving it an unusual flavor—a definite plus in today's mass-produced malls where store interiors look so much alike that customers literally forget where they are.

This section is directed to museums toying with thoughts of beginning a store and to those planning to build a new wing, information center, or other structure that might include a store. In working with the architect, initial concerns should be:

1. Placement of the store.
2. Size of the store.
3. Other needs (office, storage, security).
4. Atmosphere of the store.

Physical Plans

Store Placement

Ideally the store should be situated where no one will miss it. The best location is near the exit (few people want to *start* their museum visit at a store). Some actually design the exit *through* the store. If there is an admissions fee to the museum, the store should be located so that you do not have to pay to shop. You hope that visitors will find the museum store a good place to shop frequently and they should be permitted access to the store without having to pay for the museum every time. If the store cannot be located outside of the paid ticketed area, you can always issue a "store

14

pass" or make some arrangements for those who only want to get to the store.

For shops located in information/orientation buildings, a large inviting opening is important; one that can remain opened to the lobby all day but that can be closed separately in the case of receptions, special events, or evening programs that are offered when the store is not staffed.

Store Size

Whether or not you have sales history to guide the decision, projecting a museum store's ideal size is highly speculative. Museum visitation must be determined or projected first as a prelude to figuring an approximate square foot per visitor ratio. This is the crowding factor. Too many people stuffed into a small space will have neither the opportunity nor the inclination to make a purchase. On the other hand, an empty store can be uncomfortably dead. Clearly the answer lies in determining a happy medium.

In the museum store world, 100 visitors per square foot seems average for small and medium-size establishments, while average sales per visitor run in the realm of $1.50.[1] This visitors per square foot number assumes equal visitation year round, because you use annual visitation totals to figure it. But your shop may close for three months in the winter or the bulk of your visitation may come around Christmas or in the summer. Whatever your visitation pattern, it is clearly *not* spread equally over 365 days. Thus any store will have its crowded days and its empty days regardless of its visitors per square foot. Note that the "average" of 100 visitors per square foot does not necessarily translate to "desirable." 200 visitors per square foot is not unreasonable. I have visited several history museum shops where the sales/visitor hovers close to $1.50 and the square foot/visitor ranges above 250.

For a history museum that expects 60,000 visitors annually, a reasonable shop size might run around 600 square feet. A reasonable gross income expectation might be in the realm of $90,000 but two or three times higher is not unusual. One well-known museum store manager recommends a minimum of 750 square feet in order to generate enough income to support some paid staff, primarily a paid manager. I prefer to see shops no smaller than 500 square feet, no matter how small the museum, but of course there are many much smaller that do quite well. Naturally a larger shop does not guarantee a larger gross income—there are so many other variables involved that these figures are only useful when dealing with the unknown.

Other Needs

Office space is a necessity, as is a stock room, a work room or work area, and a safe area. All should be located directly off the store, not down the hall or upstairs. All should be secure (lockable) because of the sensitive nature of some records and information as well as the obvious concerns about theft of cash or merchandise. The stockroom should have an outside entrance for receiving deliveries and trash disposal.

One option is to locate the office off one end of the store with an area in it for the safe. A lockable closet where the safe is not visible to people visiting the office is practical and doubles as storage for small valuables like jewelry. Locate the stockroom off another side of the store with a separate work room off that or a work area within the stock room. The work area is used for pricing merchandise, wrapping, unwrapping, cleaning merchandise that arrives unfit for display, making signs, displays, and props, etc. A utility sink is nice; it is essential if the staff is going to handle food or do their own light housekeeping chores. You should not need a

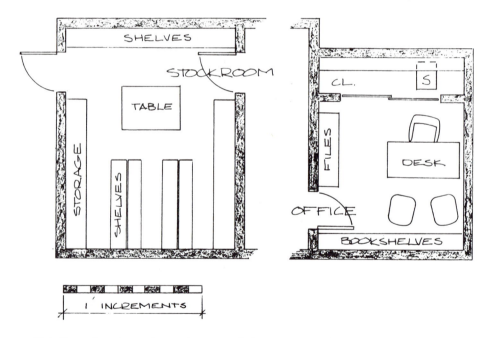

This floor plan shows the stockroom and the manager's office on opposite sides of a central sales floor. The closet in the manager's office is lockable and contains the safe. Bookshelves opposite the desk go to the ceiling. File cabinets could have shelves over them if need be. In the stockroom adjustable shelving and storage cabinets with interior shelving go to the ceiling. The center table provides a work area; stackable chairs can be added. The stockroom exits to the outside to facilitate deliveries and trash removal. *Designs courtesy—Joanne Miley, A.S.I.D., Northbrook, IL.*

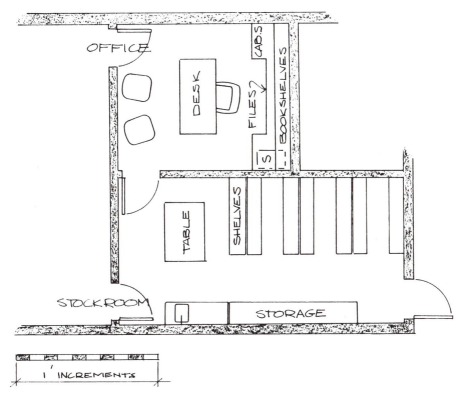

In this floor plan the office and stockroom are contiguous. The stockroom contains a utility sink, a work table, and adjustable shelves that rise to the ceiling. The storage cabinets could be of a similar height or could go desk or counter height to allow for more countertop work space. The office contains two lockable cabinets with deep interior shelves, one with the safe, file drawers in the center, and several shelves across the top. The tops of files and cabinets are the same height which allows 10 feet of additional work space. Other cabinet configurations are possible: notably raising cabinets to ceiling height, leaving 5 feet of shelving and file cabinets between them. *Designs courtesy— Joanne Miley, A.S.I.D., Northbrook, IL.*

separate break area or bathrooms for the store. Sales people can share the facilities that are provided for the rest of the museum staff.

The office should be large enough for a manager's desk and at least two other chairs for visitors, such as manufacturer's reps or other museum staff. It should have room enough for file cabinets and book shelves.

The stockroom/work area should be $1/4$ to $1/3$ the size of the shop. A well-run shop will not have excessive amounts of inventory. Adjustable shelves are a tremendous space saver. A work area involves a large table or counter space—it could be a separate room or just a space in the middle of the stock room that has its adjustable shelves along all four walls; it could be located at the end of a long, rectangular room (the end nearest the door to the shop) with the adjustable shelving on both sides in a "hall" type arrangement. A work area like this can double as meeting space for training sessions or staff meetings.

Now to insert a note of reality. While all of these features are desirable, in many museums the shop has nothing other than itself and no prospects for expansion. Profits are possible without these amenities. Where selling space is at a premium, it should not be sacrificed for office space or stockrooms—merchandise does not sell out of offices and stockrooms. There is also a tendency to spend more time off the floor in a comfortable, quiet office or a well-appointed stockroom when on-the-floor time is critical for successful management. A small museum store can make do, if it must, without back-up space.

Atmosphere

Obviously you will want the store kept within the overall theme, tone, or atmosphere of the museum itself. Whatever you decide, be sure the store is brightly lit and cheerful. Science museums and art museums will usually opt for an open, contemporary look with lots of glass and metal. Unless you want to re-create a historic shop such as a ship's chandler or period general store, you probably want a modern shop that reflects the atmosphere of the museum. Re-creating a historic shop of some sort like Colonial Williamsburg, Old Salem, or Sturbridge Village have done should be approached with caution. No matter how hard you try, its appearance will never be as authentic as a exhibition store can be and the historical restrictions will have you turning handsprings trying to minimize modern intrusions like cash registers, electric lighting, charge card equipment, price tags, and packaging. Despite the inordinate amount of time spent on limiting these intrusions, the resulting shop cannot be termed a valid depiction of any historical precedent. Your best bet is a modern shop that pretends nothing. One North Carolina historic house, the Hezekiah Alexander House in Charlotte, strikes a good balance by re-creating in the exhibit area a static 19th-century general store scene, then locating its own, modern museum store near the entrance/exit.

A modern store need not be decorated in a contemporary style, although I find most science and art museums favor this sort of shop design because it coincides best with their atmosphere or themes. History museums need to consider continuing their period style or historic theme through to the shop in a manner that will result in a unique appearance. The visitor wants an unusual shopping experience, not another airport gift shop. When Mystic Seaport's shops were renovated some years ago, Director Tom Aageson decided to use materials sympathetic to the museum's nautical environment, like dark mahogany, taking care to mix this

The Hezekiah Alexander House in Charlotte, North Carolina, exhibits a recreated period store (or part of one) in its display area. Their museum store, located nearby, is a modern shop and does not attempt to approximate the period. Separating the two store functions like this is probably best in terms of practicality and authenticity, and will avoid visitor confusion over which parts are accurate and which are modern intrusions. *Photo by author.*

with good lighting. When The Hermitage, Andrew Jackson's home in Nashville, moved its rustic little sales operation into the new visitor's center, Director George Anderjack felt that the store had lost its visual connection to the site. The slick, contemporary design of the new shop was "too urban," he explained. "It could have been anywhere." Sales did increase at the new shop, but that was most likely due to the increased space, the improved displays, many new products, and the reduced crowding factor. "We started removing the terribly sophisticated upholstered risers, and bringing in reproductions or period country pieces to tone down the design." Since the "toning down," sales have further increased from an average of $2.00 per shopper to $3.00, but again, there are too many variables to credit ambience alone for the boost. The staff is far happier with the store's atmosphere now that it compliments the museum's historic theme.

Try to fit the store into whatever color scheme the museum as a whole chooses for its logo, stationery, brochures, etc. Historic Charleston uses dark hunter green on buff paper for its museum's stationery, business cards, newsletters, and brochures as well as for its shop's bags, product information cards, and promotional literature. If appropriate, carry the color scheme to walls, carpet, and fixtures, and to employee aprons, name tags, advertising, and whatever else lends itself. The overall look is a coordinated and professional one.

Before you buy store fixtures (tables, counters, racks, shelves, etc.) a detailed list of intended merchandise should be prepared. Obviously a store planning to carry significant amounts of books and jewelry will require shelving and counter space entirely unlike one with mostly toys and clothing. How much shelf or counter space each item will occupy should be determined. This is called a planogram, and diagrams exactly how merchandise is to be displayed in your store. Simply declaring "We'll put all the pottery on shelves on the west wall" will not suffice. The exact location and number of facings need to be determined. Different shelf configurations must be sketched and each piece of pottery positioned on paper. This requires measurements of every bowl, platter, and mug so that you can determine the number of shelves, their depth and length, the amount of space between them, and the lighting needed. No doubt this sounds tedious but it is essential if your shelving is to be fixed (not recommended but all too common) and still a worthwhile endeavor for those with adjustable shelves.

Also consider the anticipated retail range of the products you will sell. Access to expensive items such as scale models of ships needs to be restricted by placing them on high shelves or behind glass. The type of customer you expect will effect your fixtures—children's merchandise

Consider your customer when locating products. Children's items belong on shelves, in bins, or in baskets or crates below the three-foot level. The children's areas in the Smithsonian Museum Shops are equipped with lucite bins to hold small items ranging in price from $.50 to $5.00. *Photo courtesy—Smithsonian Institution.*

needs to be closer to the floor. I recently visited a wonderful historic military museum that had a disastrous shop with just this problem. The inexpensive children's merchandise was totally inaccessible, almost hidden, behind the counter. One of each item was displayed behind locked glass shelves. A sign read **HATS $4.** None were visible. "Oh, you're out of hats?" I remarked, more as a conversation starter than question. "No, they're here," she replied, pulling one out of the box beside her. Lest you infer that the shop was routinely besieged by mobs of shoplifting children, I hasten to add that visitation was very modest at this particular site. So were sales.

Used store fixtures are available. Look through the classifieds in a large metropolitan newspaper or ask for donations from local department stores. Seldom will secondhand fixtures fill your exact needs but in the real world, many museum stores must rely on hand-me-downs, at least in the beginning. Check the Yellow Pages under "Store Fixtures" and "Display Fixtures and Materials" for local companies dealing in new and used equipment.

Take care in the planning stages that your store's shape and the arrangement of the fixtures allow salespeople a clear view of the entire area at all times in order to minimize shoplifting.

If the shop has a few thousand dollars to spend on a professional designer, it is well worth the money. Do-it-yourself may be your only option, but make the effort to seek out a professional interior designer with a store specialization and find out what he/she would charge to handle your shop's design. Do this even if you are convinced that it is out of the question financially. Maybe the complete job is out of your budget, but after discussing the project, you find that you can afford the designer's help with a portion of it. How do you locate a good store designer? Try Mystic Seaport Museum Stores' trick: send your staff to the newest mall or most popular shopping area in your town on a quest for the best looking shop. Consider in particular lighting, shelving, counters, and that all-important intangible, mood. Ask for a vote, notify the "winning" store, compliment them on their design, and ask for the name of the person or firm that they employed. It may have been an in-house design job, especially if the favorite store is a department store. If so, you may be able to hire that employee on a free-lance basis to advise or plan your space.

I know of only one design firm that specializes in museum stores, but this one may be all you need to know. The firm consists of two talented and experienced museum store experts, Eileen Ritter, formerly of the Smithsonian, and Sue Anne Elmore, formerly of Monticello. This team will evaluate your needs and handle new designs or renovations from start to finish—or do only a portion of the work if you prefer. Although their basic assessment fee of $5,000 may be out of the range for many stores, it costs nothing to call and discuss your needs. The firm's name is Gxero (pronounced zero) and it can be reached at 202-332-8442 or by writing General Delivery, Boyd's Tavern, VA 22947.

Staff Needs

What should a museum look for when hiring a sales manager or shop manager? Managing the sales program involves the shop itself, its promotions, product development, buying, employee training, product interpretation, inventory control, hiring, and employee or volunteer management, to name the major responsibilities. Managing all of this *well* demands a combination of experience and education—experience in retailing and an educational background in (or a demonstrable interest in) history, art history, science, education, or museum studies. Larger operations with several shops, mail order programs, wholesaling operations, production facilities, rental properties, etc. are run by people with a different background, usually a financial one. The heads of such conglomerates usually have an MBA, or a degree in finance or economics, and come with years of experience in the world of big business. There are only a handful of such people in museums today and we are not talking about them in this book, but about the shop manager of a small or medium size museum shop.

A former student of mine provides a good example of this experience/education combination. This young woman had her BA in American history with a minor in urban planning. She had taken several undergraduate courses in museum studies and historic preservation, and completed a collections internship at a history museum. Her senior thesis involved an interpretive plan for a historic building belonging to the university. She had worked her way through college as a sales clerk at a local department store. And now she was looking for an entry level position in the museum world. She found it at a small history museum, managing their small, but busy, shop. A bright "people person," she has taken the shop from $149,000 to $250,000 in three years, upgraded the mail order brochure, and recently hired an assistant manager to help with her future plans.

The mistake most museums, large or small, make is in hiring people away from department stores and gift shops without considering their background in museum related fields. Beware. They may be the cream of the crop at Macy's but without a demonstrated affinity toward museums, usually gained through formal education in a museum-related discipline (history, American studies, art history, and education are the ones most relevant to history museums), there is a substantial risk that the museum will get a slick sales program that pays uncomprehending lip service to the institution's legitimate educational, historic, and aesthetic goals. They are perceived by the main stream museum professionals as not "on the team" or as people who will do anything for a buck. This is unfair, but it exists.

Some will think that these qualifications eliminate too many good candidates. "Our bookstore manager has built the leading maritime bookstore in the country with a strong retail background alone," protested one multi-store sales manager. These qualifications are not meant to exclude anyone, just to describe the ideal. Unfortunately there are far too few candidates with both strong museum and retail backgrounds, and one must realistically hire the best one can find. If I could only hire one set of qualifications, either a great retailer who had no interest or background in anything related to the museum, or a person with a great museum background who had no retail experience, I admit I would choose the former and hope that I could guide that person toward an understanding of the museum's mission and stimulate that person's interest in the museum's topic. Museum directors who hire a manager with only a retail background should make it clear that he or she needs to become conversant in the topics of the museum and sensitive to its not-for-profit mission. The director should include the new manager in any appropriate training programs that would impart an overall knowledge of the museum (such as a training program for tour guides) and take the time to draw up a reading list that will give the newcomer the basics on the museum's topics and educational mission.

Sadly, the small museum shop often has *neither* of these two sets of qualifications to choose from. For example, I know a small historical society that recently hired a part-time manager for its new store after months of advertising the position. The best choice was a bright, personable woman who had a medical/clerical background and whose only retail experience was a few months work in a crafts supply store twenty years earlier. No retailing background, no museum or history background. But she was excited and eager to learn. She plunged into relevant history books and spent hours of her own time learning about bookkeeping. What this "self-starter" did have were "people skills," a sense of organization, and a mature approach to her work. While no one would characterize this as the ideal store manager background, she will probably work out reasonably well for this small operation.

In summary, a good candidate for a museum store will have museum or relevant historical experience or education and sales experience and store management experience, including personnel management, display skills, and retail finance exposure. You may not find all that in one candidate of course, but aim high and hire the person with the best combination of those abilities, filling in the gaps with your own on-the-job-training.

What follows here is a job description menu containing far more, or perhaps far less, than your situation demands. It can guide you in tailoring a job description to your museum's individual needs. Choose which provisions apply to your particular circumstances, modify those that need it, and add others. Perhaps your store manager has duties beyond the shop. At one deep south historic house the store manager also gave tours and scheduled tour guides (—and quit in a state of exhaustion after two years). A Nebraska museum has its shop manager handle many secretarial functions during the slow season. Add whatever non-store duties your job requires.

Museum Store Manager Job Description

The museum store manager reports to the museum director or to the board member responsible for the shop or to the chief financial officer.

I. *Store and Managerial Duties*

▪ Maintains attractive shop appearance with effective merchandise presentations and regularly changed displays.

▪ Maintains and evaluates all shop records including daily sales receipts, monthly profit analyses and work sheets; prepares annual report to Board on profit picture.

▪ Takes inventory twice a year; maintains inventory at most efficient level, keeps inventory storage areas orderly.

▪ Develops and implements annual budget; monitors performance.

▪ Hires sales staff or volunteers.

▪ Conducts annual performance appraisals on all store personnel; takes corrective or disciplinary measures when necessary.

▪ Schedules staff efficiently.

▪ Arranges volunteer appreciation program if applicable.

▪ Trains staff in store procedures; arranges for staff training in substantive museum related areas and interpretation techniques.

▪ Develops packaging materials: bags, boxes, gift wrap, etc.

▪ Handles mail orders, develops brochures or mailers to reach larger audience.

▪ Handles wholesale of suitable products to other museum stores or gift shops.

▪ Maintains good customer relations.

II. *Administrative Duties*

▪ Attends regular museum staff meetings to coordinate shop activities with museum programs and events.

▪ Promotes shop through public relations program.

▪ Reviews insurance policies for shop, merchandise, and products liability annually.

▪ Anticipates IRS audit by keeping accurate records and distinguishing between related and unrelated merchandise.

III. *Product Responsibilities*

▪ Buys appropriate merchandise for store, related to museum's purposes and adapted to visitor profile.

▪ Develops appropriate educational products based on the collection or on subject matter or time period related to museum.

▪ Attends trade shows and fairs to buy merchandise.

▪ Works with museum staff on product development with multidepartmental purposes such as posters, publications, and donor gifts.

▪ Responsible for pricing and markdowns.

▪ Produces educational product information for merchandise in the form of product cards, tags, or package information.

▪ Handles trademarks, logos, or copyrights of merchandise when necessary.

IV. Background

▪ Education: prefer college degree in _____ (whatever fields relate to your museum) or museum studies, or education; business courses helpful. Equivalent experience can substitute for degree.

▪ Experience: professional experience in gift shop, department store, or similar retail establishment at a level that included shop management, buying, visual merchandising, budgeting, price setting, personnel management, public relations, and other such marketing and merchandising responsibilities.

▪ General knowledge or abilities: Candidates should have a general knowledge of standard retail concepts and practice, buying and product development experience, knowledge of merchandising concepts and strategies, experience with budgeting, accounting, advertising, promotions, staff supervision, and customer relations, the ability to interact with a wide variety of people, and good communications skills. Candidates should be well-organized and amenable to change. Candidates must possess genuine interest in learning the museum's subject matter thoroughly, must understand the importance of relating merchandise for sale to the collections of the museum, and must have a retail philosophy compatible with the purpose and goals of the museum.

Locating and Hiring Staff

If you have a lead time of several months, one of the best ways to locate good people is to advertise in the AASLH's "History News Dispatch," in the AAM's "Aviso," and/or on the Positions page of the magazine "Museum Store," published by the Museum Store Association. A couple years ago, classified ads looking for shop managers were practically unheard of. Today it seems that every issue carries at least one or two. These ads are not expensive to run and the response is usually overwhelming. Typically these ads are trying to fill jobs at a middle level or higher, where salaries are respectable and responsibilities broader than managing one small shop. If the job you seek to fill is a more modest one in terms of responsibilities and salary, such an ad is unlikely to entice someone to move to your town, and your best bet is local newspapers, your own museum's newsletter, the placement office at the nearest university, and word of mouth. These are also your best options if the position needs to be filled quickly as the lead time on the national publications will cost you at least two months.

Volunteers vs. Paid Employees

After selecting the shop manager or person responsible for sales operations, he or she should hire the remaining staff. The biggest issue for museums planning a new store is volunteers vs. paid employees, or a combination of the two. Which is best for your museum? The answer lies buried in your projected gross revenue, the nature of the museum's existing volunteer group (if any), the volunteer "pool" in your area, community response to and interest in the museum, the going price of retail sales help in your area, and the availability of quality part-time employees. Generally speaking, as sales volume rises, the need to use volunteers declines. As the business becomes more sophisticated, volunteers cannot keep up to date working two afternoons a month. They are still needed, but perhaps in an altered role. If sales are budgeted in excess of $125,000, you should probably look for paid staff. On the other hand, shops with a dedicated, active volunteer group can expect an additional profit of from 17–22% of their gross sales—a significant amount by any standard.[2]

Do not underestimate the time and effort and the hidden costs in using volunteers! In a sales operation of any significant size, a paid part-time volunteer coordinator will be needed to recruit, train, schedule, supervise, locate back-ups, and organize volunteer appreciation events. Even the smallest shop that can manage with one on-duty sales person at a time would require a minimum of 28 reliable people to work two half-day shifts every month, and that would suffice only if there were no illnesses, turnover, vacations, or other absences.

Most museum shops that use volunteers require a commitment of one to two days per month, often broken down into one morning or afternoon each week or each two weeks.

To calculate the worth of your volunteer program, add up the number of volunteer hours worked or projected and multiply by the hourly rate for sales clerks in your area. Add 7.65 social security that you would pay (1990 figures), your state's workman's compensation contribution, your state's unemployment tax if any, federal unemployment tax (actually .008 of the first $7,000 of each person's salary, but you can be accurate enough if you just multiply the total wages by .008), the cost of any benefits your institution offers such as health insurance and the cost of vacation replacement. You will probably have another 20–25% of the base salary when you are finished. Use this percentage in future calculations.

Next subtract the cost of a volunteer coordinator (half-time is usually sufficient for smaller operations), and any major volunteer appreciation activities budgeted (for instance, an end-of-the-year dinner party or summer family picnic.) Don't subtract the little niceties that you would provide for any worker regardless of status, such as coffee and donuts.

The remaining figure is your true savings, the actual value of your volunteers. Don't be secretive about it. Announce to the museum administrators and the board, to the newspapers, and to the volunteers themselves. "Our volunteers contributed work valued at a total of $136,700 last year!"

The recruitment of volunteers for stores usually differs somewhat from recruitment of tour guides, library aides, or fundraisers. It should not. Too often those recruiting for shop volunteers settle for less. "We're desperate," sighed the volunteer coordinator for one museum. "We need certain types of people for the docent program and we have high standards, but I can fill those slots with little trouble. I'll take almost *anyone* for the shop—it doesn't take any special skills to punch a cash register—but we are always short staffed!" The coordinator's any-idiot-can-work-in-the-shop attitude was coming through loud and clear. Who wants to volunteer for a job that "any idiot" can handle? The museum's low expectations were contributing to low performance, poor morale, and rapid turnover.

The beleaguered volunteer coordinator quit shortly thereafter and was replaced by someone who correctly assessed the situation. She began by combining the volunteers into one program, keeping the time commitment at two eight-hour days per month, or four four-hour mornings (9–1) or afternoons (1–5). She equalized the perks: the 25% discount which had been reserved for shop volunteers in a vain attempt to lure more people was extended to all volunteers, even to the two who came in irregularly to help with typing and mailings. Each former docent was required to devote at least $1/4$ of his or her time (or one four-hour slot per month) to the shop and each former sales clerk was similarly required to spend at least one slot giving guided tours. To forestall the anticipated rebellion, an evening meeting was held to explain the changes and discuss the expansion of the duties at the shop. No longer a "register puncher," the newly defined position of Shop Assistant involved the regularly scheduled arrangement of attractive displays and shop restructuring, periodic checks to compare pricing and products in other shops, a multitude of hitherto neglected projects such as the design and purchase of a shop bag to replace the plain Kraft paper ones, the research and writing of product information cards to accompany designated educational merchandise, the implementation of active spoken product interpretation that picked up on the themes stressed during the house tour, and, yes, ringing up sales at the cash register. In addition the shop manager (paid position) offered to take along a different group of three volunteers on the twice yearly buying trips to the gift show in nearby Atlanta. Hesitant at first, she was converted when it became clear that the viewpoints, tastes, and ideas offered by the volunteers were bringing new enthusiasm and a fresh perspective to the buying process.

The volunteer training program was modified and consolidated to support these changes. Everyone now attended the sessions on history, interpretive techniques, and hospitality and courtesy, resulting in a marked improvement in the shop volunteers' ability to impart educational information and to answer visitor questions, as well as the new sessions on shop merchandising, creative display, and accurate sales transactions. Most training was scheduled at 9:00 AM, one hour before the shop opened. Previous training of shop volunteers consisted only of on-the-job training.

In essence, only two changes were required to improve the volunteering situation at this particular historic house: consolidation of the two programs and the upgrading of the sales clerk job status. While this is not the automatic solution to all volunteer problems, the lesson is clear nonetheless. If shop volunteers are hard to come by, lowering standards and limiting the job is probably not the answer. Whether paid or unpaid, shop workers have long been the stepchildren of the museum. Don't permit that attitude to cripple your sales program.

The Smithsonian Institution operates one of the largest and most successful volunteer programs in the country. Although it does not encompass the shop personnel, who are paid, it is worth examining, for its underlying principles are applicable to any volunteer circumstance.[3]

Guidelines for a Successful Volunteer Program

Five Basic Rules

1. Review and assess the goals of the museum to determine if or how a volunteer program can best aid in their achievement. In doing so, pay strict attention to the parameters of budget, professional personnel, and space. A viable, self-perpetuating volunteer program cannot be established without the money to support and sustain it, the staff to develop and manage it, and the space to house it.

2. Employ a volunteer manager. This should be one who has a demonstrated ability to work with and respond to a myriad of individuals—staff and volunteers—whose personalities, levels of ability, and adaptability vary substantially. The volunteer manager's role is that of a friend, supervisor, counselor, teacher, employer, and co-worker.

3. Outline thoroughly the mission of the museum. This should include the objectives of the volunteer program and the qualifications for program participation, emphasizing the commitment of time required of the volunteer on a regular basis. Be sure that the work to be done by the volunteer is clearly stated and understood by the prospective participants.

4. Set high standards for your volunteers and their supervisors. High standards clearly explained and consistently applied will result in high levels of performance. Conversely, low expectations will result in poor morale and a poor level of performance.

5. Establish a system for review and recognition. Evaluation of performance and rewards for work well done are essential to an effective program. Because volunteers receive no monetary compensation, it is especially important that the value of their service and the quality of their work be consistently acknowledged.

Much has been written about volunteer appreciation. Expensive banquets and awards ceremonies are nice, but they are not the only options. Benefits can include privileges similar to those accorded the paid staff, such as invitations to special museum events, shop discounts, a newsletter, free copies of museum publications, etc. The most valued form of volunteer appreciation is also the cheapest—sincere thanks. Acknowledge your volunteers and their contributions in a specific and genuine manner. "Oh, I'm so pleased to see *you* this morning, Ruth. Eight busloads of junior high students demolished our spring displays yesterday and we need your creative touch to rework them." Or "I'm glad we had *you* here today Bill with this crowd. No one rings that register faster than you. Thanks for the herculean effort!" Thanking volunteers (or paid employees, for that matter) for a specific bit of help is far more effective than a vague, "Thanks for coming—good night!" at the end of the day. However there is no substitute for sincerity. Better to say nothing than to fake it with some phony flattery.

While staffing the shop with paid employees is preferable, it is not an option if revenues won't support the salaries. Many shops operate successfully on a combination plan: part paid, part volunteer. The paid employee is hired for the times that volunteers are unwilling to work, typically weekends, summers, and school vacations. College students are often considered first for the obvious reason that they are available during those times, however they should be approached with caution. The shop manager who hires a college student must realize that the shop does not come first (and maybe not even second or third) on the student's list of priorities. School is first, and when exam time comes or a big paper is due or job interviews are scheduled, they are unlikely to come to work. If you have some back-up, they may be worth the risk. Paid college students generally have a better success rate in the summer when some volunteers are reluctant to commit and when vacations cause excessive absenteeism.

The least preferable staffing option is to use the existing tour guides for "double duty." This is viable only where visitation is minimal and controlled. In some museums the bulk of the visitors come during two or three months, leaving the rest of the year with a trickle. During sparse times, one person may act as the ticket seller, the tour guide, and the sales person, accompanying the group to the shop at the culmination of the tour and handling any transactions. The *Elizabeth II,* a historic ship museum in North Carolina that is required by the state to be open all year long, uses this plan very effectively during the slow winter months. The ticket seller is located next to the shop and he or she rings up sales as well. Sales usually amount to less than $50 a day during the winter, clearly not enough to cover a paid employee and not enough to warrant a volunteer's time.

Whatever staffing option your store selects—volunteers, paid workers, or a combination of the two—the general principles of employee motivation will apply. Hundreds of research projects have been undertaken and volumes have been written over the past several decades on motivation in the workplace and your public librarian will be able to direct you to any number of examples.[4] Although many aspects of the topic are quite controversial, most experts agree on the basic principles outlined here.

Management Principles

People often say that a good manager motivates his/her people. This is misleading. No one can motivate another person. Motivation comes from within and, try as you might, you cannot make someone else want to succeed. All a good manager can do is prepare the conditions that will allow and encourage employees to become motivated. A challenging and rewarding job will motivate most people. When the job is neither, aspects peripheral to the actual job take on increased significance. For example, an employee who finds her job exciting and stimulating will not be overly concerned about sharing a small office with two others. When the job ceases to provide adequate reward, her crowded working conditions take on greater importance. This otherwise peripheral factor now moves to center ring and becomes the source of constant complaint.

Museums are fortunate. Although the physical environment of the workplace and other tangible elements peripheral to the job itself (employee benefits and salary, for instance) usually lag considerably behind comparable positions in the private sector, people choose to work in museums because they perceive great challenges, excitement, opportunities for personal growth, prestige, and other intangible rewards that motivate them to labor hard and long for relatively meager physical benefits, or even for free! Therefore museums tend to receive more than their fair share of strongly motivated people from the start. Maintaining an environment that nurtures this motivation involves several management principles.

1. *Positive reinforcement.* This must be appropriate to the person and to the situation; it must be sincere and deserved, and it should occur as soon as possible after the desired behavior is noticed. Positive reinforcement is very personal. What appeals to one employee may not to another. A congratulatory announcement at a staff meeting could mortify a shy, private person (quiet acknowledgment in the manager's office might be preferable here) while it may be exactly the boost that someone suffering from low self esteem needs. Make sure that everyone's accomplishments are adequately recognized, not just those of the superachievers.

2. *Two-way communication.* Be accessible to your employees, willing to listen to work-related problems. Ask for their ideas in solving them and in improving work conditions. No one knows the job better than the person doing it! Some museums offer a small cash reward or gift to employees whose valid suggestions result in improvements or cost savings. The boost to morale is an added benefit. Allow your people to participate in decision making as much as possible.

3. *Provide support when needed.* This does NOT mean acting as a counselor. A manager can best help people with personal problems, whether financial, marital, psychological, or alcohol and drug related, by giving them the name of community counseling or treatment centers, many of which are free or prorated to one's ability to pay, and strongly encouraging them to seek professional help. A good manager will provide job support in the form of resources, training, positive reinforcement, and honest evaluations. It is often said that a manager's most important job is making his or her employees successful.

4. *The big picture.* Let your people know how their efforts relate to the significant whole. Make them feel part of the museum staff, part of the museum's important goals, part of the revenues generated by the store.

5. *Job reviews.* Managers should provide each employee with a work evaluation once or twice a year. This need not coincide with a pay increase although the evaluation will certainly have direct bearing on the

results of the next scheduled salary review. The evaluation covers what is expected of the employee, both in terms of quantity and quality of work and how he/she is meeting the expectations. Always include both positive and negative ("needs improvement") comments. Some managers prefer the Positive-Negative-Positive approach, starting with a positive comment, then reviewing what needs improvement, and ending with a positive. Negatives should never be couched in personal terms: substitute "Your work is—" for "You are—." Criticize behavior, not people. "Your handling of charge card transactions is too inaccurate," not "You are sloppy in your charge transactions." If there is a specific aspect of the job that needs improvement, let the employee offer suggestions as to the solution. Ask, "What can I do to help you improve the accuracy of your charge transactions?" People have a greater commitment to a plan that they help to develop. Plan to meet again at a definite time to evaluate improvement. "I'll ask Betsy to go over the charge procedures with your tomorrow at 9:00. We'll meet again next Tuesday at 11:00 to see whether any improvement has occurred."

6. *Personal growth.* Encourage your employees to become involved in new aspects of the job, to learn and to grow in the job. Provide opportunities to try increasingly difficult tasks. Someone who is very interested in books, for example, could be encouraged to develop an expanded list of appropriate publications for the shop by visiting local libraries and bookstores and contacting university presses for publications lists.

Management Growth

Do not neglect your own personal growth: good managers never stop improving their "people skills." Continued readings and seminars are extremely helpful, even if they appear redundant. Most large museums offer their own in-house courses; if you are located near such an institution, you might ask to participate in their upcoming session. Many university business schools offer reasonably priced seminars on management and business skills that are tailored to the needs of the community.

Continued growth for the shop manager can also come through museum store seminars. The best has been the Smithsonian's three-day program that covers most aspects of museum stores. The seminar was "cancelled temporarily" in 1990 and I can only hope it will be revived in some form soon. Call 202-357-3101 for information.

Additionally the Museum Store Association annual meeting offers seminars on a variety of store topics. Since this meeting is held in a different city every year, it is likely that it will come near you now and then. Sometimes the AASLH and the American Association of Museums

(AAM) annual meetings, which also change location every year, have one topic of interest to stores. As it is probably not financially prudent to attend for the benefit of one presentation, I recommend purchasing the recorded cassette tape of relevant sessions. Write for a list of topics of the past few years and see what sounds relevant. The cost of each tape is only a few dollars.

> AAM (American Association of Museums)
> 1225 Eye Street NW
> Suite 200
> Washington, D.C. 20005
> 202-289-1818

> AASLH tapes produced by:
> Vanguard Systems, Inc.
> 4210 Shawnee Mission Pkwy.
> Suite 100A
> Shawnee Mission, KS 66205
> 913-432-6520

Your state or regional chapter of these organizations may also offer seminars and workshops. The main offices can refer you to their regional affiliates if your director is unable to supply the information.

Notes

1. Thomas H. Aageson, *Financial Analysis for Museum Stores* (Doylestown: Museum Store Association, 1986), p. 21.
2. *Ibid.*, p. 30.
3. What follows is quoted from the booklet "Management of Museum Volunteers" prepared by the Smithsonian Institution Visitor Information and Associates' Reception Center. A free copy is available by sending a self-addressed stamped envelope to:

> Visitor Information and Associates'
>   Reception Center
> Smithsonian Institution
> Washington, D.C. 20560

4. *The One-Minute Manager* by Kenneth Blanchard and Spencer Johnson (Berkley Publ., 1987) is one that has received much attention recently, as did its sequel, *Putting the One-Minute Manager to Work* by Kenneth Blanchard and Robert Lorber. Other good ones are Peter Drucker's *Managing for Results* (Harper & Row, 1964) and Robert F. Mager's *Analyzing Performance Problems* (1970) and Richard Plunkett's *Supervision: The Direction of People at Work* (Brown, 1979).

3

Merchandise

Some museum stores pay lip service to the term *related*. "There is an antique fan in our collection," joked one Virginia museum executive, "so we sell fans." He referred to the cheap Hong Kong imports that the store retailed for one dollar. No one is fooled by comparisons like that and unfortunately such practices cheapen the term *related*.

Institutional Purpose

A product must make a genuine contribution to the museum's stated educational purposes or overall mission to qualify as related. A museum must first have an articulated purpose or mission statement before anyone can begin to judge whether or not the products contribute to it. Museum store managers need to become familiar with their institution's purposes so that they can evaluate their merchandise accordingly.

History Museums

If the products in a history museum store are to contribute to the institution's goals they must be related to the museum in some fashion. There are three possible directions for history museums to take in developing or buying related products:

1. Products can relate to the museum's collection.
2. Products can relate to the museum's historical period.
3. Products can relate to the actual structure of the museum or its location if these are historically or architecturally significant.

Products that relate to the museum's collection are the ones that first come to mind when the public thinks of museum products. Such items are copied from or are based on antiques, art objects, or artifacts in the possession of the history museum.

35

History museums can look to products that relate to their period or specialty. A Civil War museum store could carry Union and Confederate caps even though its collection contained no such antique. An eighteenth-century farm might sell baked goods made from recipes of that period; a maritime museum could sell a print or painting of a seascape or ship, even though it did not own the original. A historic house portraying upper class life in the mid-1700s might choose to sell molded beeswax candles or a modern day reproduction of a Chinese export porcelain bowl copied from an example in another museum's collection. Such items are all authenticated through research to the museum's time period or particular specialty.

Historic houses and buildings or their architectural details can provide inspiration for an abundance of products, as can old books and documents. Excavated artifacts, such as this button found behind a tavern in Williamsburg, are an excellent basis for related products at historic sites where archaeology is part of the research effort. *Photo courtesy—Colonial Williamsburg Foundation.*

Those museums that occupy or own historically significant buildings can include products that relate to these structures or their architectural features. These can include two-dimensional renderings of the structure: old or new photographs or drawings made into posters, postcards, note cards, framed prints, or transferred onto ceramic plates, tiles, calendars, or linen towels, as well as three-dimensional items like a miniature house in wood, ceramic, tin, or cardboard. Historic Savannah has an attractive and unusual cardboard gift box in the shape of one of their historic houses. Colonial Williamsburg's restored and reconstructed buildings serve as a basis for authentic paint colors, interior moldings, miniature houses, and framed sketches and watercolors, to name only a few.

Art and Science Museums

An art museum can take the same three directions in developing or buying related goods as the history museum, with slight modification:

1. Products can relate to the museum's collection in terms of the artist(s) or the works of art.
2. Products can relate to the museum's artistic category or categories, such as "twentieth-century art" or "American portraits."
3. Products can relate to the actual structure of the museum if it is historically or architecturally significant.

Science museum stores will find the first two directions more applicable than the third. Relating the sales item to the collection itself or to the general topic of the museum (botany, astronomy, zoology, or general science) is very probable. The actual structure of the science museum is not likely to be relevant to its educational mission, even if it is a rehabbed train station or architectural treasure.

Product Development: A Group Effort

It takes time, money, and a sincere commitment to develop tasteful, authentic, and educational products that will sell. The most important component is the sincere commitment. Everyone in the museum— director, historians, craftspeople, curators, shop manager, public relations people, interpreters, and others—must be prepared to allocate a portion of their time to this ongoing effort. It is neither possible nor desirable for the shop manager or product developer to accomplish anything alone. It requires the unstinting support of the entire museum staff and, as with any program, more support in the early stages than later when the process has gathered momentum. If the curators are too busy, if the director isn't sure she really wants a store, or if the educators can't see the interpretive potential, even the best program for product development will fizzle.

This is why one of the first steps in this process is the formation of an advisory committee with representatives from many areas of expertise. Six to eight people chosen from the following list might be included: an educator, a craftsperson, one or more curators, someone from public relations, a research historian, a fund raiser, and any other specialist pertinent to the museum (musician, architect, archaeologist, etc.)

The committee members should serve on a permanent basis with maybe a rotating member selected from the ranks of the tour guides, volunteers, board members, or anyone with an eye for quality and good design. The committee should be chaired by the shop manager or the person responsible for the shop.

An advisory committee adds professionalism to the program and increases involvement and support from the staff. It reduces the possibility of error based on one person's taste or judgment and provides a forum for the exchange of ideas. The result is a better product and a stronger program. Do, however, keep in mind the old adage, "The camel is a horse designed by a committee." The committee is there to advise, to guide, to judge, and to suggest, not to rule. The chairperson would be well advised to heed consensus opinions but the final decision must remain his.

There are three ways for a museum store to obtain related products. One is by way of a *licensing program* wherein a designated manufacturer is licensed to develop the product, wholesale it through all of its regular distribution channels including the museum's stores and mail order program, and pay royalties on all sales. A second method involves *contract product development,* wherein the museum undertakes the development and inventory costs of the product which is then sold exclusively at the museum's shop. The third way is by means of judicious *buying on the open market* products already developed that happen to relate to the museum's purposes.

Licensing Programs

The good news about licensing is that it frees the museum from most of the financial obligations of product development while providing the museum with tax free income. Once licensed, the manufacturer incurs all the product development costs—and they can easily run in the thousands of dollars—as well as the inventory investment. The museum acts as a control throughout the process, insuring that quality and authenticity are not compromised while bearing in mind that the realities of modern manufacturing may prohibit most handwork and certain aspects of the product's design from being copied precisely. The museum purchases the product at wholesale, subject to the same conditions as any other wholesale customer (price, minimums, price breaks for quantity orders, etc.)

The selected manufacturer is licensed under a formal contractual agreement to develop specified products that are deemed marketable by the manufacturer and educational by the museum. For instance, a museum may authorize (license) one company to develop products in the fabrics category and another to develop note cards. Seldom is more than one company licensed in any one category but you can define your categories very narrowly if need be. One textile manufacturer could be licensed to produce silks, another for cottons and linens; one card company could do original black and white sketch note cards while another handled color photograph note cards. This is not being sneaky. Many manufacturers specialize and would be unable or uninterested in venturing beyond their area of expertise. Be sure to define clearly from the beginning the product category being licensed. It is easier to broaden the scope of a license later to include additional categories than it is to restrict or take away from a licensee's "territory."

Royalties are usually calculated as a percent of the revenue generated by every product sold at wholesale by the manufacturer, less returns and including the sales to the museum itself. Royalties range from four to twelve percent depending upon the manufacturer, the industry, and the museum's bargaining power. They are usually paid on a semi-annual or quarterly basis; monthly is preferable if the company is large and the amounts of money significant. The manufacturer is permitted to use the museum's name in its marketing efforts for that museum's products. Best of all, the IRS has ruled that royalty earnings are not taxable.[1]

The bad news about licensing is that manufacturers are really only interested in tying into museums whose names are nationally recognized by the public at large, such as the Smithsonian, Colonial Williamsburg, or the Metropolitan Museum, or at least those with strong regional customer recognition such as Winterthur, Historic Charleston, or Old Sturbridge Village. It just doesn't make good business sense for a manufacturer to enter into a licensing agreement unless there is the potential to develop salable products that will be enhanced by the museum's prestige. The idea is for manufacturers to identify themselves with the excellent reputation of a well-known museum in order to give their products an edge in today's highly competitive marketplace. In many cases, the royalties are added to the cost of the product rather than being absorbed by the manufacturer, resulting in a higher retail than other similar products. This is not generally considered a liability. It has been proven over and over that customers are willing to pay for a "name," be it a brand name, a designer label, or a museum association.

One possible exception to the rule of customer recognition is in the category of wallpaper and fabrics, often developed together by one manufacturer for coordinated decorating purposes. Here it is conceivable that a manufacturer would agree to pay royalties on one or two designs borrowed from a textile or wallcovering collection even if the museum has limited name recognition value. They may incorporate these few designs into a larger book of historical wallpapers taken from several unrelated museums. But generally speaking, if your museum is the only place the product would sell, it is not worth trying to license. The purpose of licensing is to reach beyond your museum's natural customer base to markets that would not otherwise come into contact with it.

If you think your museum has licensing potential in certain product categories, first identify possible licensees. One way is to check what companies other museums are using. Most museums will not object to sharing their list of licensees and they may even give out the name of the contact person (usually the Director or Vice-President of Marketing or the President of the company). A partial list of companies currently licensed by at least one museum is presented in Appendix B.

The advantages of dealing with a company already licensed by another museum are several. There is a track record to examine. Did the company fulfill its commitments? Is the museum happy with the arrangement? The marketing strategies and procedures are already in place. In other words, licensing is not new to this company and it presumably has an appropriate distribution network of sales reps and showrooms already in place and a viable market niche. The company has already shown an interest in historical or museum related products, relieving you of the need to persuade them that a relationship is to their advantage.

There are disadvantages too in being one of several museums to which a manufacturer owes allegiance. You may be less important. You may find that the company already has products in their line developed with another museum that are similar to the ones you wanted developed, and is not willing to compete with itself. For instance, a ceramic dinnerware manufacturer that already has a blue and white Canton pattern on the market is not likely to care about reproducing your museum's prize Canton, even if it is different from, superior to, or more attractive than the existing pattern. Your collection may be used to "fill in the gaps" left by the other museums' collections.

After having settled on a short list of companies, check their Dun & Bradstreet rating and contact the appropriate executive. The president is the best place to start. He or she can refer you to the correct person if need be. An interested company will want to visit your museum to see the range of your collections before negotiating particulars.

A lawyer is a necessity—just be sure to find one who has experience in commercial law. If you must use the free services of the attorney on your board, at least make certain he or she has a copy of the sample draft of a licensing agreement found in the *Connecticut Law Review,* 10, No. 3 (Spring 1978) to work from. Part of it is reprinted with permission in Appendix C.

Small- and medium-size museums can benefit from licensing programs without becoming directly involved in one themselves. Investigate the products that are reproduced for other museums and buy those that relate to your own collection or historical period. A piece of eighteenth-century Chinese export porcelain owned by a large museum and repro-duced by their licensee may be identical to a piece in the small museum's collection, or it may be similar enough to merit its inclusion in the small museum's store. Maybe there is no similar porcelain in the small muse-um's collection but the style or pattern relates to the time period or social lifestyle that institution depicts. By and large, the products developed through museum licensing programs are among the best available in both quality and educational merit. They bear further investigation.

Try "creative piggybacking." Is there a large museum similar to yours that has a licensing program? Is your museum a smaller version of an American decorative arts museum like Winterthur or an early nineteenth-century town like Old Sturbridge Village? If so, ask for a list of their licensees—most museums are delighted to share it since that will lead to greater sales and greater royalties—and explore those product lines. Fol-low their development activities. Do they have a wholesale program for any items they develop in-house? Get the name of a contact person at the museum and call or write every few months to keep up with their activi-ties. Since it means increased sales or royalties for them, most museums are happy to cooperate.[2]

Contract Product Development

Contract product development is suited to all museums regardless of their size. It differs from development through licensees in several ways. The museum generally pays the development costs, such as molds, tool-ing, and artwork, and may be obliged to guarantee an initial order larger than the store manager would like to inventory. Owning the tooling gives the museum some leverage. If it becomes necessary to change suppliers—and there are many reasons why this happens—ownership of the tooling enables the museum to start up production with another manufacturer without incurring the development costs again and again.

The manufacturer or craftsperson is not permitted to use the muse-um's name in any promotional efforts since no royalties are being paid. The museum should require exclusivity for the product for the same rea-son. After all, museum funds are paying for its development.

A contract should be drawn up for every manufacturer or craftsper-son with whom the museum works. It need not be a lengthy legal docu-ment. A simply worded statement in letter or memo form is sufficient. Have the craftsperson or manufacturer sign and date two copies, one for their files and one for yours. This sort of concise agreement spelling out everyone's responsibilities will help avoid conflicts later on. A sample con-tract is provided here for use as a point of departure.

Sample Agreement between Museum and Craftsperson

To: (Craftsperson's name and business name)

From: (Museum's name)

Subject: (Product Development and Supply Agreement)

With regards to any products developed by _____ on
(craftsperson)

behalf of _____, the undersigned craftsperson/artist
(museum)

agrees as follows:

All reproductions, adaptations, interpretations, or creations that are made from

_____'s art objects and/or antiques, or that are de-
(museum)

veloped from specifications provided by the _____
(museum)

are to be produced exclusively for the _____.
(museum)

Under no circumstances may the craftsperson/artist sell or give away any

item developed in conjunction with the _____.
(museum)

The _____ is the sole judge of whether the pro-
(museum)

posed prototype meets the standards of the museum. Once approved, the
prototype becomes the standard against which all future production is judged.
Production pieces which, in the sole opinion of the museum do not come close
enough to the prototype are to be rejected and destroyed, not sold or given
away to any other source.

If special tooling costs or other start-up expenditures are necessary, they must

first be approved by the _____. Once they are ap-
(museum)

proved and paid for by the museum, these tools and/or equipment become the
exclusive property of the museum and must be returned to the museum whenever requested or when the business relationship is terminated.

_____ may not use the fact that he/she is a supplier
(Craftsperson)

for the _____ in any advertising or promotion.
(museum)

_____   _____
(Craftsperson's signature)   *(Date)*

_____
(Signature of authorized museum employee)

_____   _____
(Title)   *(Date)*

Buying at Trade Shows and Craft Fairs

Buying on the open market is something every museum store does. The trick is to ferret out those vendors who have products that relate to the museum's educational purposes.

Attending one or more trade or craft shows each year is the ideal way to acquire a good overview of the marketplace, current trends, and comparative costs. Trade shows also provide inspiration for future development and will introduce you to potential custom manufacturers. They will contribute new display ideas and other merchandising techniques to your mental repertoire.

Attending shows can be expensive, even if your museum is located near a large metropolitan area like New York City where many are held. You may find that the costs of airfare, hotel accommodations, meals, and ground transportation put such buying trips out of the range of your meager budget.

There are ways to minimize costs. If you go to the big shows, be aware that promoters, the people who run the show, often make special airfare and lodging arrangements for out-of-town buyers. Realistically, few small and medium size museums are able to afford the big trip, but most museums are located within a few hours' drive of a metropolitan area large enough to host an occasional smaller trade show or craft fair. Some shows travel—the Museum Store Association show is one—making it possible for buyers to attend every three or four years when it comes to their region. A few shows are experimenting with video tours, enabling buyers to preview the market by video cassette. It is a new idea that seems to be catching one, so inquire whether this is available. Video previews could be the answer for stores with no travel budget at all.

Trade Shows

The Museum Store Association show is an excellent choice for buyers on a tight travel budget. It is held in conjunction with the organization's annual meeting in a different city every year. Sites are not determined years in advance, so call 303-329-6968 for locations and more information. Though recommended for all museum types, science museums will probably find it the most relevant.

The National Stationery Show, held every spring in New York and each summer in San Diego, is a good one to attend. Call 212-686-6070 for dates and details. Don't be put off by the name of this show—it transcended mere stationery long ago. Today it features publications and small gift items as well as all sorts of paper products. Several museums wholesale their merchandise here, in past years Mystic Seaport, Worcester Museum of Art, Boston Museum of Fine Arts, the Museum of Modern Art, and the Philadelphia Museum of Art have been represented. While an excellent show for all museum types, art museums will probably find it the most relevant.

A relative newcomer is the New York International Gift Fair's section called Museum Source. Created in 1988 especially for museum stores and for those gift shops that target a similar quality-conscious market, the Museum Source is located at the Passenger Ship Terminal. This show is held twice a year, usually in January and August. Specifics are available by calling the promoters, George Little Management Co. at 202-686-6070.

When attending any show throw fashion cares to the wind and wear your most comfortable clothes and shoes. Take a notepad—your brain will be saturated within an hour—and a shopping bag for vendor brochures. One with a shoulder strap is best. Pre-registered buyers avoid long lines at the entrance so call ahead and the promoters will mail you a registration form. Bring a calculator, your tax number, and credit references with you to any show. Bring dozens of business cards to leave with prospective vendors. There are always vendors who run out of catalogs or who offer to mail literature if you leave a card. Strangely, most do not follow through with their promise, so get *their* business card or circle that booth in the show catalog so that *you* can get back to *them* after a month has gone by. Take a colleague if finances allow—two heads are better than one.

It is probably better for an inexperienced buyer to wait to place orders until after returning home. It is easy to get carried away in the excitement and bustle of the show and place orders you later regret. At least wait until you have seen the entire show before going back to the booths that interested you most. If you are going to place orders at the show, know in advance how much money you can spend and stick to this budget. Naturally vendors want you to place orders right then and there, and may entice you with gimmicks or special promotions, such as a 10% discount off all orders placed at the show. This is nice if you are certain you want the product, just be cautious. Take small risks. Buy a few of the new item, not a truckload. If you have identified your customers, you will be able to target each segment of your customer profile with suitable merchandise at appropriate price points.

Think about Your Product in Broad Terms

From the moment they are purchased or developed until they leave your store with the customer, ideally your products should all:

- be easily stored;
- keep forever, not spoil or become outdated;
- never break;
- stand a good markup;
- be easily displayed;
- be easily packaged;
- bring in repeat business;
- promote your museum;
- come with educational information;
- further your museum's educational purposes;
- sell fast!

Evaluate Individual Items

- Quality (always critical).
- Whether there is room for the product on the shelf? in the stockroom?
- Product safety: is it sharp? poisonous? lead-free? small enough to swallow?
- How the item relates to the shop's overall sales plan.
- How it will look with other merchandise on the shelf? in a display?
- Country of origin, a sensitive topic for some cases or in some areas. Remember that it is against the law to remove those country of origin stickers and yes, it is enforced!

Don't presume that the cost quoted by the vendor is firm. There is often some room to wiggle. Keep in mind that your shop is a desirable account to any vendor because of the prestige in selling to a museum, no matter how small a museum it is. Listen to the name-dropping when vendors are trying to impress a potential customer—if there is a museum store account among their existing customers, they will flaunt it. Another reason companies are partial to museum accounts was summed up by one vendor at a recent gift show. "They pay their bills," he said bluntly. "It may be slow but you know the money's coming." When the trendy little here-today-gone-tomorrow gift shops go bankrupt, it is usually the vendors who take the loss in the form of unpaid bills. There is virtually no such risk doing business with a museum store.

As a valued customer, you should not hesitate to ask for better prices, discounts, and favors. Remember those prophetic words, "The worst they can do to you is say *No*." Always ask for a **better price,** then move on to request **free shipping,**[3] a **liberal return policy** (when the vendor agrees to allow you to return what doesn't sell for cash or credit, also called a guaranteed sale),[4] **dating** (where the vendor agrees to hold off billing you for a month or two or three or six after you've received the merchandise), and an **advertising allowance** (you *could* run an ad in your museum's magazine or newsletter, couldn't you?). *The worst they can do to you is say No.*

Craft Shows

Craft shows are another good source of products. The ACC Craft-fairs in Baltimore, San Francisco, West Springfield, MA, and St. Paul, MN are among the largest. Regional shows abound, particularly in areas with strong craft traditions such as Tennessee and Kentucky (the Kentucky Craft market) and the Carolinas (the Southern Highlands Handicraft Guild Fair in Asheville, NC). Avoid the so-called craft shows in malls, parks, churches, or schools which tend to attract spare time hobbyists, not professionals.

Trade Publications

Trade publications are another good source for products and development ideas. Check your local library before you commit to a subscription. Popular magazines can provide product sources if you are willing to do some detective work. History museums will find many of the "shelter magazines" relevant. *Americana, American Heritage, Colonial Homes, Country Home, House Beautiful,* and *Victorian Home* are a few to look over. The last few pages of advertising may prove the best. Professional journals can help too. Ask the curators who already subscribe to circulate their copies to you.

Trade or Related Publications

GR: Gift Reporter
George Little Management Inc., Publisher
2 Park Avenue, Ste. 1100
New York, NY 10016

Free subscription to qualified store managers; excellent monthly publication with good articles and information on sources and shows.

Gift and Stationery Business
1515 Broadway, Rm. 3201
New York, NY 10036

Monthly magazine.

Giftware News
1414 The Merchandise Mart
Chicago, IL 60654

Monthly publication for gifts, stationery, collectibles, and tabletop.

Gift and Decorative Accessories
51 Madison Ave.
New York, NY 10010

Advertisements for merchandise, articles on gift shop operations, and an annual buyers directory; monthly publication for gifts, tabletop, gourmet, home accessories, greeting cards, and stationery.

Playthings
51 Madison Ave.
New York, NY 10160–0406

Monthly, targeted for mass merchants, occasionally ads feature items suitable for museum shops; expect to be inundated with marketing literature from toy manufacturers if you subscribe.

The Crafts Report
700 Orange St.
P.O. Box 1992
Wilmington, DE 19899–9962

Monthly; good source for craftspeople and craft show dates and locations plus free listings in "Crafts Wanted" for shops seeking specific work to sell.

Party and Paper Retailer
500 Summer Street, Ste. 300
Stamford, CT 06901

Monthly; mostly greeting cards, stationery, plus topics of little interest to museum stores, like balloons.

Ornament
P.O. Box 35029
Los Angeles, CA 90035–0029

Quarterly magazine on jewelry and costumes; ancient, contemporary, and ethnic.

Catalog Age
Six River Bend
Box 4949
Stamford, CT 06907–0949

Mail order industry.

BOOKLIST
American Library Association

Excellent, expensive, twice monthly; check your public library; this publication critiques new titles.

New York Times Book Review

Check your public library.

Some of these publications are free to the trade, so be prepared to supply some basic information about the type of shop you operate.

Product Categories Defined

Whether you are dealing with a licensed manufacturer, a jobber, a craftsperson, or the IRS, or talking with a customer about a product, definitions and categories can provide the basis for good communication. It has become commonplace to hear customers, and all too often museum people, refer to nearly everything sold in the store as a "reproduction." This confusion is extremely unfortunate. It cheapens the real thing and hurts the credibility of all museum sales programs. Standardized terminology would benefit museums and consumers alike but thus far there has been little interest. In its absence, the following terminology is recommended for history museums.

Reproduction or Replica

A copy of the appearance of the original antique or object, accurately duplicating the size, color, and material of the object. It is often, but not necessarily, made in the same manner as the original object but its function may not be the same. Example: a reproduction weather vane used today as a piece of table sculpture rather than on a barn.

Adaptation

An alteration to the size, color, and/or material of the original object. Examples: a reproduction fabric also offered in a dozen adaptation colorways; a harvest jug scaled down to one-quarter size; an antique linen tablecloth copied in a cotton-polyester blend.

Interpretation

The use of a design or an element on an antique, artifact, or other object in a totally different context. Examples: a quilt design on a paper napkin, a fabric design produced as a wallpaper, the decorative carving on a chair as a silver brooch.

This antique Noah's Ark toy at the Abby Aldrich Rockefeller Folk Art Center in Williamsburg, Virginia, inspired a die-cut notecard. Similarly, the design of these paper napkins was copied from quilts in the museum's collection. *Photos courtesy—Colonial Williamsburg Foundation.*

Creation

Something new created from research or by an artist or photographer for the museum. Examples: an educational board game relating to the museum; a book written by the curator; paper dolls in period costumes; sealing wax developed from a formula found in an eighteenth-century encyclopedia; a toy horse developed from a nineteenth-century genre painting; a poster, postcard, or photographic image of the museum or of any part of its collection. Although these products are based on research instead of on actual antiques or other objects, products recreated from a period print, recipe, formula, instructions, or painting can be as historically authentic as a reproduction. Others can be totally modern in function and design, as in a poster that is composed of a photograph of a porcelain figurine with the museum's name and exhibit dates below.

Termed *creations* because they are created from research as opposed to being reproduced from surviving antiques, the drum and the noisemaker show up quite plainly in this print by William Hogarth, as well as in Catchpenny Prints, in several period oil paintings, and in eighteenth-century store inventories. *Photo courtesy—Colonial Williamsburg Foundation.*

The terminology is inappropriate for science museums and for museums of natural history, zoos, aquariums, nature centers, botanic gardens, parks, and planetariums because it is not possible to reproduce or adapt their collections. Live animals, geodes, flowering plants, battlefields, and stars make unlikely candidates for the reproduction process! All products would of necessity be classified as creations or interpretations.

Art museum professionals would faint at the thought of marketing a reproduction painting that attempted to copy exactly the size, colors, and material of a work of art—the accurate term for *that* is a forgery. In fact, many people connected with art museums *do* use the word *reproduction,* but in a different sense, meaning a photograph of a painting or sculpture in the form of a postcard, print, or poster. This is where some of the confusion comes into play.

The numerous advertisements that survive from colonial American newspapers commonly list such items as "children's Toys of all Sorts," "Babies of all prices," and even "dressed and undressed Babies" for sale in stores. An antique doll was selected as the basis for a carefully handmade reproduction, from her gesso face and flax hair to her wool petticoat under the linen skirt. The Colonial Williamsburg collection included no antique gentleman doll, but by applying the construction details of existing female antiques to the outward appearance of a male doll depicted in a mid-eighteenth-century John Collet painting, a gentleman companion was created. Thus, one of the pair of dolls would be called a reproduction; the other is better termed a creation. *Photos courtesy— Colonial Williamsburg Foundation.*

Notes

1. Passive income sources (dividends, interest, royalties, etc.) are excluded from taxable income since theoretically they pose no threat of unfair competition to for-profit businesses. However, legislation is currently (1991) under consideration to eliminate these exclusions. See A. Worley's "The Unrelated Business Debate: Wait Until Next Year" in *History News,* 43 (Nov./Dec. 1988) for more information.

2. A partial list of history museums with licensing programs would include Colonial Williamsburg, Henry Ford Museum, Historic Charleston, Historic Deerfield, Historic Newport, Historic Savannah, the Library of Congress, Monticello, Mystic Seaport, the National Trust for Historic Preservation, Old Salem, the Smithsonian, the Society for the Preservation of New England Antiquities, Old Sturbridge Village, and Winterthur. There are many others.

3. Freight terms are often negotiable. FOB (freight on board) varies:

   > FOB Baltimore—the vendor pays shipping to Baltimore, your store pays it the rest of the way.
   >
   > FOB origin—you pay shipping from the point of origin, usually the manufacturer's plant.
   >
   > FOB destination—the vendor pays shipping all the way to you.

   These freight terms also determine when you take ownership of the shipment. This becomes important if an accident should occur in transit, since the owner will be responsible for any losses not covered by insurance.

4. Publishers and book vendors are most likely to offer returns but obviously this practice is not to the vendor's advantage. Many publishers have instituted a dual discount system, one discount for a regular sale with return privileges, and a greater discount for a straight sale with no returns allowed. On a new item your store has never tried, take the first option and order a few with return privileges. After you see that it sells well for your shop, reorder at the no-returns discount level from then on.

4

The Educational Role of Related Merchandise

R elated merchandise is not automatically educational. Oddly, most museum stores seem to have missed this point. It is unexpected because museum professionals have long been aware that objects don't talk and they have developed many ways of conveying or "interpreting" the educational message to the visiting public. In galleries, period rooms, historic houses, and historic sites, exhibit labels interpret the antiques and artifacts, docents conduct guided tours, self-activated films and slide presentations and audio guides give background information, historical markers explain what occurred on this spot long ago, living history programs permit a glimpse of lifestyles in years gone by, and printed guidebooks and reading material abound. Science and art museum galleries rely heavily on labels, guided tours, demonstrations, participatory events, guidebooks, films, public lectures, and dozens of other methods to pass along their educational message.

The store is no different from the rest of the museum in this respect. Its related merchandise cannot contribute to the institution's educational goals without interpretation. While some products, like books, *are* intrinsically educational, most need some sort of interpretation to perform their educational function. The first step in that direction is the compilation of product information on each item or on each group of items for the purpose of employee training.

Product information is nothing more than a summary of all the relevant facts to be used when interpreting the item. History museum directors and educational specialists who are accustomed to preparing interpretive information on specific antiques and on social, economic, and political topics will find this no different. For every sales item some or all of the following apply:

- How was the product made?
- Is this different from the way the original antique/artifact was made?
- Where was the product made? The original?

55

- Do we know who made them?
- Elaborate on the original, its function and qualities.
- Where is the original located today? Can visitors see it?
- Background information on the craftsperson or manufacturer.
- What is the cultural, artistic, or historical significance of the item?
- How does the customer care for it?

For art museums, this information will focus on the original painting, sculpture, or work of art, its artist, and that artist's time period or school. It may well include the materials or techniques used in creating the original, such as pastels, ivory, or fruitwood, or the function of the original, especially with prehistoric art and artifacts. Science museums will aim their product information more toward the animal, plant, or natural phenomenon to which the sales item relates.

Arrange a concise summary of the product information in a three-ring binder divided into topical categories such as Jewelry, Toys, or Ceramics. Add any pertinent articles gleaned from books, magazines, or research reports, and a photograph of the antique, artifact, or architectural feature on which the product was based. There you have it—a product reference book!

The book belongs on the sales floor where employees can refer to it when responding to visitors' questions. A convenient location will make it easy for salespeople to review unfamiliar portions during slow periods. You may want several copies, one to lend to new employees for home study, one in the break area, the master copy in your office. Volunteers who only work once or twice a month will find this reference book indispensable. Post new product information on the bulletin board for a week or so until everyone has had the chance to notice it before filing it away in the reference book.

The product reference book also functions as a sales tool. Telling a visitor that the doll she is examining is copied from a rare antique not currently on display is weak; showing the visitor a photo of the doll and reviewing the specifics of its manufacture are better. The extra effort will generate considerable more appreciation for the doll and its price. *Product knowledge always increases the likelihood of a purchase.* If you want to sell more, teach more!

Verbal Interpretation

What is the first greeting we hear whenever we enter a store? "Hi, can I help you?" And what is the knee-jerk response, even when we *do* need help? "No thanks, just looking."

THE EDUCATIONAL ROLE OF RELATED MERCHANDISE

So how do you begin your product interpretation in a store? After all, it is not like a guided tour where you gather up your captive audience and begin in a prearranged, formal manner. Making matters more difficult is the passive role to which most retail store employees are accustomed. Using the counter as a protective shield, they wait to be approached before talking at all.

Re-training people into new habits is *very difficult* and cannot be accomplished with an isolated training session. Encouragement and training must be continual. Demonstrate your sincerity by adding interpretive requirements to the sales person's job description. Use it as one of the criteria by which employees are evaluated.

Sales floor interpreters cannot wait for the visitor to pose a question. They must take the initiative and approach the visitor. There are easy ways to do this, only a few of which are described here.

The sales person can refer to something the visitor may have seen on exhibit. "Did you know that bowl was copied from an antique on exhibit in the Egyptian Gallery?"

They can refer to the historical significance of an item. "The candlestick you are admiring is a reproduction of an 1862 brass antique owned by General Robert E. Lee."

Mentioning an activity or craft can whet a person's interest. "Our basketweavers tell us that it takes about four hours to weave this style basket, but that it is not as difficult as some people think. Have you ever tried basketmaking? There is a good 'how to' book on the third shelf there."

To the customer buying a piece of wrought iron: "Have you been to the blacksmith's forge out back yet? They are making hinges today and it is fascinating to watch."

The social use of an item can be a good point of departure. To the child buying a mob cap: "This little cap was worn by girls like you indoors as well as outdoors. And when they went outdoors, they often put another hat on top of this one. How would you like to wear two hats at once?"

A reference to another educational product can lead to a longer interpretation and another sale. "These preserves are made from an early nineteenth-century recipe. This cookbook gives many old recipes from that period that you might like to try. Its been updated to include modern measurement equivalents as well."

During busy times, product interpretation can be as little as one or two sentences spoken while the purchase is being rung up, wrapped, or bagged. It is not hard, it is simply a different habit to develop.

In the beginning, grooming one experienced sales person to act as "lead interpreter" will smooth the process considerably. He or she will by example provide encouragement for the hesitant and act as a model for the new employees. There is probably more than one talkative, outgoing personality working in every museum shop already. Sell that person on the value of product interpretation and the work is well begun.

Training Museum Store Employees

In a museum store the employees are expected to function both as salespersons and as educational interpreters. They are responsible for accuracy in cash handling and courtesy to the customer, as are employees at any other retail establishment, but if the salespeople are to contribute to the museum's educational goals they need to be trained accordingly.

This need not mean developing an elaborate new training program. Simply include store personnel in your museum's existing interpretive training for new tour guides or other "front-line" people. This applies to paid staff as well as to volunteers. Incrementally some of the existing staff should attend each training session, perhaps in order of seniority, until all have participated. Newly hired staff can then be scheduled for the next available session.

Why go to all this trouble? Why bother with the effort and expense of training store employees as carefully as you train the museum's front-line personnel? First because they need a solid historical (or scientific or art related) background on which to base their interpretation in order to feel confident when cast in the role of an interpreter. Second, salespeople are asked as many or more questions, both substantive and directional, than are tour guides, often by those who hesitate to speak up in a group for fear of looking foolish or bothering the guide. For many museum visitors, the salesperson is the first human being they encounter and may provide their first and only opportunity to ask a question.

The third point may be the least important or the most: morale. Long the second class citizens of the museum, store employees tend to feel less a part of their institution than any other group. Pride in themselves, in their jobs, and in their museums will grow as the institution recognizes the importance of their educational contribution and demonstrates a sincere commitment to training them for it.

One way to indicate this shift in attitude is to change their job title. What are the store employees called at your shop? Sales clerks, most likely. While that may be appropriate for most retail establishments, it does not indicate the scope of their responsibilities in a museum store. Sales comprise half their job. The titles *sales interpreter* or *shop interpreter* more accurately reflect the dual nature of their responsibilities and signify a determination to transform the ideal into reality.

Written Interpretation

Another form of product interpretation that is as effective and essential as the verbal method is the written one. *Some form of written interpretive material should accompany nearly every article sold in a museum store.* This is ambitious but not unrealistic.

Ideally written interpretive material reinforces the message that the customer heard in the shop. Teachers know that the more senses used in teaching, the greater the retention level. Apart from that, written material gets the educational message to the customer when the sales staff is too busy to talk or when the customer is too rushed to listen. It delivers the educational message to the third party when the item is purchased as a gift. It can help make an inexpensive souvenir into a distinctive gift. The customer may not buy Aunt Rachel a soap ball, but package three with an interesting card explaining soapmaking in rural nineteenth-century America and the item is transformed into a suitable gift.

Product information is not just educational, it is good business. Once upon a time, a museum offered a small reproduction delft dish that limped along for years at an uninspiring pace. Then someone thought to add a product information card to it with an eighteenth-century candy recipe and some history about delftware. Sales tripled.

The best option is to incorporate the product information into the package. When developing the package for an item, plan to include product information. It can be printed on the box, tied to the product by the vendor, sealed in a plastic bag with the product, or in some fashion permanently or semipermanently attached to the product or the package. The few manufacturers that cater to museum stores have begun to do this as a matter of course and it is to be hoped that more will follow. Some manufacturers will, if asked, print or devise a custom package for the product you order at little or no extra charge. Ask! The worst they can do to you is say No.

Failing the "on package" route, the next best method of disseminating product information is by printing a card or tag yourself. Either put it with the product on the shelf (tied to a basket handle or placed inside a mug) or drop it in the bag at the point of purchase.

During the colonial period in America, foreign coins made of precious metals came from Spain, England, Portugal, Holland, France, and elsewhere. All were legal tender. By far the most commonly circulated coin in the Virginia colony was the Spanish milled dollare of eight reales. The coin was divided into eighths, or "bits" — hence the slang "two bits" to mean a quarter of a dollar. The patterned milled edge of the coin was designed to prevent dishonest people from shaving silver from the sides unnoticed.

This copy of a Spanish milled dollare, the original of which was minted in 1757 in Mexico City, was made by Colonial Williamsburg craftsmen using a hand-cut die to strike the impression into a cast nickle silver blank. On one side the Spanish royal crown sits above the coat of arms of Spain. On the other side, the Pillars of Hercules and the two orbs symbolize Spain's worldwide empire.

More than 20 million dollares were minted each year during the two decades before the Revolution. When the new American nation established its own coinage in 1792, it was this coin that became the basis for the American dollar.

SPANISH

MILLED DOLLAR

Cards can be specific or categorical in their approach to the topic. A museum store just beginning to use product cards would be well advised to start by identifying a dozen or so related merchandise groups such as baskets, hats, glass, or candy, and writing a generic treatment for each group. The top-selling items in the store probably deserve their own product cards.

The ultimate goal is NOT a specific card for every product—that would be too cumbersome and costly for most stores to implement. A more reasonable ambition is the creation of a mixture of categorical cards, where the categories are not so broad as to make the context meaningless, and specific cards for the better-selling items. Keep in mind that one of your store's largest product categories, books, needs no accompanying product information and those items you develop or purchase with information on the box or in the package need nothing further at store level. It is probable that less than half your store's merchandise actually needs store level product information.

Product cards (some museums call them provenance cards) can be arranged in an open file box next to the cash register and slipped in the bag with little fanfare along with the sales receipt. It is easy to manage several dozen cards from the register; more than that is cumbersome. The more that can be put with the product on the shelf or printed on the package, the better.

A third form of written product information targets a different group. This is the short informative article, captioned photograph, or flyer that goes to other museum employees, especially the tour guides, to inform them about the products in the store, the new arrivals, and their interpretive possibilities. If they are familiar with the merchandise, tour guides and other museum employees can refer visitors to the shop. Tour guides can also make valuable suggestions since they hear visitor comments and are frequently aware of what items the visitor wants to buy. Such employee-oriented information can add substance to the assertion that the store is as concerned about education as the rest of the museum.

If your museum publishes a magazine or newsletter for members and friends, consider including shop topics regularly. Short articles, a column, or photos featuring interpretive information already amassed add another dimension to the museum's educational outreach. Price should be mentioned only if it can be done discreetly as this is not to be confused with an advertisement. It may well result in added sales but the larger purpose here is to increase interest in the shop and spread the educational message. You may want to run advertisements in your museum newsletter as well, but don't mix the two.

S H O P · T A L K

FROM THE HISTORIC AREA SHOPS

SOAP

Eighteenth-century Virginia Gazette advertisements indicate that Williamsburg merchants imported and sold many varieties of soap. The finer quality soaps were usually scented with a pleasant fragrance and colored. Some typical soap colors of the period were red, black, green, brown, white, marbled, purple, blue, and speckled. Soap could be purchased by the pound, in boxes, or as individual washballs.

One of the earliest written documents referring to a soap-like product dates to the first century A.D. However, the use of soap as a cleansing agent was not actually recognized until sometime in the second century. It was the Greek physician Galen who pointed out the importance of soap as a cleansing agent and a disease preventative. The earliest soaps were made exclusively from animal fats. These soaps possessed good cleansing qualities, however they had the distinct disadvantage of an unbearable smell. By the eighteenth-century this terrible odor had been overcome by replacing animal fats with vegetable fats (i.e. olive oil). Soaps were also scented with various fragrances by working in oils of lemon, orange peel, cloves, orris root, rose, and other flowers and herbs.

Eighteenth-century engravings, illustrations, and other period references provide insight to the methods and techniques used in soap making. Basically, a fat and lye mixture was boiled into a liquid form. It was then poured into large square or rectangular molds and set to dry. Once the soap hardened, the large blocks were cut with wires or wedge-shaped blades into smaller cakes. The round soap balls were hand molded into assorted sizes, or as a 1796 reference states "a size agreeable to your mind." The better quality cakes and balls of soaps were stamped with the manufacturer's trademark or some type of artistic marking such as suns, lilies, crescents, and bear claws. The markings increased the commercial value and assured a good quality product.

Records indicate that a soap and candlemaker, Morto Brien, set up a business in Williamsburg in 1776 and advertised soap for sale. Some of the colonists purchased their soap directly from soapmakers, others made their own at home. The soap used in household cleaning and laundry activities was generally produced at home using lye made from wood ashes and animal fats from cooking. Many preferred the finer imported soaps offered by the local merchants. Today the Historic Area stores offer several types of soaps for sale. One recent addition is a box of three soap bars with each bar bearing an eighteenth-century sun design. The soaps are scented with lemon, wildflower, and lavender. Cakes and washballs of lavender and bayberry fragrances are also available in the stores.

Castile soap, formerly known as castle or Spanish soap, will soon be for sale in the general stores. This soap was available in white or mottled cakes; however the stores will carry only the white cakes and balls. The hard soap is made with olive oil and was considered one of the finer types available in the colonial period. It was known for its medicinal qualities and used as a base for pills and a cure for various ailments. Castile soap as well as the others sold in the Historic Area stores today were listed for le by merchants in eighteenth-century Virginia.

5/84

~ with the finest of wares ~

Educational information also needs to reach the employees of the museum—especially those who do *not* work in the store. They can be of great help by referring visitors to the store, if they know about the products there.

Accomplishing the Tasks

Do all these projects—interpretive training, product information cards, product reference books, articles for newsletters, employee flyers—sound overwhelming? Just when is the typical shop manager, already mired in retail management problems, going to accomplish these tasks?

Actually many are already being done and the only change necessary is to have the shop included in existing programs. If your museum produces a newsletter or magazine, the person responsible for it could meet briefly with the shop manager as each issue is being prepared to solicit ideas and pick up copies of any new product information.

The creation of a product reference book from scratch is a big project. Once completed, however, it takes little effort to keep the manual up to date. A brief form can help to make the process smoother and consistent. As a new product is developed or purchased, information is gathered on the form and added to the book.

Originating a product reference book is an ideal project for a college intern or apprentice. It requires scholarly skills such as writing and research, it can be done outside normal working or classroom hours, it is finite, significant, highly visible, a good learning experience, and exciting! Your local college or university is likely to have a student placement service that will delight in helping you; if not, post a notice on a jobs bulletin board in the appropriate departments (history, biology, fine arts, or whatever) plus the English and education departments. Run an ad in the student newspaper. There are usually many applicants interested in an unpaid internship, in no small part because of the popularity of museum work as a career and the difficulty of acquiring that first job without previous museum experience. Of course if you can pay something, so much the better. Payment need not be couched in terms of an hourly wage. You could offer a flat sum for the satisfactory completion of the project within a specified period of time.

In continuing praise of interns, let me suggest having one around permanently. College juniors, seniors, and graduate students are usually enthusiastic, hard-working, and fun to have in the office. They can generally spare the equivalent of one eight-hour day per week. With appropriate supervision they can take on the preparation of product information cards and even draft short newsletter articles.

Your use of volunteers need not be limited to students. Retired people are fast replacing the homemaker as the backbone of the volunteer movement. The "young old" in particular (those in their 60s and early 70s) are playing a significant role in our schools, hospitals, and cultural organizations. A retired teacher/professor could be the answer to your prayers.

NEW PRODUCT

APPROVED FOR SALE IN   Tarpleys, Greenhow

PRODUCT NAME   Fruit Basket and Stand

PRODUCT IRIS NUMBER   126201

RETAIL PRICE $86.00

SPECIFICATIONS   Height 2 3/8", Diameter 5 3/4"
Creamware

HISTORY

Creamware is a modern term for a refined earthenware known
as "cream-colour'd earthenware," "queen's ware" and "queen's
china" in the eighteenth century. Around 1760 the light-
colored pottery began to supplant white salt-glazed
stoneware. Like its predecessor, cream-colour'd earthenware
was made of a white clay mixed with ground flint but had a
lead rather than salt glaze and was fired at a much lower
temperature.

Although cream-colour'd earthenware is most closely
associated with the factory operated by Josiah Wedgwood,
other potteries working in South Staffordshire, Derbyshire,
Liverpool, Bristol and Yorkshire produced creamware. Our
fruit basket and stand is based upon an illustration in a
1783 catalogue produced by Leeds, a pottery that was
Yorkshire's answer to Wedgwood's great earthenware business
in Staffordshire. While the basket is a copy of a period
design, a modern lead-free glaze has been applied so the
product can safely be used with food.

MARKETING FEATURES

Oval circular basket with flared
sides and intertwined cord
handles. Heavily pierced.
Stand not shown.
A modern lead free glaze has
been applied so the product can
safely be used with food. Not
recommended for use in a
dishwasher or microwave.

DATE AVAILABLE
10/22/86

Writing Product Information Cards

The Ideal

Drafting copy for product information cards comes easily to some but for many it is intimidating and laborious. First, the ideal: a succinct paragraph or two containing three components. This is one I wrote years ago for an adaptation silver coin, the Spanish milled dollar.

Part One—General Historical Background

During the colonial period in America, foreign coins made of precious metals came from Spain, England, Portugal, Holland, France, and elsewhere. All were legal tender. By far the most commonly circulated coin in the Virginia colony was the Spanish milled dollar or eight reales. The coin was divided into eighths or "bits"—hence the slang "two bits" to mean a quarter of a dollar. The patterned milled edge of the coin was designed to prevent dishonest people from shaving silver from the sides unnoticed.

Part Two—Specifics of this Particular Item

This copy of a Spanish milled dollare, the original of which was minted in 1757 in Mexico City, was made by Colonial Williamsburg craftsmen using a hand-cut die to strike the impression into a cast nickel silver blank. On one side the Spanish royal crown sits above the coat of arms of Spain. On the other side, the Pillars of Hercules and the two orbs symbolize Spain's worldwide empire.

Part Three—Historical Significance of the Item

How does it relate to the museum? This should answer the question, "So what?" If all you write is a string of facts, you and your customers will miss the big picture. Put the item in the larger perspective of your museum's educational program. Here is the answer to the "So what?" question on Spanish milled dollares.

More than 20 million dollares were minted each year during the two decades before the Revolution. When the new American nation established its own coinage in 1792, it was this coin that became the basis for the American dollar.

Imari Porcelain

THE IMPORTANCE OF THE CHINA TRADE TO THE eighteenth-century colonists cannot be stressed enough. In Virginia's colonial capital as well as in England and continental Europe owning something oriental was very desirable and most fashionable households contained a few Chinese imports. Porcelain was a regularly imported product simply because at that time some of the finest porcelain in the world was made in China, at prices attractive to eighteenth-century pocketbooks. The process was a closely guarded secret and it took many decades of experimentation before the Europeans could even come close to matching the quality of oriental porcelain.

Imari was quite popular in Williamsburg during the colonial period. Archaeologists have excavated thousands of fragments of this blue and red porcelain at different sites throughout the town. Many fragments came from the site behind Wetherburn's Tavern, and several pieces of antique Imari are on display inside the Tavern.

To make Imari, each piece of porcelain is fashioned by hand. The artist then paints the design, firing the piece after each color is applied. This is the same process that was used over two centuries ago, resulting in the same exceptional quality that our ancestors enjoyed. These pieces of porcelain were made near Peking exclusively for the Colonial Williamsburg Foundation.

Bracelets

EIGHTEENTH-CENTURY silversmith die plates were used to design these dainty bracelets. The tools originally fashioned the decorative moldings so popular on silver holloware of this period.

SALTGLAZE STONEWARE

INSPIRED by fragments excavated in Williamsburg and by antiques in the Colonial Williamsburg collection, this utilitarian pottery is made today much the same way as it was in the eighteenth century.

Saltglaze stoneware requires only one firing, since the glaze is produced by the action of common salt introduced into the kiln when the pieces are partially fired and the temperature is above 2000° F. The salt chemically combines with the silica present in the clay to form a durable glaze impervious to liquids and acids. The saltglaze technique was invented by German potters in the fifteenth century and adopted by English potters in the late seventeenth century. It was brought to the colonies from England by immigrant craftsmen.

This piece of pottery was hand thrown and fired in a saltglaze kiln in the eighteenth-century manner by a local potter.

RINGS

The storekeepers, jewelers, milliners, and silversmiths of eighteenth-century Williamsburg imported significant amounts of jewelry to meet the local demand for high-fashion merchandise. Finger rings were among the items advertised frequently in the newspapers. "Fashionable diamond, topaz, emerald, saphir, amethist, and garnet mens and womens rings," boasts one pre-Revolutionary War advertisement; "a great Variety of rings" reads another.

The friendship rings and the wider band rings are typical of the "plain gold rings," the "hoop rings," and the "wedding rings" that appeared in Williamsburg shops during the latter half of the eighteenth century. The signet ring is copied from an antique in the Colonial Williamsburg collection. The enameled rings and those set with precious and semi-precious stones are adapted from eighteenth-century mourning rings also in the collection.

These examples give historical information about a *group* of products.

Part Four—Care and Cleaning of the Item

Can it go in the dishwasher? the oven? the microwave? the freezer? You may have to undertake a few experiments on your own. How do you polish it? Is the paint nontoxic? Is it suitable for young children? Does it need assembly instructions or directions to play with or use it? Be clear.

Is there any set recommended length for these information cards? No, in fact, the example above tends toward the long side. In some cases, two or three sentences may suffice.

Flint:

A small piece of very hard quartz used with the flint striker to start a fire.

Flint Striker:

Flint and steel provided an economical and portable method of starting a fire. Grip the steel across the knuckles with the left hand and hold the flint between the thumb and index finger of the right hand, with the thin edge of the flint out. Vigorously strike the flint in a downward motion across the steel. This creates sparks, which are tiny bits of steel cut by the flint and heated to their ignition temperature by the friction. Direct the sparks into the tinder to start a fire. Tinder can be several substances: one of the most successful is partially charred and crumbled bits of linen.

The Colonial Williamsburg Foundation

Pencils

CEDAR PENCILS, IMPORTED from London, were sold by many eighteenth-century colonial stores. Typical merchants' advertisements indicated that "large and small black pencils" and "red and black lead" were among the many writing supplies available. The pencils are made by placing a long piece of lead between two slices of cedar glued together. These pencils, unlike modern ones, remain in the unfinished wood and do not have erasers. To sharpen the pencil, one end was cut into a point with a knife.

The Colonial Williamsburg Foundation

Glass Bottles

BOTTLE STYLES IN THE EIGHTEENTH CENTURY changed nearly as often as clothing fashions. From a very squat profile at the beginning of the century, the wine bottle grew taller and more cylindrical toward the end. This bottle represents a typical mid-eighteenth-century shape.

The mouth of the bottle was generally sealed with a cork and wire. Most bottles were unmarked, but some carried their owners' initials or a date on a seal placed just below the shoulder. Bottles were used and re-used—and not only for wine. Williamsburg archaeologists discovered over a dozen with cherries in them buried near Wetherburn's Tavern.

Both the antiques and today's modern versions are made of soda glass. Impurities in the glass—nickle, potassium, and copper—account for the green-black color. Most such bottles were imported from England in the eighteenth century, as there were no glass blowing operations in Virginia at that time. Our modern bottles are hand blown exclusively for the Colonial Williamsburg Foundation.

These examples give historical information about a *particular* product.

Short Cuts

Ask a curator or research historian, scientist, or art historian to write product information for you. As experts, they won't need to spend the time the manager would in researching the topic. Emphasize *short* and

Eighteenth-Century Beverages To Make With Loaf Sugar

AN ARRACK PUNCH

Pour the strained Juice of two large Oranges over three-fourths of a Pound of Loaf-sugar. Add a little of the outside Peel cut in very thin Slices. Pour over it one Quart of boiling Water, one Pint of Arrack and a Pint of hot red *French* Wine. Stir together. This may be served when cold and will improve with Age.

(Arrack - An alcoholic beverage of the Near and Far East distilled from the juice of the coconut palm, or from rice and sugar fermented with the coconut juice.)

A NEGUS

Rub a small Lump of Sugar over a Lemon until it is well-flavored. Put it in a heavy Glass and add two Teaspoons of Lemon Juice. Pour into this a large Wine Glassful of Port or Sherry. Fill the Glass with fresh boiling Water and serve up with grated Nutmeg on Top.

(Recipe derived from one first popularized by Colonel Francis Negus, who died in 1732. This popular Drink was known in England and her Colonies by this Name.)

Recipes from *The Williamsburg Art of Cookery* by Helen Bullock.
The Colonial Williamsburg Foundation

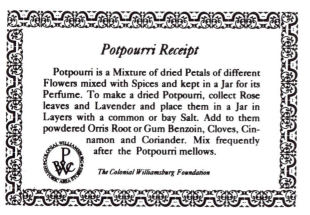

Potpourri Receipt

Potpourri is a Mixture of dried Petals of different Flowers mixed with Spices and kept in a Jar for its Perfume. To make a dried Potpourri, collect Rose leaves and Lavender and place them in a Jar in Layers with a common or bay Salt. Add to them powdered Orris Root or Gum Benzoin, Cloves, Cinnamon and Coriander. Mix frequently after the Potpourri mellows.

The Colonial Williamsburg Foundation

DELFT QUILL HOLDER

The antique prototype for this WILLIAMSBURG® delft reproduction is an English quill holder made in Liverpool about 1750.

In the eighteenth century when handwriting was admired as much for its beauty as for its legibility, goose quills were carefully shaved with a knife to form a point that would produce a fine, shaded line. One English copybook of the period, published in London about 1743 to provide examples of calligraphy for penmanship practice, urged young gentlemen to perfect their hands with the utmost care:

"Ye British Youths, our Age's Hope & Care,
You whom the next may polish, or impair;
Learn by the Pen those Talents to insure,
That fix ev'n Fortune, & from Want secure,
For Ease and Wealth, for Honour & Delight,
Your Hand's your Warrant, if you well can write.
True ease in Writing comes from Art, not Chance;
As those move easiest, who have learn'd to Dance.

24178

Use quotes or recipes from period publications. Cite modern publications as well: encyclopedias, reference books, and others.

basic. Should they evince something less than total enthusiasm, ask them to tell you a little about the item or topic, jot down relevant points, and you've all but finished. The Spanish dollare is an example of this short cut. A referral from one of the museum's curators led to a brief interview with a local Spanish professor who was also a published scholar and collector of Spanish antiques. The result was more than enough information to compose an interesting product card.

An alternative is to find an encyclopedia or authoritative book on the topic in your bookstore or library and lift an excerpt, appropriately cited of course. Don't overlook period publications such as encyclopedias, newspapers, and books from which an interesting quotation can be extracted.

General Instructions

Use recipes for items that relate to food, like kitchen utensils, dishes, drinking vessels, and food itself. There are cookbooks galore dating from the 1600s onward—no doubt several fall into your historical time frame. Most are not copyrighted or the copyright has long expired, so they are available for use as part of an product's educational information. Otherwise ask permission from the publisher and give credit.

Some words of caution: do not put the manufacturer's or craftsperson's name on a printed product card. The life of your card will be only as long as the association with that supplier and many products go through a dizzying succession of suppliers. If it is important to have the craftsperson's name on the item (and this *does* tend to enhance its perceived value) ask him or her to sign or mark the product itself, a tag attached to the item, or the back of the product card.

Print your museum's name and shop logo, if you have one, on the bottom of the card. In small print add something like, "All profits from the sale of this merchandise supports the museum's educational purposes and activities." It doesn't hurt to remind people where their money is going and it makes customers feel as if they are contributing to the museum. (They are!) However, be aware that they are *not* contributing in the eyes of the IRS; they cannot take their purchase as a tax deduction. Store staff members are occasionally asked whether the purchase constitutes a tax-deductible gift to the museum and the answer is an unequivocal "No." Do not unwittingly play into the hands of tax cheats by accepting checks made out to your museum instead of to your shop.

Always have someone review your proposed draft for your product information card. Better to deal with any objections or errors before you go through the time and expense of having something printed. When you buy products that come from the manufacturer with a product information card, run one by the appropriate expert at your museum to double check the information. The shop manager at the Science Museum of Western Virginia in Roanoke gave a copy of the pre-packaged product information that accompanied the trilobite fossils to the curator only to learn that it contained gross inaccuracies. The manager forwarded the curator's memo to the company whose president replied immediately,

CREAMWARE DOLL DISHES

Doll size dishes have long been popular with little girls. George Washington ordered a tea set from London for his step-daughter Patsy, and several Williamsburg merchants advertised such toys in the <u>Virginia Gazette</u>: "a Variety of Queen's china for children, sets complete," said one; "complete sets of china toy tea ware," said another.

Creamware, also called Queensware in honor of Queen Charlotte, is a sort of earthenware. These doll dishes were copied from antiques in the Colonial Williamsburg collection.

Earthenware

These earthenware dishes are copied from an English antique shaped by pressing the clay on a mold and decorated by using a mixture of clay and water called "slip."

thanking the curator for her comments. He changed their product information at once.

Typesetting and printing costs for these cards can mount up, and while such efforts do result in a nice, professional looking card, they are not necessary. Take short cuts here if need be. Type the information on a regular office typewriter, perhaps with a distinctive typeface, and photocopy four or eight to a sheet. Calligraphy or even exceptionally nice handwriting can work well. Experiment with a light colored paper instead of white in the copier.

Product Promotion

Promote your products, your shops, and your museum at the same time. If your museum already has a staff member with responsibility for public relations, suggest that he or she work with the store manager to broaden the scope of existing promotional efforts. If no one else handles this task, the store manager should pursue it.

Product promotion consists of getting your ideas to the public by way of the media. It begins with the development of personal contacts with reporters and writers from local, regional, and perhaps even national newspapers, magazines, television and radio stations, and with talk show hosts. That may sound intimidating, but keep in mind that, while the *Wall Street Journal* or "60 Minutes" may not be interested in your story proposal, local opportunities abound. Most reporters appreciate any ideas you have to share. Local morning or noon TV talk shows might pick up on your "show and tell," the town newspaper may run a feature or a captioned photo about your unusual new product, a radio station might interview the craftsman who makes a product for your shop. No matter how small your museum or shop, national magazines are a possibility. Look at the magazine's masthead on one of the first few pages to choose which staff member to contact. Many publications prefer to feature the small, lesser-known museums rather than the big ones that have been done to death.

Once you know the names of the appropriate people to contact locally (and a quick phone call will give you those), invite the likeliest candidates individually to the museum for lunch and a tour. Discuss how they prefer to work. Periodic press releases, accompanied by 8″ x 10″ black and white glossy photos if you can afford them, are a typical method of maintaining regular communication. Address any mailings to a specific person, not to the newspaper or magazine, or it may go straight to the circular file.

When your first attempts do not result in front page articles or even in tiny back page inserts, keep trying. Reporters are inundated with press releases and feature ideas and very few make it to air time or to print. You never know when your story idea will surface. A newspaper writer may love your idea for a feature article on a particularly talented volunteer in the shop and file it away for use next spring.

Whenever you are successful in having something published, write a brief thank you note to the reporter responsible. A second note from the museum's director or board chairman wouldn't hurt either.

Product promotion is not advertising. Promote the product's educational value with historical references or social significance. Mentioning price is probably inappropriate. Don't push a sale. Promote the product, promote the store, promote the museum and the wonderful work everyone is doing. Sales will follow.

Story ideas and photographs should be "human interest" and go beyond bare facts about a new or existing item. Here are a few ideas to get you thinking:

- An interesting craftsperson who makes something for the store.
- A handicapped citizens group that packages your merchandise.
- A talented employee or volunteer.
- A local collector who has something from the shop in his collection.
- The live plants, seeds, or horticultural items your shop sells with planting tips and their historical significance.
- Herbs: how to cook with them, how to grow and dry them.
- A recipe from your museum's cookbook. Select a good one! If people like it they may seek out the book.
- The antique you have reproduced with comparative photos of the original and the reproduction.
- Seasonal products. Not just Christmas! Remember Mother's and Father's days, graduations, Easter, Thanksgiving, June weddings, Veteran's Day, Hanukkah, Labor Day or any of the dozens of days or weeks set aside to commemorate some particular interest or person that relates to your museum's products.

Include information on interesting products in existing museum publications: newsletters to members, employee flyers, or the museum's magazine. A regular column or an occasional article makes a good, high visibility project for an intern or volunteer with research and writing skills. A photo with a descriptive caption may be enough and will likely attract more editors and readers than an article.

Examine your merchandise for its relationship to various holidays and commemorative days or themes. Valentine's Day was the catalyst for this simple promotion of heart-related products. *Photos courtesy—Colonial Williamsburg Foundation.*

5

Product Development
on a Budget

This section is based on the premise that your museum has practically no money to spend on product development, but that your shop wants to begin or extend such a program. It makes financial sense for a fledgling development program to start with those product categories that require the least amount of investment and experience, leaving the others for later pursuit.

Avoiding Disaster

Most museum stores that have had trouble with product development have made the same error. A well-meaning person with a good idea for a new product singlemindedly pursued its development, focusing on the unit price and disregarding the manufacturer's minimum orders. One case in point: a museum shop developed a charming tin box to resemble their historic mansion. There were six on the shelf when I first visited and 5,000 in the basement. At a sales rate of approximately two per week, this shop is the proud owner of a 48-year supply of tin house boxes and over $10,000 worth of inventory—all the development money the institution had to spend.

This scenario is pathetically common. There is probably not a museum shop manager in business today who doesn't have a similar tale of woe. In many cases, the disaster was inherited from the manager's predecessor and served only to convince everyone that product development was the way to wrack and ruin or at least that it was only for the rich. Neither is true.

A Rule to Follow

Never develop products that require a large purchase to get a unit cost low enough to stand an adequate markup (more on "adequate" markups in the next chapter). If it necessitates an inventory investment of more than two or three years (an overly generous length of time, by the way), *run in the other direction!*

Printed products are a prime example. Notecards, prints, stationery, and especially posters are lovely to look at but deadly to develop. Printing is a world unto itself that deserves investigation, but the quantities needed to cover start up costs and get the unit cost down to a reasonable level may be too large for the small or medium size museum. For instance, the fewest posters one would realistically print would be 2,000 to 3,000. If anticipated sales are less than two a day, 365 days a year, posters are an expensive luxury for your shop.

The Buddy System

Find one or more counterparts, similar in historic time frame to yours or with a collection, historic house, or educational purpose that resembles yours. Art museum stores can look for another museum that shares their artistic focus (American impressionism or ancient Egypt). Zoos and aquariums across the country overlap significantly in their purposes and collections; science museums can locate other institutions with kindred collections, such as space, rocks and minerals, or insects. I've often wondered why every Civil War museum shop in the country doesn't have direct and frequent contact with all the others, at least within its general region; the same with the shops of every railroad museum, every antique car museum, every maritime museum, every air and space museum, every aquarium, every botanical garden, every zoo—you get the idea. Certainly there is some contact between many of these similar institutions, but there is very little between their shops. Working together on developing items that similar shops can share saves time, money, inventory, and aggravation. List everyone's product needs and see what the group has in common. A cookbook? Develop a recipe book of shared historical recipes from each museum. A doll? Create one clothed in period costume and share the minimum order. Cocktail napkins or beverage glasses? It is no more costly to design one with two or three historic houses (or airplanes, or Civil War generals) on it than with only one and you can split the development costs and divide the inventory. Some themes are fairly generic and can apply to most museums of a particular genre. For instance, a bookmark with a rendering of a dolphin could be developed by a group of aquarium shops. Each shop would sell the same bookmark but in a customized paper holder with their own name on it, or they could use the same paper holder that listed all their names.

Swap excess inventory. Send half of your slow-moving maps over to your partner museum store in return for some of their excess tie tacks. No money changes hands, only inventory of equal value.

Promote visits to the other shop(s). One group of three museums in Virginia located within walking distance of one another launched a very successful program where they even sold block tickets. They developed tote bags, shopping bags, and other items with their three historic buildings on them and encouraged visitors to see all three. Attendance increased everywhere. Breaking out of the suspicious siege mentality that afflicts most retail establishments benefits everyone, particularly the visitors, so share your sources, your display ideas, your product ideas, and your management successes with others.

How to get started. One way to begin is to arrange a meeting of museum store managers working within your city or within a two-hour drive. If there are many, group them into related topics, either the basic three: science, art, and history, or whatever fits your group. Collaboration is often possible between history museum stores and those of nearby art museums, children's museums, botanic gardens, natural history museums, and libraries. Occasionally there is overlap of theme or purpose between history museum stores and those in science museums, planetariums, aquariums, and zoos. Try to hold regular meetings twice a year or every quarter. Discuss product development, inventory excesses, bags and boxes, vendors, etc. Keep other stores in mind when you go to shows. Those painted wooden parrots might be just what the zoo shop in your city was looking for and the local Victorian house may be interested in that attractive line of reproduction Victorian cards and ornaments. Pick up product literature to pass along to your "partners" if you can do it without interfering with your own shopping.

Temporary Exhibit Products

Developing products that relate to temporary or travelling exhibits is unwise. Too much time and effort and money is invested in product development to waste it on merchandise that can only be sold for a few months. However, buying related merchandise already on the market is a necessity. Your museum's upcoming temporary exhibit on American samplers would suggest all sorts of reproduction kits, books, framed pictures, coloring books, and notecards; that travelling exhibit of Revolutionary War firearms due next fall would lend itself nicely to a variety of adult and children's books, activity and coloring books, flags, toys, and miniature soldiers. This merchandise should be grouped together in a prominent location for the duration of the exhibit, displayed under a special banner, poster, or sign indicating its relationship to the exhibit. Any remaining stock can be marked down to sell quickly the last week or so, with the intention of having it all gone by the exhibit's last day.

A few years ago, I learned of a disturbing merchandising practice. When the museum contracted with a private company for a travelling exhibit, it automatically committed the store to a pre-determined group of related merchandise and sometimes to a pre-set quantity. Last year I was present when a group of science museum directors were ruefully discussing their experience with a merchandising package that was part and parcel to a travelling dinosaur exhibit. They were for-profit exhibitors, not connected with another museum. The science museum shops had to take what turned out to be excessive amounts of dinosaur related products at inflated cost prices, with a no-returns policy. "We were had," admitted one director. "We had to buy their merchandise that went with the exhibit in quantities far greater than we could ever sell. Not only that, my store manager told me she could have bought the same merchandise directly from the manufacturer for much less," but everything had to come through their middleman at a considerable markup. These shops, and there were several there that had been taken advantage of by this scam, were not buying anything special that had been developed for this particular exhibit. It was nothing but regular dinosaur merchandise that they could have bought directly from any number of manufacturers at prices and quantities they could afford. The result in each case was a tremendous overstock in dinosaur products that now had to be literally given away.

Exhibit deals should not include a mandatory merchandise purchase for the shop. There is certainly nothing amiss, indeed it can be a distinct benefit, when exhibit promoters offer related merchandise to shops in museums where the exhibit is scheduled, but no shop should be forced to buy merchandise as a precondition to the exhibit.

Handcraft Product Development

Working with Craftspeople

Handcrafts are the ideal development pursuit for museum stores, particularly for those with no money to invest in product development. Working with local craftspeople has many advantages beyond the low minimum orders typically required.

A craftsperson near your institution can pay frequent visits to examine the collection, to help select a reproducible item, to transport it personally to the studio, or to return periodically to study it if necessary. When you deal with a craftsperson, there are no middlemen involved to boost the final cost, so you receive greater value for your dollar. Custom made, handcrafted products created exclusively for the museum store enhance its image.

There are definite drawbacks to working with craftspeople however, difficulties that must be recognized and overcome. Finding the right crafts-person can be time-consuming, as can dealing with the one you finally choose. Often their enthusiasm for the project results in unrealistically low price quotes. Subsequently finding themselves unable to make a profit on the original estimate, they must quote a higher figure. The store may no longer be interested in the product at the new cost level and a good idea languishes after considerable investment in time and money on both sides. When craftspeople undervalue their work, it is often due to a lack of familiarity with standard business practices, particularly overhead.

Nor do all craftspeople understand wholesaling. Some have only one price and it is the same whether they retail the item at a local craft fair or wholesale it to the shop. If you cannot persuade them to make a distinction, it is doubtful that you can afford to do business with them because they are in direct competition with you at half the price.

Retails are the sole concern of the store manager. Do not allow a craftsperson, or any vendor for that matter, to set your retail price. Never agree to pay anyone a percentage of your retail. When unsure of what to charge, some craftspeople will suggest, "I'll just take 50% of whatever you can get." With this kind of pricing, you have lost control over your profit and the craftsperson is being paid on a basis unrelated to his time and investment. What if you need to reduce the item substantially, will he take half of the reduced price or all of it? What if you can wholesale the item, will he take half of the wholesale price? Soon someone else is participating in your business decisions. Negotiate a fair price with the vendor and do not discuss retails except in general terms. "I don't think I could get more than $18 to $20 for a product like we've discussed."

Variety and handcrafts go hand in hand—theoretically, no two objects are exactly alike. The store manager or developer must know enough about the craft to be able to distinguish valid variations inherent in the process from controllable variations. A quality control check is essential with handcrafts, whereas manufactured mass-produced goods are less likely to vary within a given production run. For example, saltglaze stoneware pottery can differ considerably in color and surface texture depending on uncontrollable circumstances that occur in the kiln during the firing process. This is an allowable variation. The shape of a handcarved decoy should not vary noticeably from item to item—carving is a controllable variation.

Small craftspeople are seldom able to provide packaging because they lack storage space and investment capital. The store is probably going to have to be responsible for developing, purchasing, and storing the box if one is deemed necessary.

Finally, it goes against the creative nature of some craftspeople to reproduce the work of others or to take an interest in the repetitive nature of "production crafts." While they are delighted to make ten, fifty, or even one hundred, some lose interest after several months of repeat orders. If you anticipate large orders over a period of many months or years, this should be discussed up front.

Shop managers or developers must be alert to some of the most common pitfalls in dealing with craftspeople so that museum stores can do a better job presenting the American craftsperson to the museum-going public. It is to the advantage of all concerned that successful museum-related products be developed and sold. Such products enhance the reputation of the store, the prestige of the association with the museum benefits the craftsperson, and the public, which has come to expect the highest quality from museum stores, is given the opportunity to buy the best.

Locating Craftspeople

It cannot be overstated—a good craftsperson is very hard to find. For that matter, a mediocre craftsperson is hard to find! Haunt the real craft shows, not the ones at the local mall. Ask other craftspeople, "Who does the best work in traditional earthenware in this area?" The crafts network is strong and they usually know who is good and who is pretending. Pay for an ad in the local newspaper or ask them to run a short "news feature" (free) stating that the museum store is searching for good craftspeople to do specific kinds of work. Check the phone book in larger towns for craft guilds. If you are prepared to work long distance, advertise nationally. *The Crafts Report* is a publication to which many professional craftspeople subscribe, or consider one of the specialty magazines like *Ceramics Monthly*. A librarian can suggest appropriate publications. Check other museum stores. They may be able to refer you to someone they have dealt with or whose work they know. Ask your curators. Often they are aware of fine craftspeople through their conservation work, professional societies, and reproduction activities.

A competent craftsperson is a treasure. Once you have found one, be sensitive to the difficulties in pricing his or her wares. Discuss as specifically as you can details such as the expected turnaround time from the receipt of a purchase order to the delivery of the product, your warehouse packing requirements, any packaging expectations, what to do with damaged items, what returns for variances are acceptable, and so on. Never forget that *it is to your advantage that the craftsperson make a decent profit,* lest he soon quit producing your item or be driven out of business altogether.

International Product Development

International product development can appear alluring but it is seldom worth the trouble. The lower cost prices may entice you but the amount of additional time and dollars wasted becoming familiar with the complexities and inevitable problems involved with overseas shipping methods, clearing customs, possible quotas, insurance, quality control, currency exchange, foreign banks, and language barriers will eat up any savings and then some. If you do import merchandise from overseas, the mark up on it will need to be at least three or four times cost, maybe more, to compensate you for the added costs and effort.

Buying something already in existence from abroad poses many of the same hazards. You are infinitely better off buying foreign goods through their established import connections instead of trying the "end run" to the source. If you are determined to buy something direct that is best made overseas, foreign trade commissions, consulates, and embassies can often steer you to a good supplier in their country. A Washington D.C. or New York phone book at your library will provide enough phone numbers and addresses to get you started. Here are some phone numbers of the New York offices of several countries' consulates/trade commissions (*GR: Gift Reporter*, August 1988, p. 100):

Austria	212-265-4506
Belgium	212-586-5110
Canada	212-586-2800
Denmark	212-223-4545
France	212-541-6720
Hungary	212-752-3060
Italy	212-980-1500
Japan	212-997-0400
Netherlands	212-246-1429
Spain	212-661-4959
Sweden	212-751-5900
Switzerland	212-758-2560
Taiwan	212-532-7055
United Kingdom	212-752-8400
Germany	212-940-9200

Consignment

Consignment merchandise—some call it the answer to a museum store's prayers, others the fool's gold of retailing. What is the truth about consignment? The answer is a firm, "It depends."

The big advantage is obvious. The museum has no investment tied up in inventory of consignment merchandise. That is the *only* advantage however, and its significance must be stacked against the negatives. For the most part, consignment leads to excessive vendor control of your business. Vendors tend to run you instead of vice versa. High vendor involvement results in disputes over setting retails (who sets them, who can adjust them, and what are the ramifications of such a change with respects to the agreed-upon split?), responsibility for the product (where and how it is displayed, what happens in case of theft or damage by customers, store staff, or natural disaster?), how many your shop takes and for how long, insurance (is it covered under the store's policy or the vendor's or no one's?), and return policies. Consignment always causes bookkeeping and inventory hassles.

Several craftspeople have told me that it is typically the weaker vendors, the craftspeople who are new, inexperienced, and looking for exposure, who are willing to sell on consignment, while the more experienced, successful people are secure enough to expect a direct sale. This is probably an oversimplification but there is enough truth to it to merit consideration. Artists usually expect to work through galleries on consignment and if your shop sells original art or has an art gallery in it, consignment arrangements may be more appropriate than with the crafts.

In some cases, consignment may be worth pursuing. An Indiana art museum carries some expensive one-of-a-kind jewelry on consignment. They put a six-month time limit on it and display it out of reach under glass. It works for them. Mystic Seaport Museum in Connecticut has an art gallery that is totally on consignment, with over one million dollars in art on display. With original art, any other format is unthinkable. Not surprisingly, art museum stores carry consignment merchandise more than other museum store types.

If you decide to succumb to the lure of investment-free profits, prepare a written agreement in advance clearly setting out your rules. Clarify the issues mentioned above and stick to them. For handcrafts or other merchandise, a 60/40 retail split is customary (that's 40% for the shop). A straw poll taken in 1990 at several east coast art galleries reveals a wider range of policies. Some determine the split in separate negotiations with each artist; others have standard arrangements of 65/35, 60/40, 55/45, and 50/50. Art galleries that get a higher percentage tend to deal in contemporary art and justify their larger portion by the extra promotional expenses incurred in handling new artists. The big city art galleries in New York and other places where the cost of doing business is greater are more likely to have a 50/50 split. Whatever percentage you determine is fair for your circumstances, keep meticulous records. Carefully separate consignment goods from the rest of the merchandise before inventories.

A very experienced manager at one of the country's largest museum store complexes calls consignment "the mom and pop approach to retailing." In my opinion, unless you are dealing in original art or in very expensive crafts, consignment isn't worth the trouble it causes.

Using Your Collection for Product Development

The only place to start is at your museum. Examine the collection— all of it, not just the portion on display. Re-examine it with a curator, asking lots of background questions about manufacture, history, significance, and the collection's strong points. Jot down all the possibilities you find for reproductions and adaptations, then look again, thinking beyond the objects themselves to their design elements. Would that weather vane make an unusual brooch? Would one motif on that quilt make an attractive notecard? Is it possible to re-create that rag rug in the painting? Will your building have appeal as a watercolor?

Listen to the curator and other museum professionals. Their advice is not a hindrance, it is an asset. Most have a wish list that might overlap with yours. Does the curator need some wooden bowls like the ones described in an old inventory for the hearth cooking program? Does the interpretation department wish for some period style clothing for the school groups to try on? Does the director want a special gift to give that retiring board member? Does the fund raising staff need an inexpensive "thank you" item to send donors? Any of these can serve double duty as sales items while providing a way to get your initial order higher (and thereby drive costs down and profit margins up) and to share any development costs, not to mention the appreciation factor.

Examine rare books, keeping a sharp eye out for cookbooks, housekeeping manuals, formulas for soaps and scents, and children's literature, all of which are particularly desirable from a product standpoint. Look carefully at old prints and paintings. Pause at portraits and genre scenes that might inspire ideas for household accessories, toys, or jewelry.

Never stop examining your museum's collection. Even if you have seen everything several times, continue periodic inspections. The next time you notice that silver tureen, you may be thinking about jewelry and spot a decorative motif that would fill the bill nicely.

Some museums have little or no "collection" per se. A children's museum or a planetarium, for instance, rely more on displays and activities for learning experiences than on objects. Shops in these museums should operate along the lines of a general science museum, concentrating on merchandise that conveys scientific principles or information to children, as they usually make up the largest percentage of visitors at these institutions. Science museums with living collections, such as zoos, aquariums, and botanical gardens, are fortunate in the wide array of merchandise available that relates to their living specimens. A thorough investigation of the marketplace, primarily through trade shows, should be undertaken before considering product development. Exclusive merchandise developed for your shop should be a part of your program, but it will probably be a less significant percentage of your total. Your shop will probably do more in the way of customizing existing merchandise, as opposed to developing new products. For example, there are already scores of plush elephants on the market, making it unnecessary for any zoo shop to develop its own plush elephant, but it may want to arrange a tag or box for the elephant with Centerville Zoological Park emblazoned on it.

Before You Develop

Don't rush into developing a product without first canvassing the marketplace for similar merchandise.

Art museum shops in particular have a reasonable selection of art-related items already on the open market from which to choose. If your museum owns a Marc Chagall print, there are boxes of Chagall notecards or Chagall calendars on the market to check before you consider any product development. Exclusive items are a must, just be certain that you are not spending time and dollars developing a custom product that already exists.

No matter what your museum's focus, books will be a major component of any museum shop. It is highly probable that you can find an adequate number of books on your subject, making it unnecessary to develop your own. The goal should be to have the area's most significant selection of titles relating to your topic. Your shop should be the first place people go for titles pertaining to your subject areas. This does not necessitate stocking a large inventory of every relevant title—one of each of the more esoteric is plenty. Nor does it mean you should carry every book published on your topic. Be selective. Only choose the best. The amount of books a museum shop should carry differs so much that generalizations are meaningless. Some small, narrowly focused museums have trouble filling one shelf with related titles (Ash Lawn, home of our fifth president, cannot locate a single biography of James Monroe currently in print), while managers of general art museum shops face a frightening task of sorting through thousands of excellent books relating to fine art, art history, artists, and arts and crafts.

If you are uncomfortable selecting books for the shop, get some help from an expert. Ask your public librarian or university librarian to sit down with you and advise. A knowledgeable local book store owner-manager (not the bookstore chains) can also render this service. Write or visit other similar museum shops for their recommendations. No doubt you have already enlisted the continuous aid of the museum's curators, historians, scientists, craftspeople, art historians, musicians, architectural historians, botanists, and education specialists. They can bring your attention to new books in their field on a regular basis.

After you are thoroughly acquainted with your museum's collection, study this chapter on product categories to see whether any of the suggestions apply to your shop situation. At the risk of sounding repetitive, no idea is worth pursuing unless it solidly relates to your museum's collection or its educational purposes. In some cases, I have provided the names of vendors whom I have found capable of producing a quality product in a reliable manner, and who are interested in working with museum stores. Generally, local vendors are preferable. I receive no kickbacks, nor do I make any guarantees!

Baskets

If your museum demonstrates or discusses basketmaking or has antique baskets in period rooms, look for basketmakers. Be selective.

Baskets are made of materials that vary regionally, like grass, vines, roots, or wood. If you are short of actual antiques to examine, go to prints, paintings, or other primary sources to learn the styles and materials that were typical of your region and era.

Baskets are wonderfully popular, quite collectible, and great to use in the store as display vehicles. They do take up a lot of space in the store (or the stockroom if you over-order) and must continually compete against the flood of cheap imports that make American-made look expensive. If you decide on the low-end retail, remember that imports come with a tag or sticker on them indicating country of origin and *it is against the law to remove it.*

Consider developing decorated baskets: stamped, stained, or painted in traditional methods. These are growing in popularity with collectors. A lidded sewing basket, with or without accessories, makes a fine gift, as do small baskets with dried herbs or flowers in them.

Native American baskets are in a class by themselves. Principally sold in specialty shops and museum stores west of the Mississippi, their scarcity and exceptional artistry seem to elevate them above "craft" to "art."

They are priced accordingly. Not surprisingly, this pricey market is being invaded by foreign (central American and South American) imitations and forgeries, so the inexperienced buyer needs to exercise great care when dealing with representatives of alleged American Indian basketmakers. After all, "American Indian" could mean South American Indian and a "native American" could refer to a native Central American. The Indian Arts and Crafts Association was formed in 1974 to help buyers and product developers locate reliable sellers of United States Native American Indian arts and crafts. This group also sponsors at least two wholesale markets each year, usually one in Denver and one in Arizona, where one can be assured of finding genuine baskets, pottery, textiles, jewelry, and other traditional Indian goods. Write 4215 Lead Avenue SE, Albuquerque, NM 87108 or call 505-265-9149 for details and their informative brochures. Also contact the Indian Arts and Crafts Board, US Department of the Interior, Room 4004, Main Interior Building, Washington, D.C. or call them at 202-208-3773 for information.

Red Bird Mission Crafts (Box 15, Queendale, Beverly, KY 40913; 606-598-2709) provides the marketing for many Appalachian Mountain basketmakers. Their products include creek willow, honeysuckle, white split oak, and grapevine baskets, all traditional in their styling.

Making their own baskets may appeal to your visitors. Wildwoods Basketry (3554 Paul Sweet Rd., Santa Cruz, CA 95065) sells moderately priced kits for several traditional basket styles. Each includes illustrated instructions and all necessary materials.

Candles

Candles usually generate brisk sales and it is easy to find people at craft shows to make them for your shop. If your museum demonstrates, exhibits, or interprets candlemaking or if it represents an era when candles were a significant source of light, this can relate well. Although most are made with paraffin or stearic acid today, traditionally oriented craftspeople will use real bayberry or beeswax on request, making candles different from the manufactured ones available everywhere.

Molded or dipped? The public prefers dipped and the pairs make an attractive display hung over a nail or peg. But molded candles and the candlemolds themselves are worth trying, as are kits for the do-it-yourself crowd. Some cotton wicking, a tin mold, a pound of beeswax, and brief instructions can make an enjoyable creative project for a school group or for adults.

Consider interpretive candles molded in the form of your historic house or other significant shape. The one-time cost for a mold is not overwhelming. Some companies stock hundreds of ready-made molds, one of which may relate to your circumstances. A craftsperson who makes candles may share his sources for supplies with you or you could contact the Association of Crafts and Creative Industries at P.O. Box 2188, Zanesville, OH 43702 for their suppliers directory. There is a small charge for this, call 614-452-4541 for details.[1] One supplier of waxes and molds is Candle Craft Supplies, 15106 10th Avenue SW, Seattle, WA 98166.

Ceramics

Ceramics is a very broad category, one that has application to nearly every museum store in the country. Before developing any ceramic item, learn something about this craft. Do you need a craftsperson who can cast creamware, press mold plates, throw stoneware mugs, or apply sprigs? Do you want porcelain, stoneware, or earthenware? What sort of glaze, what kind of decorating techniques are required? Ceramics are complicated but even a superficial overview will help immensely in developing an authentic product.

Appropriate concessions must be made when working with ceramics. Clay differs from region to region, even within the same clay pit. It reacts differently to firing. It shrinks differently. Certain glazes and coloring agents that were common in past centuries are known to be dangerous or poisonous today. You must be prepared to accept some degree of variation in handcrafted ceramics, more so than in any other product category.

Consider reproducing or adapting such products as cups and saucers, mugs, figurines, vases, tiles, small containers, inkwells, small dishes and bowls, doll or miniature china. Utilitarian stoneware and earthenware are experiencing a surge of appreciation today. Think of interpretive products made of clay: small ceramic houses and ornaments for example. Believe it or not, there *are* such things as quality mugs, ashtrays, and souvenir plates and tiles, if *you* supply the quality!

Several companies, some international, produce historical ceramics—Mottahedeh, Wedgwood, Royal Doulton, Foreign Advisory, Rowe Pottery, and English Faire to name a few. They reproduce for various museum programs so check their offerings for merchandise appropriate to your period or similar to your antiques. Their merchandise is apt to be a bit pricey and minimum orders may be high—certainly more so than with local handcrafts—but they could add a needed dimension to your shop.

Mottahedeh and Company (porcelain, other)
225 Fifth Avenue
New York, NY 10010
212-685-3050

Rowe Pottery Works, Inc. (stoneware)
404 England Street
Cambridge, WI 53523
800-356-POTS

Jensen Turnage Pottery (porcelain, earthenware)
8529 Hicks Island
Lanexa, VA 23089
804-566-1989

Foreign Advisory Service Corp. (delft, other)
P.O. Box 549, Polks Road
Princess Anne, MD 21853
301-651-0600

English Faire (staffordshire repros)
701 East Bay Street
Charleston, SC 29403
800-826-4473

Holdcroft Stoneware Co. (saltglaze stoneware)
Rt. 1, Box 130, Holdcroft
Charles City, VA 23030
804-829-5665

Food and Beverages

Your shop might be suited to selling fresh baked goods if your museum demonstrates baking like Old Salem or Colonial Williamsburg. Check period cookbooks and manuscripts for appropriate recipes. Baked goods are fraught with problems, however, so approach with caution. Spoilage, pests, and health department regulations make this product category more difficult than it would seem.

Nonspoiling foods can be profitable, related, and much appreciated by the visitor. Jellies and preserves, pickles, and syrups made the old-fashioned way are available from small local operations, craftspeople, or a "homemaker business."[2] Stoneground meals are available from small mills around the country but avoid them unless your shop has refrigeration capacity. The amount thrown out due to insect infestation will more than consume your profits.

History museum shops are in a perfect position to offer period candies since most nineteenth-century confections and some from the eighteenth century are still being made today. Licorice sticks, rock candy, dried fruits, horehound, benne brittle, nonpareils, chocolate covered almonds, and marzipan are among the eighteenth-century varieties that may have been available in your area. The assortment possibilities are greater for the nineteenth century: add licorice, candy sticks, peppermint, gumballs, and chocolate to the list.

Some candies can be purchased in bulk at significant savings if your shop has the staff available to weigh, count, bag, or wrap them. If employees handle unwrapped food the shop manager needs to check with the area health department for permit requirements. It is likely that the employees will have to attend a short class to become certified food handlers.

> William Bernstein Company, Inc.
> 15 Park Row
> New York, NY 10038
> 212-233-5922
> *Licorice sticks, vanilla beans,*
>   *cloves, herbs & spices,*
>   *potpourri ingredients.*
>
> Wythe-Will Distributing Co.
> P.O. Box 8, Route 60
> Lightfoot, VA 23090
> 804-565-0352
> *Rock candy, period candies.*

Include a recipe, modern or historic or both, with any food related object you sell: bowls, kitchenware, rolling pins, copper pans, candy dishes, cookie cutters, etc.

Serving beverages is better left to the cafeteria, but bottles of cider and packages of tea or coffee with a historical relationship to your museum can be profitable. One firm, Pelican Bay Ltd. (639 Chestnut St., Clearwater, FL 34616; 800-826-8982) will custom package historical beverage mixes like mint juleps, wassail, glogg, and sangria, for your museum shop. Another, First Colony Coffee and Tea Co., Inc. (204–222 West 22 Street, Norfolk, VA 23517; 804-446-8555) wholesales historical blends of teas and coffees packaged with historical information cards.

The interest in wine in museum stores is growing. Monticello has had some success with its custom labeled bottles of Virginia wines but it has a strong historical tie-in with Jefferson and his vineyards that few other museums enjoy. Because of the complications and up-front costs involved in obtaining a liquor license and designing and getting federal approval for a label, and because of the potential for controversy over selling alcohol, such a product is probably better left to others, or at least to programs with a strong track record.

Furniture

At first glance this may seem like an unlikely category for all but the largest history/decorative arts museum. There are several notable furniture reproduction programs: Baker has relationships with Colonial Williamsburg and Historic Charleston, Kindel with Winterthur and the National Trust, smaller Eldred Wheeler Co. works with the Abby Aldrich Rockefeller Folk Art Center. Here again, products already in production may suit your sales program if you feel that furniture has a place there.

Regional craftspeople and small workshops can copy one or two of your museum's antiques on a contract basis. Start modestly: a small-scaled chest, a tool box that can be used as an end table or coffee table, a lap desk, doll furniture, shelves, a mirror, a candlebox, or a spoonrack could be relatively simple and inexpensive places to start. Children's furniture—chairs, cradles, and high chairs—appeals to everyone. Check with your museum's curators and tour guides to see whether there are any items of particular significance or that visitors regularly admire.

If you graduate to larger pieces, consider chests, pie safes, and corner cupboards. Informal country pieces and painted or decorated furniture are very popular now and interest in things Victorian is growing. I have been surprised at how many quality Windsor chair makers I have encountered at craft shows during the past few years. Museums located in parts of the country where furniture craftsmanship is a tradition, like the Carolinas or Pennsylvania, are lucky to have many small workshops in their backyards. Others may have to look a little harder or farther to find one.

Glass

Glassblowers interested in traditional work are rare and manufacturers capable of doing such work are likely to require too high a minimum order for most museum stores. If you are fortunate enough to locate a supplier, consider reproducing or adapting wine bottles, medicine bottles, glasses, vases, pitchers, sugar & creamer sets, paperweights, and small dishes, bowls and plates.

Horticultural Materials

This category can do wonders for your shop's appearance, authenticity, and profits. Bunches of dried herbs, live plants, seeds and bulbs, garden kits, and dried flowers are all worth considering, particularly if the museum shows a period herb, flower, or vegetable garden or has a greenhouse.

Dried herbs and flowers are fragile and therefore best obtained locally to minimize shipping damage. This is another product ideally suited to a "homemaker business."[2] Seeds and bulbs can be ordered in bulk and packaged by a sheltered workshop. Be sure to comply with your state's laws on dating seed packages.

Plants and trees take a lot of care and are probably not worth the trouble but if you have the outdoor space to run a seasonal project or a once-a-year sale, either could be feasible. A local nursery could help with this sort of project. This is a natural focus not only for the botanical garden shops or nature centers, but also for a science museum or natural history museum that involves botany, an agricultural museum, a county historical society that includes the natural history of the county, and a historic house with significant gardens. For years the small shop at Berkeley Plantation in Virginia has prospered selling small boxwoods. At the other extreme, in Delaware, Winterthur Museum and Gardens runs a large scale sales operation offering a remarkable array of flowering trees, shrubs, and flowers, along with such garden accessories as bird baths, fountains, bird houses, containers, and outdoor furniture.

The biggest problem with seeds and bulbs is that the seasons are backward: when the tulips are in bloom and interest peaks, you have no product to sell; when the bulbs are available for planting, there are no tulips blooming in the garden to excite visitors. Overcome this as best you can by taking orders in the spring or by forcing bulbs to bloom indoors in the fall. Another difficulty arises from the "dated" nature of the product. Leftovers cannot be held to sell next year. At the end of planting season, plant them yourself in the museum's garden or give them away to employees to plant at home rather than throw them out. You *can* try to sell seeds the next year, but the germination percent will be off drastically. Customers know this and show little interest in last year's seeds, regardless of the attractive price.

Farm museums no doubt realize that crops like tobacco, flax, and cotton can be fascinating to city folks and suburbanites. Shops should note that such seeds may be even more desirable than traditional flower seeds, especially for school projects. Orchards on your property can make fruit trees a good related item. Develop detailed instructions for the planting and care of your seeds and live plants. Protect the customer from purchasing an outdoor plant or tree that won't grow in his part of the country. Note on the product information which climate zones are appropriate for each specimen.

Sell related products with your horticultural materials: bowls, vases, jars, flowerpots, watering cans, and herbal cookbooks. Combine them for a display or group together on the shelves. A packet of seeds may not be terribly "gifty" but packaging it with an attractive vase and product information will make it so.

Jewelry

Do not expect much of the antique jewelry in your museum's collection to be reproducible or salable but do examine all possibilities. A talented craftsperson can copy certain types of jewelry. Rings are probably the easiest item to reproduce from antiques; the drawback is the inventory necessary to fit all size fingers.

Most of your jewelry will of necessity fall within the "interpretations" category. You may spy an attractive shell motif on a silver salver and transform it into a brooch and earrings. Other three-dimensional designs can provide similar inspiration. Don't overlook the portraits in the collection when scouting for jewelry ideas. An appealing cross pendant or stickpin shown in the portrait of an original resident of your house or town can be transformed into an authentic "creation"; so can renderings in a jeweler's design book or an old advertisement. Two companies, Liberty Workshops (30 Wensley Drive, Great Neck, NY 11021; 516-487-0457) and Design Master Associates (P.O. Box 212, Williamsburg, VA 23187; 804-565-2500) design and produce custom jewelry for museums and package them nicely with historical information. Liberty distributes to museum shops throughout the country; Design Master products are available exclusively to your museum shop.

Some large jewelry companies have a comprehensive selection of chains and charms. Almost certainly one of them will be appropriate to your historical time frame or collection. A charm in the shape of the state in which your museum is located does NOT relate to your museum, but surely some of the thousands of existing designs will. (Maybe if your museum is the New York State Museum in Albany, a charm of the state of New York *would* relate, but relationship is established by your museum's mission, not by the state in which it happens to be situated.) Several charm companies can make a custom charm for you, usually for a reasonable minimum order with no mold charges. This may be worth pursuing if you have something so unusual that it is unavailable anywhere else. Charm bracelets tend to bounce in and out of fashion. Being "out" does not necessarily mean your shop should discontinue them; it does mean to be conservative about purchases.

Souvenir pewter or silver spoons don't have to be tacky, although most of them are. Remember that souvenir spoons with your state or museum's name or logo are NOT related products. A period style spoon or one with an educational relationship to the museum's building or collection can relate, and reproductions are always excellent if prototypes exist.

A good project for the program with some money to invest and a good track record is reproduction coins. Copied in copper or adapted in "nickel silver" for silver coins or in "new gold" for gold ones, these are tremendously popular, inexpensive, and educational. They lend themselves to a host of other products such as keychains, jewelry, or paperweights (the coin encased in lucite). The Colonial Williamsburg Foundation reproduces coins for their shops and for other museums. Contact the Silversmith Production Shop (P.O. Box C, Williamsburg, VA 23187) for current information.

Metals: Brass and Silver

Developing sterling silver and brass products is better left for the distant future. Silver items are simply too expensive to be worth development time and money, at least in the early stages of a shop's development work. Brass foundries are few and custom products are difficult to make at a salable price. Virginia Metalcrafters (1010 East Main Street, Waynesboro, VA 22980; 703-949-9400) and Baldwin Brass (841 Wyomissing Blvd., Box 82, Reading, PA 19603) are two large companies with period style items and of course there are others. With Virginia Metalcrafters, minimum opening orders can vary regionally from $300 to $1,000, so you may find yourself priced out before you start. (Subsequent minimum orders are much less.) Examine the product lines of these two and of any other brass companies for related items if you feel that brass would be a good addition to your merchandise mix.

Metals: Pewter, Copper, Tin, and Iron

Pewter is popular, inexpensive (relative to silver and brass at least), and can be purchased from companies like Kirk-Stieff (800 Wyman Park Drive, Baltimore, MD 21211) that manufacture traditional styles and museum reproductions. Small craftspeople are hard to come by in this field.

Proven sellers in pewter include spoons, candlesticks, small bowls, cast objects like animals or figures, and small cups that can double as punch cups and baby gifts. If your museum's collection includes any of these items, copying them is worth considering IF you can locate a local manufacturer or craftsperson.

Copper and tin are experiencing a surge of interest these days. Copper kitchenware like molds, kettles, and pans are likely to sell well, particularly if your museum uses them in its kitchen or cooking program.

Tin is becoming very collectible: antiques that could be had for a few dollars ten years ago command hundreds today, creating a market for reproductions (and, unfortunately, fakes). Tin cookie cutters are "hot." Candle molds, coffee pots, cups and mugs, and sconces have been strong sellers and painted tin (A.K.A. tole) is rather trendy thanks to the surge of interest in the "country" look. Be sure that the craftsperson from whom you buy is using pure tin solder, not lead, on products that might hold food or beverages. I know of one crafts family, the Cuklas of Hammersong Country Tinware (221 South Potomac Street, Boonsboro, MD 21713; 301-432-4320) that uses eighteenth- and nineteenth-century tools to fashion their wares, turning out true collector's items.

Wrought iron (really wrought steel nowadays) is a good category for product development. Mediocre blacksmiths abound and good ones are out there if you look hard. You are better off locating someone fairly local as shipping costs on wrought iron can amount to more than the wrought iron. Stay away from developing cast iron products for now. There are cast iron kettles and kitchenware, irons, and firebacks galore on the market already and developing your own may be an expensive redundancy.

With curatorial assistance select a simple iron object with which to begin. Nails, hooks, brackets, or horseshoes are good starter projects. Work up to kitchen utensils, fireplace tools, footscrapers, candlesticks, and the more elaborate items.

Maintaining the finish is a serious concern for all metals, but especially for iron/steel which rusts so quickly. Accompanying product literature must include instructions for polishing, cleaning, and outdoor care. A wax, oil, or paint coating on the iron will retard rust formation while in stock or in the store but further instructions are obligatory.

Paper: Postcards, Notecards, Prints, and Posters

The cost of anything made of paper has skyrocketed in the last few years and the nature of printing is such that large quantities are needed to offset initial expenses. These two facts suggest that ideas for printed products are best reserved for the future.

Don't misunderstand—paper products are great for museum stores, probably the most educational, most related, most profitable product category of all. But don't venture into paper first, start with something that involves less investment and less expertise and when you have a little more money and a successful track record, forge ahead into the printer's world.

Certain printed products are unavoidable from the start: all museums need an assortment of postcards. Increase your assortment through the buddy system; exchange a few hundred of your postcards for an equal amount from a nearby museum, thereby increasing you selection and promoting mutual visitation without adding to your inventory dollars. When creating new postcards, consider locating an amateur photographer willing to donate a few hours or to work for a small honorarium. One eastern zoological park found a talented college student who spent his afternoon photographing the animals. The student received a small fee and his first professional job for his portfolio; the zoo got several decent pictures to use for postcards and notecards. Don't know of a local postcard printer? Call any printer and ask who does postcards in your area or look on the back of existing postcards for a name. One quality company that deals with a number of medium size museum stores is Herbert K. Barnett, 3995 Mount Royal Blvd., Allison Park, PA 15101; 412-486-7172.

It is seldom feasible to produce a postcard of a temporary exhibit. Cards must be timeless which is why people or cars should never be included in the photography. Hairstyles, hem lines, and other fashion indicators date a picture too quickly.

Notecards are reliable sellers and are particularly educational when information is printed on the back. If expense deters you from proceeding, think about developing notecards bearing images from several museums in your area. Dividing the inventory and start up costs three or four ways makes this type of product manageable for even the smallest establishment.

One midwestern museum store group hired local talent to do pen and ink sketches of four separate historic houses in their city. The group purchased the drawings outright to preserve their ability to use them for future projects without renegotiating with the artist each time. The members elected to do this first notecard project in black and white to keep printing costs low, even though they were aware that color sells better. They got bids from two local printers, asked for the printer's assistance in selecting an appropriate paper, and printed enough for 1000 boxes (five of each of the four sketches for a total of twenty per box). A short history of each house was written for the back. The box was selected from among the standard sizes available at a nearby package manufacturer. A community sheltered workshop sorted the notecards, counted the envelopes, boxed them, applied the printed box label, and delivered 1/4 of the order to each museum shop. The shop manager coordinating this project paid all the bills (artist, printer, box, typesetter, label, workshop) and billed the other three for their share when the project was complete. Each shop started with 250 boxes, agreeing that whichever shop sold out first would purchase from the shop that had the most left until all were ready to reorder. The second order should cost considerably less since the artist, typesetter, and some of the printing charges will not be repeated. If I had been involved, I probably would have recommended that the cards and the box be in color and that the box design be a bit more sophisticated. This would have brought the retail up, but the price they had was too low. One has only to look through some of the big museum's mail order brochures to see what a nice box of notecards is fetching these days, and then aim to stay at that or a bit under. But all in all, the effort was laudatory, and the product did sell fairly well. The sad part of the story is that no further joint development projects were attempted after the woman who had organized it (and done the lion's share of the work) moved on.

Reproductions of prints, maps, and paintings in the collection should not be undertaken without some market research. Beware of selecting on the basis of one person's likes and dislikes. Items that sell well are usually colored and have a strong appeal to an identifiable buying group, such as parents for children (used as baby gifts or in children's bedrooms or bathrooms), cooks (food and kitchen subjects and botanicals hung in the kitchen), professional groups (lawyers, teachers, architects, dentists, nurse, doctors, etc.), and sports enthusiasts (golf, hunting, tennis, horses). Humorous topics can have wide appeal and occasionally you can take advantage of a trendy subject like the Metropolitan's product line focusing on cats. When the painting or print is attractive and has one of these appeals, it is more likely to succeed. Consider offering your prints framed as well as unframed for a higher price point item.

Many history museums and historical societies have significant photography collections that contain old pictures of the town or region. These can be very appealing and educational sales items when reproduced and framed. The Valentine Museum in Richmond, Virginia, noted for its extensive photograph collection, selected several easily recognizable scenes of old Richmond, and matted and framed them in an inexpensive contemporary manner. It is a peerless product. It is attractive and reasonably priced, fits into any home or office, appeals to virtually every segment of the adult population currently residing in Richmond or originally from the area, has a direct relationship to the collection, is highly educational, and is squarely in line with the museum's mission, which involves the interpretation of the history of the Richmond area.

Reproducing a significant map in your collection may be unnecessary. The same map or one similar to it in subject and date may already be available. Historic Urban Plans (Box 276, Ithaca, NY 14851; 607-273-4695) published excellent quality colonial and nineteenth-century reproduction maps at reasonable prices, with something for nearly every state in the U.S. as well as some early maps of Canada and the Caribbean. Every history museum shop should browse through this catalog for related maps and views. If your museum has an unusual map that will appeal to visitors (the appeal usually comes from a map that shows the area where they live), you may have a popular sales item. Colored maps, like colored prints, sell better than black and white.

After the selection process comes the printing. Start by learning the printer's language. Obtain a copy of *Pocket Pal* published by International Paper Company. It is available through most printers or ad agencies or can be ordered from Pocket Pal Books, P.O. Box 100, Church Street Station, New York, NY 10046. The *Pocket Pal,* updated every few years, will help you deal with your printer and understand how to structure a job in the most advantageous manner.

Shops that already have assorted notecards should consider packaging them for different purposes. Suppose that in a box of assorted notecards there is a snow scene and a painting of a mother with her baby. Print these two images separately and pack them in tens for Christmas cards and baby announcements. No greeting inside is the safest course, in fact, many people prefer the blank space for their own message or invitation. Without a message to limit its use, the snow scene could be used as a Christmas card, a Hanukkah greeting, a party invitation, or a thank you note; the package of mother-and-baby cards could be used for new baby announcements, shower invitations, or thank you notes. There is a distinct trend toward more sophisticated baby cards, attributed to the increase in the average age of women giving birth and the higher income level of these "older" parents.

Consider multiple uses for the color separation of a popular image. When the DeWitt Wallace Gallery in Williamsburg found that its best selling postcard was the detail of a genre painting showing a kitten playing with string, it used the same image for a notecard and for the cover of a small blank book.

Make certain your envelopes fall within the standard size mandated by postal regulations. An envelope that is not "machineable," explains the post office, is subject to a surcharge. Customers forced to go to the trouble of a visit to the post office and the expense of additional postage will not likely return for more.

The fast-growing field of paper party goods has captured the interest of many large museum reproduction programs. This is an interpretive category that uses designs from antiques, artifacts, or art objects to decorate a coordinated line of paper napkins, cocktail napkins, party invitations, paper plates, cups, tablecloths, and gift bags.[3] This type of product should probably wait until the easier and less expensive development work is completed. There are good manufacturers around the country but minimum orders are usually high. Unless a manufacturer is willing to enter a licensing agreement with your museum, the start up costs are probably prohibitive. This relatively new industry has its own monthly trade publication called "Party and Paper Retailer" (500 Summer St., Suite 300, Stamford, CT 06901; 203-964-0900).

Posters are simply out of reach for stores with modest traffic. For one thing, printing fewer than 2,000 is not economically worthwhile; for another, the cost of good photography or artwork and design is substantial. While students, amateurs, and volunteers can be very useful in certain types of product development, poster design in NOT the place to economize this way. A knowledgeable, experienced, professional designer who specializes in this sort of work is a must. Creating a poster is akin to creating original art—a good one that will sell well and do justice to your museum's reputation is probably not going to come about by enlarging an existing color transparency and placing the museum's name in big letters beneath it (although it *has* happened). Keep in mind that to sell posters, a store needs a selection, at least three, preferable six or more. The markup on posters is what lures many but this markup, roughly four to twelve times the unit cost, reflects the considerable investment in time, money, and inventory that was made for each one.

In the real world however, posters are considered a prestige item and it often happens that the museum wants one or several regardless of the business aspects. At one Virginia museum where the shop was in the planning stages, the Board insisted on spending one-third of the merchandise seed money to develop a poster that was unnecessary by any measure other than ego. If a premature poster deal is imposed upon the store, first try to work the costs into the budget for the upcoming exhibit or event to which it relates, including poster costs as part of the marketing plan. Some of the run can be used for pre-event publicity, the rest can be purchased by the shop as inventory. Ideally the shop buys only what it realistically expects to sell within the allotted time span. I know of one museum that, when soliciting grant money to underwrite special exhibits, routinely includes the development cost of one poster in the total.

Consider looking outside the museum for financial assistance for posters. Joanna Smith, the shop manager at the Stonewall Jackson House in Lexington, Virginia was able to parlay her good customer relations into some free product development. A former teacher, she has maintained a good relationship for years with Civil War buffs all over the country, especially book collectors. "I let them know when out-of-print books become available and when new titles come on the market; they alert me to look for certain titles." When she wanted to create a poster from a Stonewall Jackson portrait but didn't have the funds, she called a Jackson admirer in Texas and asked for a sizeable donation. She got it, and the poster bears a discrete inscription at the bottom crediting the donor.

Now it goes without saying that store managers should clear such forays into fundraising with their directors, but this is an area that deserves more thought. Managers with strong relationships with the business community and with their customers have an opportunity to use that good will in a substantive way to help with store projects. Remember—all they can do to you is say No.

Publications

Publications should definitely be reserved for those museum stores with a full-time development staff, several thousand dollars to invest, and an established wholesale network to help move the inventory. However, the museum itself, if not the store, is likely to enter the world of publishing in pursuit of its educational goals, so the issue is not so easily dismissed. The best publishing option is for the museum to co-publish with a university press or a for-profit publisher who will produce the book and sell it through its regular channels. However, no publisher is likely to take on your guidebook, exhibit catalog, or books with limited appeal. If the museum feels that these are important to the achievement of their educational mission (and most do) then the museum will have to foot the bill alone.

Some commercial publishers like Dover will develop a product for a museum in return for the rights to that product. This is like licensing without the royalties and it is not recommended. But realistically, it may be the only way for a small museum to get a product and the choice could boil down to an unfavorable deal with a product versus no product at all.

The major complaint from store managers from museums small and large is that *they* do not generate their museum's publications yet *they* must pay the consequences. What usually happens is this: the museum publishes books, catalogs, or research reports, prints large quantities (their eyes on unit price, not total expenditure), and charges them to the store's inventory. The store manager, then, is stuck with a forty-year supply, a grossly inflated dollar inventory, and unsympathetic superiors who complain about poor inventory management. Comments like "With $50,000 tied up in inventory we just can't authorize your request for a $5,000 product development expenditure" are made all too frequently, ignoring the origin of the offending inventory. Often when the books do not sell, the store manager is held responsible even though he has no control over the retail price, the product's appearance or content, or the quantity produced.

There is no easy solution to this dilemma. That part of the museum's mission is to promote and publish research or other scholarly materials is not in dispute. Unfortunately the expertise of store management is seldom tapped during the publication process. If a knowledgeable shop manager's influence is brought to bear on the appearance, length, and retail price of the book and of the quantity ordered, a more salable product may result. Would the curator's two brief treatises do better combined into one publication? Would the paleontologist's lengthy manuscript sell better for less if broken into three smaller paperbound pamphlets rather than one hardbound volume? Color photographs are always nice, but will the extra expense bring a commensurate increase in anticipated sales? The museum has to decide what is significant enough to publish, but once that decision is reached, the store manager can help in the "packaging" and marketing of the work to maximize its sales potential.

The total inventory of the museum's publication should not be charged to the store but to a separate account. It should be paid for by the store only as it is drawn out, volume by volume. Museum publications departments should treat the store as if it were a customer and sell to the store at a regular 40% discount. As Tom Aageson, President of Mystic Seaport Museum Stores, points out, this method places the responsibility for the dollar investment with the department that made the decision to spend the money.

Whatever bookkeeping arrangements are made, the bottom line is that educational museum publishing should be done for educational purposes with no profit expectation. If the museum chooses to publish a book with the anticipation of appealing to the public at large, such as an address book with color illustrations of the museum's interiors, it should be developed by or in conjunction with the shop's product development staff, subject to the same rules and expectations as other products. Good-selling publications for well-established development programs include address books, cookbooks, blank books, coloring books, and activity books.

At some point during a meeting of your Board of Trustees or your product development group, someone is bound to say brightly, "How about a cookbook?"

Well, how about a cookbook? Many a museum store and plenty of other not-for-profit clubs and organizations derive all or most of their income from successful cookbooks. Even more have been defeated by the unexpectedly laborious process before they ever reached print; others have successfully self-published their masterpiece only to find its appeal limited to the members of their organization who, having purchased copies for themselves and their mothers-in-law, purchased no more. A direct donation of $10.00 from each member would have brought the same financial result with none of the work.

And have no illusions, it is work. But because cookbooks are a staple for many museum stores, the basics are worth considering here. First and foremost, does a cookbook relate to your institution's mission? A compilation of the trustees' favorite desserts does *not* a museum cookbook make. History museums can reprint selected period recipes or an entire book, although the appeal will be limited to hearth cooking hobbyists. Adapting historic recipes to modern kitchens is a better route, or at least print both versions side by side. A historic house, like a president's home, could devise a cookbook based on the family's recipes; a governor's mansion could compile recipes from several governors whose families lived there; a state museum could gather recipes from various parts of the state or its historic sites; a Civil War or Revolutionary War site can put together meals based on soldiers' or civilians' fare at that time.

Non-history museums will find cookbooks less obviously related, or not related at all. I've yet to come across a cookbook related to an art museum (*Mrs. Picasso's Favorite Meals* just doesn't make it), although there are probably some out there. An ethnic museum can focus on their group's native cuisine; a children's museum could publish a children's cookbook; a maritime museum could gather seafood recipes; a botanical garden might develop an herb or vegetarian theme cookbook. A nature center could even compile a short "cookbook" for the birds, highlighting the different seeds and ingredients (peanut butter, suet, etc.) that various species prefer.

Of course, any museum store can put together a top-quality cookbook unrelated to its mission, using superb recipes collected from people in town, trustees, or volunteers. The income from such an item should be tracked so that Unrelated Business Income Tax can be paid on the profits. I don't recommend this—I don't recommend developing *any* unrelated merchandise—but the option is certainly there.

Once you have decided upon your recipe source or theme, and while you are in the process of collecting and testing every one for accuracy and good results, you are ready to begin with format. One of the first major decisions that will arise is whether you can afford a full-color product. Full-color pictures come from four-color printing. Why only four colors? These are the so-called process colors: yellow, black, blue, and red (in printer-speak that's yellow, black, cyan, and magenta) that are combined for the final full-color effect. The printer works from a transparency (what we call a color slide, only larger), not from a print. The transparency is "separated" into four copies called separations, each in one of the four process colors. Then all four separations are printed separately, one on top of the other in transparent inks and voila! A full-color picture. This printing process is about three times as expensive as black and white.

The less expensive alternatives include:

1. Use no illustrations whatsoever. This is the cheapest and easiest, and really, who needs them? A great many successful cookbooks do not include pictures and while this makes them less appealing to browse through in the store, it affects the recipe not one whit.

2. Use pen and ink drawings. Perhaps you know an amateur artist who can sketch your historic house or draw attractive borders around each recipe. Keep drawings simple. Too much detail clutters the page. It is safest to draw them to the exact size they will appear on the page. That way you can avoid the minor costs of blowing up or reducing the art work. It is also easier for inexperienced artists to draw to the exact size needed, since they may be unaware of the effect that reducing or enlarging their work can have.

3. Use clip art and borders from copyright free art books. Dover Publications, Inc. produces dozens (31 East 2nd Street, Mineola, NY 11501).

4. Use existing art from old cookbooks "in the public domain," meaning that the copyright has expired.

5. Use black and white photographs. If your images are of people or places from the past, this could be charming, but

black and white pictures of food seldom look very appetizing. Just as you should exclude people or cars from postcards, exclude current photos of people, kitchen interiors, or appliances from cookbooks. This sort of image will give your publications an out-of-date look sooner than you think.

6. To give the illusion of color in your cookbook with less of an investment, consider selecting a light colored paper stock with a dark colored ink. The contrast needs to be strong or readability will be compromised. Colored ink is not significantly more expensive than black. You might even choose two colors of ink: one for the actual recipe and one for the border, sketches, or non-recipe text.

Typesetting is definitely the more attractive and professional way to go, but it costs. If financial constraints are severe, a typewriter with a clear readable typeface (not script or anything unusual) can suffice. Binding involves another expensive decision. Keep in mind that cooks prefer the book to lie flat, so spirals are best. If the book is more of a booklet, a saddle stitch binding that sews or staples the pages together at the fold works quite nicely.

The multitude of *quick printers* that have sprung up over the past few years may be acceptable for your job if your quantity needs are small, like 50 to 500. My experience, however, is that their work is markedly inferior to full-service printers who do not charge much more, if anything, on larger runs. In addition, a full-service printer will have far greater selection in paper stock: more colors, and a variety of weights and textures. He will offer a greater choice of ink colors and binding methods and will also be able to advise on format and on ways to achieve the look you desire. Do make sure that the store retains the printer's plates. As in the crafts field, owning the "tooling" gives the store the ability to get bids and switch to another printer on subsequent printings.

If you have applied for a Library of Congress number and an ISBN (International Standard Book Number) early on in the process, you can now have these printed on the reverse of the title page. Write R. R. Bowker Co., 1180 Avenue of the Americas, New York, NY 10036, sending your book's title, author (the museum's name), and the publisher (name and address of the museum). A paragraph, page, or chapter about the museum should appear prominently somewhere in the book. Copyright the book. (See chapter 9 for details on copyrighting.) If other museums share your educational theme or mission, their shops make good wholesale targets. Advertise through the appropriate museum publications. You are a publisher now, so offer a discount schedule, typically:

COPIES	DISCOUNT
1–5	20%
6–50	40%
51–250	45%
250 +	48%

It is easy to have a *No Returns* policy but many places are more willing to take the risk if you do. If your cookbook is really good—and most aren't—you could go national. Try to sell to the book chains like B. Dalton and Waldenbooks, and to wholesalers.

The best book I have seen on this topic is Sara Pitzer's *How to Write a Cook Book and Get It Published* (Writer's Digest Books, 1984). Pitzer covers self-publishing as well as commercial, and touches at length on identifying your audience, and the do's and don't's of illustrations. She has good advice formed from long experience in this field. As the creator of one small cookbook, I found myself wishing her book had been available several years earlier—it would have saved me from having to learn the hard way. Another good publication is Judy Rehmel's *So, You Want to Write a Cookbook!* (1982) available from Box 1002, Richmond, Indiana 47374. Study both the minute someone chirps, "How about a cookbook?"

Do not be cajoled into developing a dated product. Wall calendars and engagement calendars are lovely and prestigious but very unforgiving. The market is flooded—surely one can be found that relates to your museum. If you simply *must* have a wall calendar, check into printing a lovely color photograph and attaching a stock calendar pad to the bottom. Printing costs for the calendar part are nil; you buy only what you want and can buy more if you run low. Discard extras when they pass out-of-date (they are quite inexpensive) or rip off and replace with a current calendar if need be. Generic calendar pads should not be hard to locate, but if you have trouble, try the Old Print Factory (P.O. Box 498, New Baltimore, MI 48047; 313-749-9498).

If your shop sells slides, assemble a set of 20 or so and package them in a sleeve with a script for home viewing or club lectures.

Finally, contact museums similar to yours and find out what they are publishing. Maybe you can work out an excess inventory trade or cooperate on future publications.

Soaps and Scents

Soaps and scents are appropriate for most history museums. To develop an authentic product look in period cookbooks and household management books for soap recipes, perfume formulas, and sachet or pomander descriptions. Soaps molded in the form of your historic house or another related shape might prove popular in the interpretive category.

The ingredients for potpourri can be sold separately or premixed. Ingredients are cheap when purchased in bulk. The Whole Herb Company (250 East Blithedale Avenue., P.O. Box 1085, Mill Valley, CA 94942; 415-383-6485) is one of many companies that wholesales potpourri ingredients. You will find others at gift shows. The ingredients can be mixed according to old recipes by shop salespeople during slow times or, if you need a more reliable supply, this can be a perfect project for a sheltered workshop. These not-for-profit institutions typically hire the mentally or physically handicapped to train them for jobs in the private sector. Sheltered workshops are wonderful to deal with, not to mention reasonably priced, as long as your project can be broken down into easily manageable segments. Mixing, measuring, sorting, and packaging are all ideal. For information, call the Goodwill Industries nearest you or your state's rehabilitative services department.

Good packaging is crucial for soaps and scents. A mundane item like soap can be elevated to luxury gift status with an attractive and educational box. There are small soap manufacturers specializing in custom soaps for hotels that will make you a customized product with a box or package designed for your museum. One of these outfits, The Greenwich Bay Trading Company (216 Spencer Ave., East Greenwich, RI 02818; 401-885-0144) makes cologne, powder, and other scented products in addition to soap balls and soap bars, and they often provide custom packaging at no extra charge. Soaps are such fast selling, inexpensive items that they make a good starting point in any product development program.

Textiles: Clothing, Weaving, Needlework, and Rugs

Most museums will find that something in the textile category relates to their collection and mission. For history museums, clothing can be a strong category. One of the best sources for period style clothing, doll clothing, or modern items in the interpretive classification is a "homemaker business." Such projects are ideal for a creative seamstress and require minimal start up investment on her part for fabric and supplies.

Handsewn 100-percent-linen mob caps, reproduced from eighteenth-century antiques, are available in Colonial Williamsburg's Historic Area stores for around $20. Machine-stitched adaptations made of a cotton/polyester blend retail for less than $5. *Photo courtesy—Colonial Williamsburg Foundation.*

Good products include period style shirts, bonnets, aprons, handkerchiefs, straw hats decorated with ribbons and flowers, christening clothing, and children's apparel. J & J Millinery Ltd. (Star Route, Box 411, Gloucester Point, VA 23162; 804-642-5081) is one good source.

Several manufacturers are willing to make customized scarves and neckties but such merchandise is most likely beyond the reach of small and medium size museum stores in terms of up-front money and inventory requirements. Check into products already on the market and those licensed by other museums if you feel scarves or neckties have a place in your store.

Eighteenth- and nineteenth-century socks and hats, straw and felt, can be purchased from any number of suppliers as can patterns for period clothing. Rubie's Costume Co. Inc. (One Rubie Plaza, Richmond Hill, NY 11418; 718-739-4040) has a large selection of inexpensive period style hats; so does the Hat and Cap Exchange (Box 266, Betterton, MD 21610; 301-348-2244). Replica Stockings (1312 Long Street #102, High Point, NC 27262; 919-882-3964) carries cotton stockings. Period patterns might be a good product at a shop whose museum plays host to frequent reenactment events or living history programs. Past Patterns (P.O. Box 7587-M, Grand Rapids, MI 49510; 616-245-9456) uses antique garments in their own collection or borrowed from museums to create a wardrobe of historically accurate clothing. The company currently works within the years 1830–1949 and plans to expand to the eighteenth century soon. If you do a good business in period patterns, consider offering natural fabrics: 100 percent linens, woolens, cottons, and silks in colors, weaves, and patterns appropriate to your period.

If you can convince yourself and your superiors that T-shirts are related and educational, there are several firms that do custom work on better-than-average quality T-shirts with reasonable minimums. I confess to a long-standing prejudice against T-shirts and was prepared to condemn them all to the Realm of the Unrelated until I saw the one developed by Ann Hanson, store manager of the Nebraska State Historical Society. Its colorful depiction of four dancing Indians was taken from a Pawnee Indian pictograph on muslin that dates from 1874. With its careful replication of the muted, but strong, original colors, the image is fresh and compelling. The graphics below compliment the design instead of floating like an afterthought or detracting from the whole. It relates to the state of Nebraska, to the museum, and to the region's original inhabitants; it can broaden one's concept of Pawnee art. It served to introduce me to the character of this tribe's artistic expression. So I was wrong—there *is* such a thing as an educational, related T-shirt and I hope one day to come across another.

Photo courtesy—Nebraska State Historical Society.

The Smithsonian's T-shirts come with educational captions printed beneath the image or on the back to lend credance to their claim to educational value. Sometimes this can work but more often it comes across as pretense. However it is far preferable to putting your museum name or logo on a T-shirt, which is the usual practice in museum stores where T-shirts are offered. I have heard many people argue that this is related to the museum because it promotes the museum. That may well be true, but promoting the museum and contributing to its educational mission are two distinct goals. This sort of logo or name product has been found unrelated by the IRS, and sales of such merchandise should be tracked so that unrelated business income tax (UBIT) can be paid on the profits.

The clothing group can have a wide range in price depending upon your authenticity requirements and those of your customers. Machine-stitched products made of polyester blends occupy the low end; handsewn natural fabrics will cost considerably more and appeal only to the reenactment crowd. A good compromise is to carry both ends with a few highly authentic articles and the bulk in the lower price range.

Sewing accessories make good gifts. Several companies produce nineteenth-century style scissors and shears and one, Gingher Inc. (P.O. Box 8865, Greensboro, NC 27419; 800-GIN-GHER) also makes an eighteenth-century pair. Thread winders, needles and pins, and thimbles (metal or ceramic) are all possibilities. Because many people collect them, a thimble copied from one in your collection or from your time period is the best place to start. Don't be bogged down by sizes. Most purchasers are buying it for display or a gift and don't know the recipient's fingertip size anyway. One or two sizes, or three at the most (small, medium, and large), will suffice.

Local craftspeople are the best source for things woven: coverlets, placemats and napkins, shawls, and blankets, as well as for handspun and dyed skeins of yarns. Mountainous regions like the Appalachians and the Ozarks and areas with significant Amish population boast well-organized quilting groups that make exceptional quilts, pillows, dolls, and other handsewn work. The Hmongs, a more recent immigrant group from Southeast Asia famous for their remarkable needlework, have started up quilting groups that attend some of the major craft fairs.

A competent needleworker (ask for references at a local needlecraft supply shop) can work up a custom pattern for a counted cross stitch or needlepoint picture. A needlework design can relate to virtually any sort of museum: art museums can adapt tapestries or other images, zoos and aquariums can create jungle or underwater scenes, botanical gardens or science museums with botany exhibits have tremendous opportunities with plants and flowers, religious museums can offer beautiful needlework patterns, and children's museums can carry beginner kits. A scene of your historic house or an adaptation of your antique sampler could be very popular with the visitors. There is so much potential in this one category that it is an easy place to start. Examine both juvenile and adult possibilities. Look into crewel embroidery, knitting, crocheting, embroidery, and candlewicking products already on the market before trying to develop custom merchandise. Several companies make products derived from antique samplers. One good, if expensive, supplier is The Examplarery (P.O. Box 2554, Dearborn, MI 48123; 313-278-3282).

Another way to deal with your museum's antique sampler is to photograph it and sell it framed. I have come across this at craft shows and gift shows. The key is the quality of the photograph. It is so good that the picture acts as a trompe l'oeil, fooling your eye into thinking it is a real sampler, even when your nose is on the glass.

Rag rugs, hooked rugs, and floorcloths are experiencing a great revival. Many craftspeople produce wonderful historic patterns and would gladly copy your antique or one from a painting. At least two importers have been licensed to copy designs from eighteenth- and nineteenth-century folk art collections: Import Specialists, Inc. (82 Wall Street, New York, NY 10005) and Thomas K. Woodard (835 Madison Avenue, New York, NY 10002). Inexpensive rag rugs made from 100% natural fabrics, usually cotton, sometimes wool, are not hard to find at craft fairs. A good source is Ragpicker Rugs (Box 95, Shenandoah, PA 17976; 717-462-4229).

Toys and Games

Successfully reproducing toys from your museum's collection is not likely unless they are wooden and you can locate a craftsperson to fabricate, carve, and paint them. Even so, their cost will make them collectibles for adults rather than children's playthings. "Creations" are a possibility if your museum has little tangible to work from, so examine those prints, paintings, and period documents for ideas.

Development in the toys and games category may be better left for a later date since several manufacturers, notably Cooperman Fife and Drum (Essex Industrial Park, P.O. Box 276, Centerbrook, CT 06409; 203-767-1779), already make good period toys which they astutely package with product information for the museum store trade. It would surprise me if there was a history museum or historic site in the country that couldn't find several related products from Cooperman. Tops, whistles, hoops and sticks, ninepins, dolls, pull toys, noisemakers, and toy soldiers are but a few of the historical toys now on the market at reasonable prices. For miniature soldiers and figures, try Reeves International, Inc. (1107 Broadway, New York, NY 10010; 212-929-5412).

Dolls can be dressed in period clothing through a homemaker business. Doll accessories such as chairs, cradles, small baskets, and hats are easy to come by from craftspeople, doll supply houses, and hat companies.

Interest in miniatures ($1/12$ scale) is declining nationally but it may still be worthwhile to carry a few unusual pieces handcrafted locally for avid collectors.

Custom designed paper dolls, possibly named after the original residents of your historic house or town and dressed in period costume are an ideal product for historical information. Ask an art student to design them for the store. Paper dolls, paper soldiers, playing cards, paper games, paper houses to assemble, etc., all require printing however and for that reason are appropriate only for development programs with a few thousand dollars to invest in up-front charges and inventory. A coloring book can be a wonderfully educational sales item and because it does not involve color printing or expensive paper, it may be affordable. History museums can tell the story of their historic home, their region's settlement, or the daily life of a child of that period. Art museums have limitless opportunities to develop coloring books that promote their theme or certain exhibits. Recently there has been a delightful trend in designing creative coloring books without pictures. Instead each page has a drawing suggestion, such as an empty picture frame and the caption, "Draw a portrait of your best friend." Science museums of all sorts have many options for coloring book themes: the seashore, farm animals, conservation, flowers, tropical fish, health, insects, whatever. Always double check the marketplace first before developing such a product. With as many coloring books as there are already on dinosaurs or trains, it is unlikely your shop will need to create its own version of these. One company, Color Us America (P.O. Box 13, Colrain, MA 01340; 413-624-8845) will develop coloring postcards for your museum shore. The postcards come packaged with felt tip markers and educational information about your museum—just color and mail to Grandma! There are no up-front costs and minimums are reasonable for most medium size museum stores. If "reasonable" is still too high for your shop, consider joint development with other museums in your locale or genre.

If your museum represents the Victorian period or later, or if it offers special Christmas programs, unusual handmade tree ornaments will sell well from summer through the end of the year. Most media are suitable for ornaments: ceramics, glass, wood, needlework, metals, straw, or basket materials. Design Masters Assoc., mentioned in the Jewelry section, produces custom metal ornaments and bookmarks attractively packaged with historical (or other relevant) information. Custom ornaments that are manufactured usually require a minimum of several thousand. A group of three or four museums in your area could develop a design that incorporated all of them, like a package of four needlework ornaments, each of a different historic house, and split the order. Much to be preferred are handcrafted ornaments which generally entail low minimums and higher unit retails. German manufacturers still make some of the old-fashioned ornaments that date from the late nineteenth and early twentieth centuries. Pore over a catalog from Whitehurst Imports, Inc. (P.O. Box F, Old Greenwich, CT 06870; 203-637-4756) for ideas.

One item popular with both children and adults is the quill pen. Goose quill suppliers are harder to locate than you might think. Cooperman Fife and Drum, mentioned earlier in this section, packages its quill pens with historical information.

Anything that makes noise is a great favorite with children. History museums have done well for years with wooden fifes, drums, jew's harps, tin whistles, and signal whistles, all available with product information from Cooperman. Historic sites with a relationship to American Indians may want to examine Cooperman's reproduction arrowheads for appropriateness.

Customized pens and pencils make good pick-up items for children and adults alike. Several companies will put your design on a high quality, colorful pencil at a low cost. One excellent manufacturer is NAPPCO (One Cedar King Road, Shelbyville, TN 37160; 615-684-9820). Another is Atlas Pen and Pencil Corp. (P.O. Box 600, Hollywood, FL 33022; 800-222-8337). An easy inexpensive place to start your product development!

Museum stores on a tight budget looking for customized merchandise would do well to contact Museum Store Products Inc. (15 Roxiticus Rd., Mendham, NJ 07945). Working from your slide, postcard, photograph, or transparency, they customize magnets in various sizes and shapes. With a tiny set up charge and small minimums, these inexpensive magnets make a risk-free new product, or even good gifts, favors, prizes, or "thank-you-for-your-donation" presents for your museum. The company also offers key chains, note cards, small plastic boxes, and other items along the same lines.

Wooden Items

A good development category is woodenware, or "treen" to use the old term. Wooden kitchen utensils are inexpensive, useful, and usually related to history museums that exhibit period kitchens or operate a cooking program. Wooden spoons, scoops, rolling pins, bowls, hooks, and such are readily available from craftspeople or small manufacturing operations. A good craft fair is likely to turn up more than one potential supplier.

Cooperage (wooden buckets, piggins, butter churns, and even small barrels) can appeal to museum visitors. The inexpensive ones that are hastily made and not water tight are found on occasion at craft fairs; authentic ones are scarce and expensive. If your museum portrays a farm, house, or site from the nineteenth century or earlier, butter churns and buckets may be popular with visitors. As in the case of wrought iron, local suppliers are preferable because shipping adds so much to the cost price. Nonetheless, Ware Neck Cooperage (P.O. Box 911, Williamsburg, VA 23187) is a good supplier of top quality genuine articles if locals cannot be found.

Wooden boxes have experienced a surge of popularity in recent years. Wooden pantry boxes, sometimes called Shaker boxes, are available from a number of suppliers. One good one is Frye's Measure Mill, a firm that has been in business since the 1850s and still makes its boxes with the original water-powered machinery (RFD #1, Wilton, NH 03086; 603-654-6581). L. E. Holt in Arkansas (P.O. Box 83, Pettigrew, AR 72752; 501-677-2529) also makes a quality product and paints them as well, either solid colors or with decoration, copying your antique. Painted designs are expensive but cost does not seem to deter the avid collector.

Et Cetera

Paper band boxes are in great demand these days, and can relate to your American history museum. Cover the cardboard with reproduction wallpaper from your time period and line the inside with reproduction newsprint. Once again, local craftspeople are your best bet, but if none are available, contact Open Cupboard (P.O. Box 240, Poultney, VT 05764; 802-287-9680).

Museums with nautical ties and maritime museums may want to sell reproductions of their scrimshaw. Fortunately, ivory has been synthetically reproduced and scrimshanders who carve and etch this polymer substance are not difficult to locate at craft fairs. Be careful before you purchase from some of the larger companies: at least one refuses to mark its products, with the result that one leading American maritime museum receives frequent requests to authenticate or purchase "antique" scrimshaw that was made yesterday. No one can eradicate this sort of fraud but museum stores should avoid dealing in unmarked reproductions that are likely to end up deceiving amateur collectors. By insisting that the reproductions or merchandise they purchase have clear and permanent markings (date or manufacturer or both), museum shops can pressure these manufacturers and craftspeople into more ethical behavior.

Horn, a ubiquitous houseware for centuries until replaced by plastics, holds a particular fascination for Americans. Horn cups, horn spoons and scoops, shoe horns, horn combs, and powderhorns are appealing and educational sales items for the museum shop with a historical relationship to them. There are few American craftspeople working with horn and no large American manufacturers to my knowledge. Most of the craftspeople are powderhorn makers for whom the artistry of the decorative process is the real attraction. Such people can be found where traditional crafts are strong or by inquiring through military reenactment groups. An appealing or historically significant powderhorn in your museum's collection can be copied by a talented craftsperson, resulting in the sort of unique product a museum store likes to highlight. Its retail of several hundred dollars will not deter the serious collector or reenactment buff.

Abbey Horn of Kendal, an English company that has been in the horn trade since 1749, manufacturers utilitarian horn items copied from period antiques in its own collection and from museums. Combs, spoons, shoehorns, cutlery, scoops, buttons, and cups make up the bulk of their merchandise. Horn's light weight makes trans-Atlantic shipping affordable and cost prices are usually reasonable unless the dollar is at a particularly low point. Those with environmentally sensitive customers will be relieved to learn that the cows are slaughtered for their meat and the horn is merely a by-product. Contact Abbey Horn of Kendal Limited for details (Kent Works, Kendal, Cumbria, LA9–4RL, England).

Leather goods are often related to a history museum: pitch-lined leather drinking vessels, pitchers, and firebuckets are popular today as gifts for men. Sign of the Harness (P.O. Box 195, Lititz, PA 17543; 717-626-0797) is a good source if you cannot locate one close by.

Tobacco products can be good gifts if related to your museum. Pipe tobacco, period style pipes, and tampers are worth exploring. However, like alcohol, tobacco has become a sensitive issue that your museum may prefer to avoid. You don't want to plunge into selling tobacco, for example, if your board has recently voted to divest itself of tobacco stocks.

Notes

1. There are also several craft and hobby *supplies* shows, if you find the need for raw materials and production supplies: the Chicago Craft and Creative Industries Show and the Southwest Craft and Hobby Association Show in Dallas. Call 614-452-4541 for information on both.
2. Increasing numbers of women are starting up their own home-based businesses. According to employment analysts there are many more out there who want to start a business but don't know where to begin. This is an untapped group of potential suppliers waiting for your project suggestions. Advertise, spread your needs by word of mouth, and interview as carefully as you would for an employee. See Janice Castro, "She Calls All the Shots,"

Time, 4 July, 1988, pp. 54–57 for details on this "gold mine of human capital," the female entrepreneur.

3. Carrying gift bags as a saleable product, not a give-away, is catching on in many parts of the country. One company, Different Looks (P.O. Box 387, Berwick, PA 18603) has a line it calls "Great Masters Collection" featuring well-known paintings by Degas, Renoir, Monet, Homer, and VanGogh. If these relate to your art museum's collection or theme, look into such a product.

6

Retails

Setting the Retail Price

Congratulations on that new product! Now what will you charge for it? Setting retails is an art, not a science, and anyone who purports to have a magic formula is an amateur. The correct response to the question is: *you charge what the product is worth,* its "perceived value." Only through experience in buying and familiarity with the marketplace can a person acquire the ability to judge the value of an item and even the most experienced buyers make mistakes.

In figuring the perceived value of a product, ask yourself whether it is unique or whether you must compete with the stores down the street. Check the retails of similar products at other museum stores, locally and nationally, and at other retail shops nearby. Ask your salespeople. Their contact with the public often gives them a good perspective on price. Finally, experiment if you must: move the retail up or down and track sales at each level. Where is the market resistance point? (Take care—too much experimentation results in chaos. This is only recommended for those few products for which the retail is particularly difficult to pinpoint.)

Generally speaking, if a vendor product (one you purchased outright as opposed to one developed by the store or customized for the store) cannot stand a "keystone" markup (sometimes called a 50 percent markup or doubling the cost), you probably should not buy it. Naturally, there are exceptions, notably books, which usually come with a discount schedule beginning at 40 percent off recommended retail,[1] but for the most part, stay away from low markups *unless the educational value truly merits making an exception.*

When on a buying trip or examining a sales rep's samples in your office, play this little game: estimate the product's retail in your head before asking the cost. Did that puzzle look like a $10 retail to you? If it costs less than $5, order it; at $6 you will have to think hard whether or not you can get $12 or $13 for it. Probably best to move on. . . . Remember too that the listed cost may not be the final price. Do you still have to pay for shipping? A box? Product information?

Many managers have trouble with the math when figuring markups. Maybe formulae in the form of a quiz will help:

Quiz Question #1. Figuring the percent markup.
    The retail price of a pair of bookends is $50.00; the cost is $28.25. What is the percent markup here?
    Answer: 43.5%
    Method: $50.00 − $28.25 = $21.75
             $21.75 ÷ $50.00 = 43.5%

Quiz Question #2. Figuring the retail.
    The cost of the game is $4.50; the planned markup is 60%. What is the retail?
    Answer: $11.25
    Method: 100% − 60% = 40%
             $4.50 ÷ .40 = $11.25

Quiz Question #3. Figuring the cost.
    The retail of the doll is $35.00; the markup is 45%. What was the cost?
    Answer: $19.25
    Method: 100% − 45% = 55%
             $35.00 × .55 = $19.25

Markups can be confusing if you are not sure whether you are dealing with a percent markup based on the product's *cost* or based on the product's *retail*. For example, if an item cost $3.00 and sells for $6.00, some will call this a 100% markup (based on the cost) while others will call it a 50% markup (based on the retail).

Markup Equivalents

% MARKUP BASED ON RETAIL	% MARKUP BASED ON COST
20	25
25	33 1/3
30	43
33 1/3	50
40	66 2/3
50	100
60	150
75	300

One shop aims for a 60% markup, the other for a 150%. They share the same goal, they are merely expressing it from a different perspective.

Setting Retails for Developed Products

Setting retails for a product you have developed or customized in-house is a bit different. A developed product is one you have researched and developed from scratch, such as a linen christening gown that has been copied from an antique. A customized product is much easier, cheaper, and faster to develop, since the basic merchandise already exists. All you do is put your museum's name or whatever on it. Pencils are an excellent customized product: the manufacturer has the colored pencils which he customizes for the museum by picturing your train on the side.

In customizing or developing a product, you have become, in effect, the manufacturer, distributor, and investor as well as the retailer. As you are taking the risk of failure and monetary loss if the product flops, you need more than a regular retail markup to compensate you for these expenses and risks. How much more? Aim for three times cost and try for more. Remember the product's perceived value. Markups on developed merchandise can legitimately range up to ten times cost or more. Such markups are possible (and necessary) in printed paper merchandise, like posters, and in food prepared on the premises, such as bread baked and served in a bakery. Customized merchandise like the train pencils can often be handled in shorter production runs, meaning you need invest less in inventory; for these a three times cost markup is reasonable.

When you originally decided to develop a particular product, you should have visualized it so clearly in your mind that you could peg its retail and the potential sales volume before you started. If your goal was to develop a box of color notecards at about a $10 retail, then you are aware from the start that your manufacturing costs should come in at about $2.50. Your one-time development costs may account for another dollar or two per box, but if your manufacturing costs begin to exceed $2.50 per box, it is time to re-evaluate the project. Put fewer cards in a box? Choose a cheaper paper stock? Change to black and white? Dump notecards altogether and work on something else?

Keep abreast of the hidden costs of developing or customizing a product. Were there:

- Up-front costs for tooling, photography, artwork?
- Mailing and shipping charges?
- Unsuccessful prototypes or errors?
- Travel costs?

- Costs in developing and printing accompanying literature such as product information, directions, assembly instructions, rules for the game?
- Costs in developing the package?
- Significant amounts of staff time spent in-house for research, writing, examination, market research, etc.?

Maintain a ledger for each product, jotting down these costs as they are incurred. (It wouldn't hurt to note the vendors names and addresses here too, so that when you go to reorder three years from now, everything is handy.) For a customized product, the only extra costs are likely to be for artwork; for a developed product, the costs usually span the list. These one-time expenses need to be tracked, totalled, and amortized over the first order or the first year's estimated sales. They are not part of the ongoing costs of the product and so are not figured in to the cost price, but they need to be watched closely to prevent the product development process from spinning out of control.

The best route is to have the manufacturer or craftsperson incur the initial development costs (other than the special tools or artwork you would need in order to change vendors) because it involves less of the museum's money. If this is the case, the cost of your initial order may be higher than future orders so that the manufacturer can recoup his development expenses. Ask what the cost will be on subsequent orders and check to make certain you get it when re-order time rolls around. It is usually not dishonesty that causes vendors to continue to charge the higher initial cost on subsequent orders; sometimes the office clerical staff merely looks at previous invoices for the unit cost and uses that on the next bill.

The amount of inventory you are obligated to carry should affect the markup. For example, a shop reproduces a popular satirical print at a cost of $2,500 for 4,000 or 63 cents each. Is it reasonable to retail the item for $1.26 when the museum has a considerable sum of money tied up in inventory? And, more to the point, is the print's perceived value only $1.26? Prints are funny products—they often sell faster at a higher retail because the public perceives their value to be higher and is wary of "cheap" ones. The expense of a decent custom frame seems absurd for a print that cost $1.26! A good quality print is certainly worth $5 to $10, perhaps more depending on its size and probable use. A large formal print that is likely to be hung in the living room is worth more than a smaller juvenile print headed for the children's bathroom, even if their costs are the same. In this instance, both the perceived value of the print and the large inventory investment necessary argue for a much higher markup than a keystone markup.

Once you learn what the approximate initial investment in development costs and inventory will be, use sales estimates to test whether the investment is a smart use of museum funds. Project your sales, both retail and wholesale, at several price points. These figures will affect the decision whether or not to go ahead with the project. Base your estimates on the sales of similar items or at least on a "best guess." If you project sales of two prints a day, you will have $5^{1}/_{2}$ years' worth of inventory; at two per week, over 38 years' supply.

How Sales Projections and Inventory Affect Markup
(minimum order 4,000)

AVERAGE SALES/WEEK	AVERAGE SALES/YEAR	APPROX. INVENTORY/YEARS
40	2080	2
14 (2 per day)	730	5+
2	104	38+

Using different retails, estimate how long it will take you to repay the initial investment. At $7.50 selling two per day you will recoup the museum's money in 6 months—not bad, not great. And of course you still have 5 years of inventory tying up space. At $7.50 selling two per week it will take over 3 years—not a good use of scarce museum funds. If you feel $10.00 is a reasonable retail and that you will sell two per day, you will recoup the museum's investment in $4^{1}/_{2}$ months. At $10.00 selling only two per week it will take $2^{1}/_{2}$ years. Will retail price affect your sales rate? Usually the answer is yes, but not always. How many do you expect to sell per week with a retail of $10.00 vs. a retail of $15.00? Don't assume equal weeks unless your sales are steady throughout the year. Maybe you expect to sell twenty-five per week during the busy summer months and two per week during the slow winter season.

Psychology of Pricing

Nearly everyone is aware that there is an element of psychology in the process of setting retail prices. Make the psychology work for you.

Avoid that "dime store" feeling. Prices like $99.95 or $97.99 just sound tacky, like low-end or discounted merchandise. Round off to $95.00 or $100.00. Avoid dealing in odd pennies, even at the lowest range. $1.99 seems gimmicky. Make it $1.95 or $2.00.

Have a price point for everyone in your customer base within every product category. The goal of price pointing is having merchandise for every customer's pocketbook. Your visitor profile will give you clues about your customer types to use when planning price strategy and where the majority of your merchandise should be priced. For example, if the preponderance of your visitation is schoolchildren, most—not all—of your merchandise will carry price points under $10.00.

Watch for gaps in your pricing. I once visited a new art museum that was selling two guidebooks, one thin paperbound volume with a few black and white photos priced at $1.95 and one lovely hardbound "coffee table" book replete with color photographs priced at $49.00. Though beautiful, it was out of range for most visitors who, like myself, would gladly have spent $10.00 to 20.00 on a nice compromise.

A hypothetical maritime museum shop that carries a shell motif jewelry line has these retails on its necklaces: $3.95; 4.25; 4.95; 6.95; 9.00; 47.40; 49.00. Two big gaps could be filled: the $10–40 range and the over-$50.00 range. As it stands, the store has price pointed merchandise for children and moderately large spenders, leaving out average spending adults and the occasional big spender. One or two higher priced necklaces at, say $100–300, would do more than target that occasional big spender. Selectively displaying spectacular, unique, or expensive merchandise often has the effect of improving sales of your less expensive products. An American Indian museum store out west displays in each section (baskets, ceramics, rugs, silver jewelry) an outstanding example of that craft priced in the thousands of dollars. Along side the showpiece is the regular line of smaller handcrafted merchandise with most retails ranging from $25–300. The universal admiration of the showpiece deflects sales to its counterparts which seem very reasonable by comparison. The showpieces sell occasionally to collectors, but turnover is not their main purpose—glamorizing the affordable merchandise is.

Underpricing can kill an item as surely as overpricing. Years ago, I remember a poor-selling print with a retail of $2.95. Almost as a joke, we raised the price to $10.00, figuring that it may as well be a poor seller at $10.00 than at $2.95. Imagine the shock when sales quadrupled. We theorized that the low price had made it cheap in the customer's mind, that few people could rationalize spending money for a custom frame for something so worthless. We subsequently reexamined the retails on all the prints, raising most substantially. There was no commensurate drop in sales, rather a small increase overall.

Marking Down Retails

No need to be embarrassed. Everyone makes mistakes. Just get rid of yours as quickly as possible!

Some museum stores have a policy of no markdowns. They argue that it doesn't look good, that it damages their reputations. Since even the most exclusive retailers in the country put merchandise "on sale" for many reasons without harming their images, such concerns seem groundless.

But who needs markdowns anyway? Simply put, everyone. Old merchandise discourages your best customer, the repeat visitor. Why come again to see the same old stuff? Markdowns free up money to buy new merchandise that turns over more quickly. Dollars tied up in old stock are not earning anything for the museum.

Don't be half-hearted about marking something down. Ten percent off won't do. There is a saying, "The first markdown is the best markdown." Reduce the item by at least 25 percent. If it doesn't move quickly, try 40 percent, then 50. You can also reduce shopworn or slightly damaged goods, but here there *is* some merit to that argument about appearance and reputation. It might benefit your museum more to send such items to the people who handle school groups or to the curators if the merchandise can be used in some way. A chipped bowl can still be of use in the hearth cooking program and a shopworn map can still be studied during next week's fourth grade field trip.

Some shops have a policy of excluding reduced merchandise from further discounts, preventing museum members or employees from applying their reductions on top of the markdown. Others allow this, rationalizing that their purpose is to get rid of the merchandise quickly, not to haggle about the few instances of double discounts.

Museum Membership Discounts

Many museums large and small have membership programs which encourage the public to "join" the museum for a modest annual fee. Benefits to members usually include special events, newsletters, magazines, and a discount at the museum's shop. The amount of the discount ranges from 10 to 40 percent, with the great majority of museums offering 10 percent. If you are wondering where your museum stands on this issue, a 1985 study of selected museum stores revealed that in the smaller operations (those with sales under $125,000) 79 percent gave a 10 percent membership discount, while 17 percent gave none at all. The remaining 4 percent of museums had discounts scattered between 5, 15, and 20 percent. The picture was similar in the larger stores with 79 percent of them offering a 10 percent discount and 12 percent offering no discount at all.[2]

If your museum offers more than 10 percent, you are probably losing money. Think of it this way—after the cost of goods is deducted from a sale and the operating expenses are subtracted, your net profit could well be (depending upon what sort of operating expenses you deduct) less than 10 percent. That means every discounted sale ends up *costing you money,* not, as most administrators think, losing you a small portion of your profit. If the manager has been able to calculate the store's net profit percent, this number can show whether the discount is taking some, all, or more than the store's net profit. Even in cases where the store's net profit is significantly above 10 percent, the museum should still not offer a discount greater than 10 percent.

	REGULAR SALE	SALE TO MEMBER
Retail	$100.00	$100.00
Discount	– 0	– 10.00
Cost of item	– 50.00	– 50.00
Gross profit	50.00	40.00
Expenses (41%)	– 41.00	– 41.00
Net profit	$ 9.00	<$1.00>

It can be a sensitive issue but the effort should be made to change to a 10 percent discount if you are above this level. You really can't afford to lose money this way.

The museum director or the membership department should be apprised regularly of the extent to which the store is subsidizing the membership benefit program. Quarterly or annually, compile the total value of these discounts for your annual report because it is one reason (maybe a significant one) why profits are not greater. It always surprises me how many administrators think of the membership discount as a big favor to the store, on the assumption that the discount is luring in sales that would not have otherwise occurred. While membership discounts may bring in extra sales, and I have never seen any study proving this is so, they aren't bringing in any profits. My gut reaction is that the reverse is often true: the membership isn't bringing in sales, rather the sales are bringing in members. There are a great many people who join the museum only for the discount. A split second of math demonstrates to shoppers who intend to purchase anything costing more than $200 that the $20 membership fee with its 10 percent discount is going to pay off.

Similar efforts should be made to track the employee discount, if there is one, so the administration will be aware of its cost. Such giveaways scrape off pure profit and, while they are usually worthwhile, they need to be understood at all administrative levels so that the store's performance can be evaluated on its own merits.

If the discount is a benefit accorded all museum employees, not just those of the shop, the museum should consider transferring the cost of this benefit to the department responsible for the discount. In a few museums, the membership or development department reimburses the store for membership discounts and the personnel department reimburses for employee discounts. This is purely a paper transfer of course, no money actually changes hands. But it is a valid bookkeeping device in that it allows the department that originated the benefit to absorb its cost, and permits the store to develop an accurate financial picture. It is unfair to burden the store with losses not of its making, especially when such losses obscure the store's true performance picture. If the cost of these discounts is not transferred at your museum, be sure to track these losses diligently and note them in your financial reports to the Board or Director.

Evaluating Retails

One way to evaluate your pricing strategy is by figuring your cost of sale at regular intervals. Cost of sale is nothing more than the cost of the product sold divided by the retail. If during one year a store sold only one item and if that item cost 48 cents and retailed for $1.00, the store had a cost of sale of 48 percent that year.

$$\text{Cost} \div \text{Retail} = \text{C.O.S.}$$
$$.48 \div \$1.00 = 48\%$$

Total the cost of all products sold during the year and divide by the annual gross revenue. Usually their freight costs are added into the equation, but if these are difficult to gather, leave them out. The important thing is to be consistent from year to year, remembering that it is the ratio's change over time that indicates your improvement or problems. C.O.S. is annualized because it varies so much seasonally: more film sold in summers, more gifts in December, for example. Be sure you are dealing with the cost of the products *sold*, not the cost of the products your store *purchased* for resale during the period. There are several ways to know what was sold.

1. Your figures will not be as precise but you can use the cost of the products purchased minus the value of the inventory on hand. This can be close enough to indicate problems and trends.

(Beginning inventory + cost of goods purchased − ending inventory + freight in) ÷ Annual Gross Revenues = C.O.S. ($4,312.00 + 35,619.00 − 3,825.00 + 1,760.00) ÷ $80,889.00 = 46.8% C.O.S.

2. Point-of-sale registers are almost a necessity for accuracy in larger operations. These registers can be programmed to tell you exactly what was sold on any given day and will compute the cost of sale for a day, a week, or a month. Remember that P.O.S. terminals are only accurate if rung accurately and if the basic information by SKU (*stock keeping unit*) is accurate. This is pertinent if your operation is staffed by volunteers who work four hours every two weeks and are not as likely to retain the complexities of the procedures as someone who is there everyday.

3. Manually track your sales. For small operations, this is the best method. Either keep a list of products next to the register and make hash marks each time one is sold or write up a sales receipt listing all purchases for each customer, retaining a carbon copy for your records. Total weekly. Enter these figures on a card or computer inventory and manually calculate the inventory value and the sales at cost and retail.

P.O.S. registers, while glamorous and fun to play with, are simply not cost efficient for some stores unless the store needs *a lot* of other information or the museum itself has other needs for it. Consider your return on investment before laying out big money for a personal computer ($2,000–3,000 for a P.C. with printer; software packages can run $250–500 for the most commonly used: Lotus and WordPerfect) or P.O.S. register system. Make sure that the benefits outweigh the cost. The benefits of computerization can be significant: stores usually find they can help with purchase orders and improve their inventory turn, tieing up fewer dollars in inventory. This savings alone might pay for the machinery. Will computerizing provide you with information you can't live without or save you payroll dollars? Unless such equipment is going to be used for other services in the museum, it is probably inappropriate for a small sales operation. It may make sense for a medium size shop.

It is more than annual revenue that defines a shop's size, however, and too many other factors go into the equation to permit any simplistic cut-offs solely on the basis of gross revenue. A shop with revenues of $100,000 and a very limited product line will have vastly different needs than another museum with three shop locations and a large number of SKUs that grosses the identical amount. The person making the decision of whether or not to buy a P.C. or P.O.S. register system must be familiar with the store's needs and with what the computers can do. A store manager who knows nothing about computers will need help; so will a computer/register salesperson unfamiliar with your store.

Even the smallest store, however, should have a traditional cash register. Select one that has the ability to ring up sales by departments: books on the Book key, jewelry on the Jewelry key, etc. This information will allow the manager to evaluate the operation by department, figuring such ratios as sales per square foot and cost of sale by department as well as for the shop as a whole. In this way you can determine that it is the jewelry department that is dragging the store's cost of sale down, and you'll know right where to start making improvements. If your shop is still operating out of a cash drawer (the "cigar box" method), and many are, you should look into a good, basic cash register before doing anything else. If finances won't permit purchasing a new one, investigate second hand registers (beware of higher maintenance costs though) or search for a store that is upgrading its registers and ask for a donation.

Back to cost of sales. With cost of sales, the lower the better. Under 50 percent is preferable. Above 60 percent indicates a potential problem: are your retails high enough? Your product costs low enough?

If a store has a high percentage of books or other low markup items that it turns frequently, a cost of sale of higher than 50 percent is fine. The "trick" to cost of sales (and most other ratios) is its relative improvement over time.

	1987	1988	1989	1990	1991	1992
C.O.S.	57%	55%	55%	54%	53%	

How do small museum stores (with gross revenues of less than $125,000) perform in reality? According to a 1985 survey, about three-fourths have a cost of sale above 51%. That means three-quarters have room for improvement. Of that three-quarters, one-quarter fell in the 51–55% category, not too bad, but half have a cost of sale in excess of 56%, a number that calls for serious improvement. The median for the smaller stores is about 55%. In larger shops, with gross revenues over $125,000, the story is only marginally better, with about one-quarter (21%) doing well with cost of sales under 50%, about one-quarter (29%) in the not-too-bad category of 50–55%, and nearly half (42%) needing drastic improvement with cost of sales over 56%. The median for the larger stores is the same as for the smaller ones, about 55%.

If your annual cost of sales is too high (over 55 percent) examine each product group by department or each individual product for areas where improvement is possible. Analyze the cost of sales on food items, for example, compared to toys. In certain areas, such as books and film, dramatic improvement is unlikely.

When you spot a discrepancy, an area where the C.O.S. is over 50 percent, resist the temptation to raise the retail without first considering whether you can take steps to lower the cost. If your price point is correct for your customer profile, it may be the product that needs altering. If a $10.00 price point is good for a small doll, ask the vendor if there is anything that will bring the cost down. Are you a valued enough customer for the vendor to pay shipping? Would increasing your orders lead to a price break? (An option only if your inventory won't exceed 3–4 months supply—six at the absolute outside.) Are there any advertising allowances the vendor could extend, even if you do not advertise or if you advertise in your museum's publication? Could the product be modified in some way to cut costs: a simpler dress design on the doll, for instance? Look around for alternative vendors who could sell you a similar doll for less. Another doll that costs $4.00 will permit you to keep your $10.00 retail.

Naturally if the existing doll is underpriced and is worth more than $10.00, raise the retail to $13.00 or whatever reflects its value. There is nothing wrong with adjusting the retail, just be sure to examine the situation from both sides before taking steps to solve it.

Merely altering the emphasis of your product mix can have a dramatic effect on your cost of sales. Look at this comparison: 60% of Store A's merchandise is in gifts (which have a 50% cost of sale) while the remaining 40% is in books (which have a 60% cost of sale). Store B has the reverse: 60% in books and 40% in gifts.

	STORE A	STORE B
Gifts	$60 \times .50 = 30$	$40 \times .50 = 20$
Books	$40 \times .60 = 24$	$60 \times .60 = 36$
	54% COS	56% COS

The moral of this story: the store with more gifts than books is more profitable, with a 54% cost of sale, than the store with more books than gifts, with a 56% cost of sale.

But why do you need to mark up products more than double? I've heard more than one museum store manager speak of markups beyond a keystone level as if they were a sin or a "rip-off." Maybe in a perfect world where you sold everything you purchased at a full keystone markup, you would never need more. But does your store offer employee discounts of 10 to 20 percent? Special membership discounts of 10 to 40 percent? Does your shop ever take markdowns on slow sellers? Do you carry merchandise like books with poor profit margins? Have your employees ever broken any merchandise that you had to write off? National shoplifting guestimates run around $2^1/2$ to 3 percent of sales with an additional $^1/2$ percent stolen by employees,[3] although it is widely assumed but never demonstrated that shoplifting is lower in museum stores due to their "better" clientele. Do you really think your store is immune to such theft? Have you ever taken a bad check?[4] Or had a newly developed product "bomb"? You need to compensate for all these factors and others by marking up more than double, and you need never apologize for it.

In summary, realistic ways to increase overall markup include:

1. Raising retails.
2. Lowering product costs.
3. Changing the shop's merchandise assortment (more gifts, less film, for example).
4. Altering the emphasis through displays and merchandising of the higher profit items.
5. Lowering shortages (shoplifting, damages, etc.).
6. Making fewer markdowns.

Selling More than One

Do you bunch products for higher average transactions? Do you sell pencils for a quarter or do you tie a dozen together with a bright ribbon and offer them for $2.95? You should do both. There are probably two different customer segments buying the product: schoolchildren who purchase one or two and adults who buy the dozen. Neither is apt to purchase in the alternate form, so both are necessary.

Everyone is familiar with gift baskets of fruits and foods. Use this concept to create your own gift baskets for year-round and holiday giving by grouping small, inexpensive items together with a specific customer in mind. Before Mother's Day try a basket filled with soaps, potpourri, cologne, and small candles. At Christmas package small toys as stocking stuffers. All year long bunch an assortment of dried herbs and spices for someone who enjoys cooking. Children on vacation would love a coloring book or activity book packaged with crayons, scissors, stickers, and tape. A basket of assorted preserves with some unusual candies makes a special treat for anyone. Historic Savannah's shop developed an imaginative cardboard box in the shape of their Federal style Davenport House and pack it with Savannah specialties. They market it to out-of-towners through hotels and convention services, and also offer it to visitors to the Davenport House. Categorize your customers and try to devise a gift basket or box to appeal to each group.

Individually wrapped bars of soap had sold well for years when the product-development staff at Colonial Williamsburg decided to put out a box of three. The product quickly became one of the store's best sellers without detracting from the sales of single bars. Customers perceived the box of three scented soaps as an ideal gift, whereas the individual bars had a more personal appeal. *Photo by author.*

Encourage the sale of related merchandise. Look for a tie-in and build a display around two or more products. Grocery stores are famous for promoting impulse sales of related merchandise: every fall Kraft Foods will move some of its caramels out of the candy aisle into the produce department next to the apples, and sales soar.

The very best tie-in for a museum store to promote is an object with a book, especially one of the museum's own publications. A book on Sandwich glass stacked on the changing display table next to an assortment of reproduction glassware, a gardening book with several vases and packages of bulbs or seeds, a book on Mary Cassatt with boxes of notecards copied from her paintings and a poster backdrop, etc. I doubt there is a book your shop carries that cannot be paired with at least one related item. Groups of books on the same subject can also be effective: several publications on the architecture of Frank Lloyd Wright or on historical wall-coverings.

Kits

Creating your own kits can sell several related items while providing a unique and educational product for your visitor. The many how-to books on the market can form the basis for such kits, or you can draw up your own instructions. One of the museum or store employees with talent in a particular field may enjoy developing instructions to be given away with the purchase of the requisite materials.

Instructions or How-To Book	Materials Needed for Kit
Basketweaving	Reed or vine
Candlemaking	Beeswax, tin mold, cotton wicking
Hatmaking	Straw braid, silk flowers, ribbon
Potpourri recipes	Ingredients
Flower gardening	Seeds or bulbs, containers
Herbs: growing, drying	Seeds, recipes, silica gel
Needlework	Fabric, thread or yarn
Music (simple tunes)	Fife, recorder, or tin whistle
Calligraphy	Paper, pen and ink, period examples
Stencilling	Pattern from examples in museum
Quilting	Fabrics or pre-cut pieces for a quilt square copied from your quilt collection to frame or make a pillow

Of course some related kits do not require instruction—paper, quill pen, powdered ink, inkwell, brass seal, and sealing wax, for example, or a slate with a slate pencil or chalk, battledore, and McGuffey's Reader.

Gift Certificates

Offering gift certificates may be an easy way to increase sales. It may just as well be a bookkeeping hassle with no redeeming sales potential. A museum shop whose customers consist predominantly of out-of-towners or tourists stopping by on their way to the beach, is not likely to find much merit in gift certificates. However, a shop patronized by locals that has a selection of high end merchandise and a reputation for interesting, unusual products may find gift certificates a plus.

The actual gift certificate should have an appealing design. You can design one yourself by using clip art borders and press type[5] or you can pay for a professional job. The certificate must include blanks for the recipient's name and for the giver's, the dollar amount, the date, the date before which it should be redeemed (after all, you don't want these hanging around indefinitely so allow at least three and no more than six months), and the museum's name and address for the benefit of those who have never visited before. Gift certificates need to be secured and treated just like money. Numbering the certificates like the checks in a checkbook makes them easier to track.

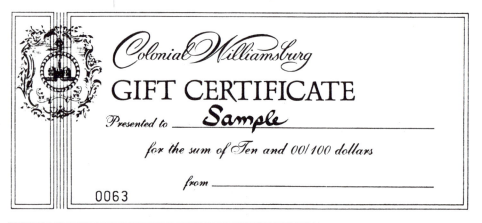

Sample gift certificate from the Colonial Williamsburg Foundation.

The salesperson will record the date sold and the names and addresses of both giver and recipient. When the certificate is redeemed, the date should be noted so the certificate can be accounted for. Some are never redeemed or only partially spent, which means free money for the store.

When the item selected costs more than the amount of the gift certificate, the procedure is simple—just take the difference in cash and ring it up with the certificate. But if the merchandise comes to *less* than the amount on the certificate, which will almost always be the case, you have several options.

1. Give the change in cash no matter the amount. This will offend your sense of what is fair when the recipient of a $50.00 gift certificate purchases a 10 cent candy stick and walks out with $49.90, after all, it is not what Aunt Gertrude intended and your shop loses its $50.00 sale.
2. Give the change in cash but require that the purchase amount to at least half the value of the gift certificate.
3. Give the change in the form of another gift certificate or store credit slip.

The second option is probably best for most shops. Circumstances may necessitate considering others or requiring a purchase of up to 75 percent of the certificate value.

Gift certificates are more suited to stores with a wide range of merchandise, like department stores. After all, the premise behind the idea is that Aunt Gertrude may not know what to give her niece for graduation but is certain that little Kathy can find something she likes at Bloomingdale's. If you feel that your shop offers "something for everyone" and that your customers would be receptive to gift certificates, give it a try.

Notes

1. Many publishers do offer greater discounts of 42%–50% but the quantity you must purchase for a discount greater than 40% is often beyond what a small or medium size museum store can afford to inventory. Some publishers offer greater discounts on the condition that you buy the books on a non-returnable basis. This is a good opportunity for extra profits as long as the book has a reliable track record at your store and you are ordering moderately. Some publishers will extend a better discount to non-profits, so always explain your status and ask.
2. Aageson, pp. 44–45.

3. According to 1988 estimates, employee theft is estimated to cost companies $40 to $80 BILLION dollars a year. This is *all* businesses, not just retailers.
4. Good advice on handling bad checks is available in a terrific publication called "It's Your $$$." The booklet is available from CEBI (Continuing Education for Business Improvement), Box 820, Asheville, NC 28804 for $5.98 plus $1.50 postage and handling. Lots of sound advice on a difficult topic!
5. Clip art is copyright free art work. There are many books of border designs alone that you can cut out and paste up to make your own "camera-ready art" for printing or photocopying. Look in art supply stores or write Dover Publications at 31 East 2nd Street, Mineola, NY 11501, or call them at 516-294-7000, and ask for their complete catalog. Dover has a veritable treasure trove of clip art books on themes as varied as Christmas, borders, children, initials, sports, and art deco.

   "Press type" is available at art supply stores as well. It comes in all sizes (called fonts) and styles (called typefaces) and sticks to the paper. Press type comes in handy for small jobs like signage where typesetting would be too expensive.

7

The Numbers Game: Ratios and Inventory

If the store manager is not tracking this data, he or she should seriously consider starting at once. There is no magic to these numbers but they are useful indications of problems and successes and will allow comparisons to be made between your shop and others and from one year to the next. They will help management to spot trends, to prepare and follow a budget, to evaluate any changes that are made, to test experiments, to plan product development, and to understand the business better.

Use graph paper or ledger paper (available from any office supply store) to set up charts. Record the following figures daily and transfer monthly and annual totals onto another chart.

Month of _____

DAY	SALES REVENUE	# OF VISITORS TO MUSEUM	# SALES TRANSACTIONS	# EMPLOYEE HOURS
1	$ 498.28	502	194	24
2	212.14	275	96	16
3	333.05	451	157	12
4	349.71	488	178	12
etc.				
30	426.52	425	203	16
31	391.94	539	185	12
TOTAL	$13,124.15	12,555	5,233	475

Summary Sales Revenue

MONTH	1988	1989	1990	1991	1992	1993
Jan	$ 3,124.15	$ 3,575.05	$ 3,478.50	$ 4,585.10		
Feb	2,881.94	2,841.65	2,141.18	3,477.23		
Mar	3,323.76	2,110.97	3,951.88	3,989.76		
etc.						
Dec	8,731.11	11,479.69	11,728.76	13,345.72		
TOTAL	$62,121.40	$75,311.12	$76,590.01	$88,358.73		

Also calculate the number of square feet of selling space, not including offices or stockrooms.

Using this data and other necessary information, compute the following each month:

1. Sales per square foot (sales revenue divided by square footage).
2. Sales per visitor (sales revenue divided by visitation).
3. Average transaction (sales revenue divided by number of transactions).
4. Dollars per work hour (sales revenue divided by hours of paid or volunteer work).

A separate chart for each item may make it easier to follow. Try something like this:

Sales per Square Foot

MONTH	1988	1989	1990	1991	ETC.
Jan	$ 6.24	$ 7.15	$ 6.95	$ 7.12	
Feb	5.76	5.68	4.28	5.65	
etc.					
Dec	17.46	22.95	23.45	21.88	
TOTAL	$124.24	$150.62	$153.18	$153.22	

If that seems like an inordinate number of pages and charts, remember that you won't be using most of them but once a month to record totals or calculate ratios. It should take about fifteen minutes each month. At first the charts won't help you much, but after a year's history is recorded, they will become extremely revealing and thought-provoking, and you will rejoice that you set up the system.

These ratios should be computed at least once a year at the end of your fiscal year:

1. Annual cost of goods (year's beginning inventory + all merchandise purchased + freight in − ending inventory).
2. Cost of sales (annual cost of goods sold ÷ annual sales revenue).
3. Gross profit (annual sales revenue − annual cost of goods).
4. Net profit (gross profit − all other store expenses).

Next we will examine what these numbers can tell you about your business and how to use them.

Sales revenue. This is the total of all money that comes through the cash register, less the sales tax (if any in your state) and less returns. *It must be tracked every day!* Remember that your store does not pay sales tax, the customer does. The store merely collects it and forwards it to the state.

Museum visitation. Most museums already track their daily attendance. The store manager needs access to these figures. To the surprise of many people, large attendance does not automatically translate into big revenue. "If your store is pushed off into a dark corner because the museum administration considers retailing a disgusting endeavor," warns one museum shop manager, "sales will be meager."[1] If your shop is chronically short of stock or so chaotic and disorganized that shopping becomes too confusing to bother with, no amount of visitation will help the situation. Of course, even an exemplary shop will do poorly if the museum attracts only a few thousand visitors annually.

Sales transactions. How many sales per day did you make? Most registers total this for you daily.

Number of hours of work. Whether your employees are paid or volunteer, count the number of hours worked per day. Two employees working all day at a shop with 9–5 hours and one hour off for lunch will work 14 total hours. You can then measure the productivity of sales per hour worked. (See *Dollars per work hour* below.)

Sales per square foot. Square feet of sales area, excluding offices and stockrooms but including behind the counter space where customers do not go, has long been used in the retailing world as an indicator of success. Size alone is meaningless. Size as compared to sales and visitation can be quite revealing. Museum stores come in every size and shape. There is no ideal.

Having said that, I'll contradict myself and suggest that if your museum is considering adding a shop or expanding an existing one, or if you are involved in the planning stages of a new museum, you try to allow for a minimum size of 500 square feet. While there are certainly successful shops smaller than this, 500 square feet is a reasonable size for even the smallest museum and can be adequate for many medium size ones as well.

As the standard indicator of store efficiency, sales per square foot is useful for your store as a whole and for the different departments if you have them. For example, compare the sales per square foot of your book section to that of your toys and games area and that of your jewelry counter. Your cash register must be equipped with category buttons to enable you to factor out your sales of books, toys, and jewelry. Stores still using a cash drawer—and there are many—would do well to consider purchasing a new or used register. Which are your best sections? Why? Consider expanding the space of your best section at the expense of your poorest. Look at the other influencing factors—space is not the only variable. Perhaps your poorest section is poorly merchandised, perhaps the products are unappealing to your customers or are the wrong price points.

What is a good sales per square foot? That depends. I know of two 500-square-foot shops that have a sales/square foot of $1,000. One is located in a fashionable resort town with a very well-to-do customer base but it is not selling high end merchandise to any unusual degree. The other is in a Civil War museum. Large retailers in general view $150/square foot as a break even point, but they typically have many more costs of doing business than museum stores. In fact, many museum stores have a sales/square foot of less than $150; the majority fall into the $50–250 range. As a comparison, department stores had a 1990 industry average of $200.

Annual Revenue ÷ Square feet = $/square foot
$102,830 ÷ 750 = $137.50/square foot

More important than the number itself is the improvement over the years.

Sales per museum visitor. Also called "average sale." Here is another figure that you want to watch increase over time.

One way to judge how successful you are at overall merchandising (buying, display, pricing, etc.) is to look at the visitation versus sales. Track your monthly sales and visitation. Divide revenue by number of visitors. Figure the trend: up, down, or steady. If sales are improving while visitation is stationary, your average sale goes up and you are doing well. However if visitation is going up by 10 percent and your sales are rising by 2 percent, you are not as successful as you could be. Don't forget the inflation factor: if inflation last year was 4 percent, then a 4 percent increase in revenues leaves you standing still. Any increase *above* the inflation level is genuine growth. If your sales are rising at a rate greater than inflation and greater than your visitation, you can be pleased with your shop's productivity, since the inevitable conclusion is that your management skills over the year have served to convince the customer to leave more of his money at your store!

A chart will let you examine these trends.

MONTH	LAST YEAR			CURRENT YEAR			
	VISITATION	SALES	AV. SALE	VISITATION	SALES	AV. SALE	TREND
Jan	459	$1,103	$2.40	511	$1,227	$2.40	=
Feb	671	1,975	2.94	622	2,456	3.94	+34%
etc.							

In general, dollar sales per visitor tend to be higher when stores have a lower visitors per square foot ratio. (Divide the number of museum visitors annually by the number of square feet, for example: 120,000 visitors last year divided by a 550-square-foot store equals 218 visitors/sq. ft.) This is logical—the customer receives more attention from the sales staff and is able to examine things at a more leisurely pace. Interestingly, institutions with the highest sales per visitor ratio are history museums. As Tom Aageson explains in his book on financial analysis:

> It is interesting that 9 out of 10 stores with exceptionally low sales per visitor are located in science museums. Science museums tend to have relatively small stores compared to their high attendance. Most have no admission charge or a very low one. Attendance in science museums is composed of a high proportion of elementary school visitors who have less disposable income. On the other hand, 9 out of 10 stores located in history museums have a higher sales per visitor. Stores in these museums tend to be rather large relative to their annual attendance. They often charge higher entrance fees which may pre-select a more affluent audience.[2]

Average transaction. Once again, a number to track over time in hopes that it will rise each year. But average transaction tells you other things too: a very low average transaction could indicate low profitability. If the average transaction is $.15, you are spending an inordinate amount of labor (and labor = time = money) ringing up sales. A sales clerk has to ring up 333 $.15 transactions just to *equal* a $50/day salary and benefits. Or put another way, if it takes an average of two minutes for a transaction to be completed, it costs the store $.17 for a $5.00/hour employee to ring up that $.15 sale. A $.15 sale has a cost of sale of .08 and a labor cost of .17, for a total of .25. You are losing .10 on every sale!

Look for ways to pull up the average transaction. Sell candy sticks at 5 for a quarter instead of a nickel apiece; bunch .10 pencils in packages of six or twelve; offer a box of assorted soap balls instead of one. Experiment with products that have higher price points to see whether there is a demand for "better" merchandise. Look at the perceived value each item and see if a higher retail is appropriate.

Dollars per work hour. This is useful in comparing the relative effectiveness of your sales staff and can help in scheduling decisions.

Revenue ÷ hours = average $/hour
$2,812 weekly revenue ÷ 84 hours paid work that week = $33.47

Following average revenue dollars per work hour will demonstrate at a glance which days of the week, which hours of the day, which seasons of the year are busiest and you can manage your employees' schedules to suit the visitors' needs. You can even break down sales by hours of the day to gather data for scheduling decisions, although small operations may find that simple observation leads to the same results. For example, if sales in the 9 o'clock to 10 slot and the 5 o'clock to 6 slot are usually less than the cost of the employee, shorten shop hours to 10–5. While it is *nice* to be open the same hours as the museum, it isn't always profitable. Since by far most visitors shop *after* their museum visit, many museum stores open one or two hours after the museum opens, and close one hour after the posted closing time. This has another advantage for the visitor: it doesn't rush the late afternoon visitors through the museum so as not to miss the store. If the decision of store hours is not the store manager's to make, he or she should present the data to the director or person responsible for discussion.

If your shop operates well with one person at a time, schedule management is not a major concern. But when you find that Fridays and Saturdays need another pair of hands, or that the hours of 10 to 2 are hectic every day, or that December's volume is triple that of September, you need to consider supplementing with part-time staff. Inexperienced managers often hire full-time bodies when part-time help would suffice. With judicious schedule management you can squeeze a little more profit down to the bottom line, and knowing the dollars per work hour can help with your analysis.

Also, knowing total labor dollars allows you to calculate the value of your volunteers' donation of time as discussed in Chapter 2 on Staffing. In addition, it allows you to figure your labor cost as a percent of total revenue:

$$\text{Labor} \div \text{Sales} = \%$$
$$\$18,312 \div \$98,103 = 18.7\%$$

Remember the "hidden" labor costs: FICA, unemployment taxes, insurance, and other benefits accorded to your employees and volunteers. Labor costs in the commercial retailing world vary according to store type (grocery stores vs. department stores, drug stores vs. shoe stores) but average around 12–20 percent. Museum stores *as a group* do better than most due to their use of volunteers.

If the number of employee hours rises at a faster rate than revenue, you need to look into ways to trim hours. Conversely, a slow decline in employee hours during a period of no change in revenue or of revenue growth indicates increased productivity and good schedule management.

Annual cost of goods. A total of the amount spent on merchandise during the year plus the year's beginning inventory, minus the end-of-the-year inventory.

Gross profit. Figured annually or monthly, this is revenue (excluding sales tax) minus cost of merchandise and its freight. It is a number to monitor closely and to compare from year to year. Figure your gross profit as a percent of revenue.

$$\text{Gross Profit} = \text{Revenue} - \text{Cost of Goods Sold}$$
$$\$40,000 = 79,000 - 39,000$$

$$\text{Gross Profit} \div \text{Revenue} = \%$$
$$\$40,000 \div 79,000 = 50.6\%$$

Cost of sale. See chapter 6.

Net profit. Also known as "The Bottom Line." Subtract all the rest of your expenses from the gross profit, including:

Rent
Utilities
Payroll
Wages for back-up services (bookkeeping, accounting)
Taxes like FICA and federal and state unemployment
Benefits like health insurance and pension
The cost of vacation replacements
Office supplies

Repairs
Paper bags
Insurance (product liability, fire, etc.)
Postage
Telephone
Credit card fees
Security
Equipment
Trash disposal
Volunteer appreciation
Business licenses
Maintenance contracts
Auditors
Advertising

A museum store may have relatively few subtractions to make here. A shop that operates with volunteers and whose museum absorbs the cost of utilities, security, administration, rent, maintenance, trash disposal, and insurance (as most do), may find its net profit coming blissfully close to its gross profit. In the real world, of course, this would never occur. As a practical matter, net profit cannot be compared from museum store to museum store because the deductions vary so much. Nor is it worth comparing to for-profit stores. It is only of value when tracked over time. To figure your shop's net profit as a percent of revenue:

$$\text{Net Profit} \div \text{Revenue} = \%$$
$$\$20,000 \div 79,000 = 25.3\%$$

In strict terms, any profit that does not take into account all the expenses, including those that the museum pays, cannot accurately be called a net profit. It is usually referred to as a "contribution" that the shop makes before unallocated expenses are applied. Be aware of this when using the term "net profit" in reports to trustees or directors, as it can be misleading to a businessperson who may not realize that there are unallocated expenses.

There are other numbers to track and ratios to calculate, the purpose of which is to help indicate strengths and weaknesses and to track your store's progress over time. Thomas Aageson's book *Financial Analysis for Museum Stores* (1986) goes into greater detail on this topic and allows you to compare your data with that of other, similar museum stores. Your inventory turn is 3.0? Give yourself a pat on the back since the study indicates that museum stores average 2.3. Is your cost of labor running 20%

of your sales? While most of the small museum stores would envy that record, two-thirds of the larger ones do better. Many other valuable conclusions can be drawn by comparing your data to the examples in this study. It is highly recommended. (See Published Resources section for details.)

Inventory

The name of the inventory game is to carry the least amount of inventory possible, without sacrificing sales or the appearance of full shelves. For obvious reasons, suppliers with no minimum order requirements and fast turnarounds are preferred. Try to order two to four months' estimated sales at a time and no more than six months' worth for a straight purchase. Certain developed products like printed matter may require as much as a two-year supply but NEVER commit to more than three years even then.

Take a physical inventory twice a year. Most museum stores own their inventories at cost, as opposed to department stores and many other retailing operations that figure inventory at retail.

Cost Method

This means all inventory is kept at the cost of the merchandise. A physical inventory is taken and extended at cost values. This method is well-suited to small stores or to stores with high dollar value items, where it is important to keep unit control. There are generally fewer items (SKUs-Stock Keeping Units) and fewer transactions.

Retail Method

This method was developed because it was becoming increasingly difficult for large retailers to track the large number of items their stores carried. It was not practical to track each SKU and its cost. The retail method is an averaging method, providing a means for reasonably estimating at any time the cost value of inventory based on the retail selling price.

The store manager is seldom involved in selecting the inventory method for the store; usually the museum's accountant, treasurer, or business manager determined long ago how the museum's inventory was to be kept, and the shop manager has merely to follow the established system. If you are responsible for setting up a new store and are starting records from scratch, you will find the cost method simpler.

The method really isn't as important as being consistent about it is. Keep all figures at cost or all at retail so you don't compare apples to oranges. A common beginner's mistake is to try to calculate turns by dividing goods sold at *retail* by the goods in inventory at *cost,* a mix up that leads to meaningless ratios.

To evaluate your own shop's inventory management, use your most recent inventory dollar total or the average of the inventories you took during the most recent fiscal year.

Annual Cost of Goods ÷ Average \$ in Inventory at Cost = Turns
\$50,900 ÷ 13,956 = 3.6

"Turns" means the number of times per year your *money,* not your physical product, turns over. Five turns means your inventory dollar investment of, say, \$10,000, has been available to purchase products five times during the year. In other words, you have had access to \$50,000 by re-working that \$10,000 so well. While I know of several museum stores that average 5 turns a year, it is unusual, admirable, and probably unrealistic for most. In the real world, three turns is the average that for-profit shops hope for. Not surprisingly, few museum stores do as well as three. Due to larger inventory requirements for products and publications developed by the museum, extreme seasonality causing many shops to close for winter months, and relative inexperience in inventory management, museum stores are in a position where a 3.0 turn is excellent, a 2.0–2.5 is fairly average. Lower than that indicates improvement needed. Again, set up a chart and track your turns over time. Comparisons and improvements are as important as the actual number.

Improving your turns is a way to measure inventory control and good inventory control inevitably leads to better profits. Lower inventories mean fewer markdowns. The less excess product you have in the stockroom, the less often you will have to reduce and clear it out at lower profit margins. Of course, lower inventories require less storage space, possibly freeing up dozens of square feet of stockroom or understock area for more valuable selling space. One museum store manager in Ohio reduced her inventory enough to divide the stockroom in half, creating a badly needed office for herself where none had existed before. If you no longer need your understock space for storage, take off the cupboard doors and turn those once-concealed shelves into selling space. It may not be the most desirable space, located as these cupboards usually are at knee level, but it could work for children's merchandise.

Museum store managers have come a long way in the past decade where inventory management is concerned. I still shudder when I recall an incident years ago where a museum executive pointed to his burgeoning inventory and boasted, "Money in inventory is like money in the bank!" Thankfully that notion seems to have faded away but there are still far too many museum stores where inventory at cost exceeds their entire annual sales revenue.

Why is that so undesirable? If we buy lots of widgets today at $1.00 apiece, after a few years they will be selling for $1.50 apiece and we'll be sitting pretty on several years supply at a bargain price. And why isn't money in inventory sort of like money in the bank—it is in storage, so to speak, and will come available when the product is sold, right? Wrong. Money sitting in inventory is better off sitting in a passbook savings account at the bank where at least it is making 5% interest. Other investments can yield more. $10,000 invested at 10 percent would produce $1,000 each year. $10,000 sitting in inventory that isn't turning produces nothing, in effect costing the museum $1,000 each year. Also, tying all your museum's money up in widgets means its not available for new merchandise, product development, and taking advantage of vendor discounts or unexpected buying opportunities.

If your inventory level is excessive, you have a lot of museum store company. Develop a plan to reduce it gradually over a period of one to two years.

1. *First identify areas of significant overstock,* perhaps merchandise in excess of a two-year supply. Consider the options:

   a) Mark down these items and position them prominently in the store. "Buy One Get One Free" may be more effective. Sign prominently. Mass the product out. Fifty paperweights on display will sell faster than five.

   b) If appropriate, contact other museum stores to buy your excess stock at cost.

   c) Use the merchandise in a give-away promotion:
      "Free map with every purchase!"
      "Free map with every purchase over $10!"
      "Free map with every purchase of a book!" (or some other related product)

   d) Put a coupon in your local paper for a free item to be claimed at the shop. This may bring in new customers and should result in some extra sales when people come into the shop to pick up their free merchandise. Run an ad in your museum's publication.

e) Use as prizes in a museum event. "All children entering the art fair will receive a free cap!"

2. *Examine your merchandise for excessive variation* in size, color, or style. I know a store that stocked nine sizes of sterling silver thimbles. I reduced that to three: small, medium, and large, but looking back on it from the vantage point of several years, I think one size, medium, would have sufficed. Ask yourself whether seven colors are truly necessary for the children's sunbonnet line. Cut to the two or three most popular colors and see if sales suffer. Too much choice can be paralyzing. "I don't know Aunt Maude's thimble size so I'd better not buy her one" versus "A thimble for Aunt Maude? Just the thing!" If a parent wants a sunbonnet for their five-year-old daughter, are they really going to walk away empty-handed if you don't have one in green? Pink, white, and possibly blue ought to please nearly everyone.

3. *Examine your merchandise for excessive duplication.* Five different Civil War theme jigsaw puzzles selling equally well could probably be cut to two without significant loss of sales. More than one book title on any topic peripheral to your museum's theme is usually unnecessary. If you find your group of inexpensive children's items numbers twelve, consider discontinuing the two or three least related, poorest sellers. Usually this will throw those sales to the remaining items, which benefits you twice: your inventory is reduced and the increase in sales of the remaining products may be enough to push you into a larger order with a lower unit cost.

4. *Ruthlessly eliminate poor selling products* unless they possess overriding educational merit.

5. *Cut orders closer.* It may feel good never to run out of any merchandise but if that describes your operation, you are carrying too much inventory. If the store will run out of railroad whistles around the end of March, reorder for April 1, not March 1. Identify your Top Ten or Top Twenty products and resolve never to run out of these. On the rest of your merchandise, stretch a bit. Take the risk of running out. Your Best Seller list should be composed of the products that bring in the most money, not the ones that sell the highest volume. Between a 5-cent candy stick that sells 200 a day

(revenue $10.00) and a $12.00 hat that sells two a day (revenue $24.00), a hat out-of-stock is going to hurt you more. The old 20/80 rule works well here: *20 percent of your merchandise brings in 80 percent of your income.* The other 80 percent of your merchandise that accounts for only 20 percent of your income is the portion that can absorb the biggest cuts with little or no loss to the store.

6. *Consider a sale.* If your inventory is pretty heavy across the board, offer 10–20% off all merchandise for a month during your busy season. If this sounds a little too department store-ish, schedule regular semi-annual or annual sales of excess stock at 25–50% off. Consider restricting the sale to members or employees, or to all employees of your city or county if your museum is operated by a governmental entity. A county historical society might offer a one-day sale for all county employees and their families where the bulk of the merchandise is excess inventory.

A serious warning about inventory: limit access to your stockroom to the smallest number of people possible. A healthy dose of suspicion is mandatory. Theft from the stockroom is not as easy or as likely if only the manager and one other have the key. I am not referring to customer theft here, but to employee theft. If you are like most store managers, you are aware that sales clerks, assistant managers, custodians, and maintenance people occasionally steal. You need to expand your suspicion horizon to include non-employees in the store on legitimate business, such as sales reps, repairmen, and pest control people, and you also need to be aware that security guards, secretaries, curators, museum directors, and trustees have been known to steal merchandise that was too accessible. This may sound paranoid but it is not. If I had a dollar for every time I ate my words, "Not Beth! I *know* Beth could never steal!" I—well, I wouldn't exactly be rich but I'd have a few dollars. The sad fact is, most people are capable of theft if the circumstances are right, and many rationalize their actions to convince themselves that what they are doing is something other than stealing. Avoid the misery of having to deal with employee theft by making employee theft very difficult. (See chapter 9.)

Taking Inventory

A physical inventory is a good housekeeping discipline as well as the only way to know for certain what you really own. No matter what the inventory cards say you have in stock, if it is not there, you don't have it. A physical inventory is used to "reconcile" your book inventory (the numbers you supposedly have as listed in the books) to the actual existing count. The two accounts *should* be the same but they never are. What causes the discrepancies?

1. Thefts account for about half of all shortages. Thefts are committed by professional shoplifters, customers of all age and description, employees, and other people in the store on business.
2. Unrecorded breakage, damage, or loss.
3. Honest mistakes, like charging the customer for 16 pencils when there were 17, or like ringing up that $39.95 figurine for $29.95.
4. Accidental discards to the trash.
5. Vendor shortages. (The box said 50 mugs but you didn't verify when it arrived so you never knew that there were only 49.)
6. Carelessness in storage that leads to breakage.
7. Loans to another department that are forgotten.

Small stores have greater "eye-ball" control and more personal contact with employees that serve to limit their shortages. No store can eliminate shortages entirely but the attitude of top management is critical to a successful shortage control program. If the director pops a sourball in her mouth and winks each time she walks through the store, the message she sends is disastrous.

The best time to take a physical inventory is at the middle and end of your fiscal year at a time when the store is closed. Some museums are closed Mondays, making that the perfect day for an inventory. Museums opened every day will have to conduct inventory at night or, as a last resort, close the shop for the day.

After setting aside any consignment merchandise, begin to count stock in a methodical way, counter by counter, shelf by shelf, not forgetting walls, floor, and ceiling. Use a different sheet of paper for each segment and label it at the top, "West Wall, Top Shelf."

Using a cost code on the price tag may speed the process along for your store. See Appendix E for cost code examples. Small businesses usually do well with a card file or PC (Personal Computer) that assigns a stock number to each item. The card then carries the cost, source, purchase history, and sales history:

Product: porcelain bowl
Stock Number: 1234
Cost Code: 924009
Cost: $24.00
Retail: $50.00
Vendor: China Unlimited
          1234 First Street
          Anytown, NY 00000
Date of first purchase: 9/28/88

Keep track of your sales and purchases like you do a checkbook, adding or subtracting, then totalling the balance remaining on hand.

DATE	PURCHASE (ADD)	SALES (SUBTRACT)	BALANCE IN INVENTORY
9/26/88	15		15
9/30/88		1	14
10/6/88		2	12
etc.			

Or less precision may be adequate for your operation:

MONTH	PURCHASE (ADD)	SALES (SUBTRACT)	BALANCE IN INVENTORY
Sept	15	3	12
Oct		7	5
Nov	10	5	10
etc.			

Whenever the stock level falls to, say, 6 porcelain bowls, the buyer places another order. For much of your merchandise, one should be the reorder point; you would not reorder until the last one was on the shelf. This will lead to brief periods of out-of-stocks, but only for products that are not on your Best Sellers list.

You can purchase pre-printed inventory cards at an office supply store or you can use index cards. The system can mesh with a PC if you have one or will need one in the near future. Inventory cards will tell you the inventory you have on hand each month (the PC can tabulate this in a flash, manually takes a bit longer) which can help you judge how much money you should spend the next month.

A manager trying to maintain an average inventory level of $15,000 may discover that April's inventory level has risen to $18,000. The manager knows to cut May's purchases back by around $3,000. A more elaborate, more precise version of this is the "open to buy" system used by most large retail operations. (See next page for details.)

When taking inventory, list the item and the cost code (or leave a blank for the cost), the quantity, and the retail. Leave space for the extension later. Any format with the basics is acceptable. Your museum's accountant may require additional information or a specific form.

Date ___ 10/30/90

Location ___ West wall third shelf from top

Team ___ Jean B. and Amelia

ITEM	COST OR CODE	RETAIL	QUANTITY	EXTENSION
Cat vase	$ 6.24	$15.00	11	$68.64
Leaf vase	43.71	95.00	2	87.42
etc.				

Pre-printed forms with the list of merchandise on the left already in place can be a big help and will ensure that nothing is inadvertently overlooked. The sales staff should write in the cost code, if you use them, but should not look up or write in costs. The store manager can fill those in when the multiplication is being done.

Assign people to work in teams for reasons of security and accuracy. If team counting is not realistic, a recount by another individual can help accuracy and avoid problems. Perhaps another museum staff member could act in the capacity of an outside auditor to spot check for errors.

Estimating is appropriate for some product counts. Stacks of printed matter for instance, yards of ribbon, or a keg of musket balls need estimating. Count an inch of paper and multiply by the number of inches in the stack; figure half of a 50-yard roll of ribbon per roll; count how many musket balls fill a smaller container and pour into that.

Don't forget products out on loan. Keep a list of everything that leaves the store for any reason. Did the curators borrow several shop items for a display at the public library? Did the product developer send samples to prospective manufacturers that are due back next month? Is there a permanent display in the visitors' center?

Open to Buy System

Having formulated a six-month buying plan specifying which merchandise is to be purchased each month, the open-to-buy plan allows the buyer to track retail activity in the store(s) in order to modify the plan. Obviously if actual sales are 20% above anticipated sales, the plan will need adjusting or the store will be severely out-of-stock; conversely if sales slump, the buyer will need to reduce planned purchases. The question is, by how much?

The open-to-buy is the main control mechanism by which the buyer learns how much money to spend for that month. The year begins with planned purchases but as time progresses, the open-to-buy becomes the method by which the buyer monitors actual performance against planned performance and adjusts spending to market conditions.

Open-to-buy is nothing more than merchandise needed minus merchandise available, including what is already on order. To maintain an open-to-buy system, the following data (in retail dollars) is needed:

- Planned sales
- Actual sales
- Planned end-of-month inventory (Yes, this system will necessitate figuring monthly inventories.)
- Actual end-of-month inventory
- Outstanding orders

To figure how much money the buyer should spend for the upcoming month, plug in your numbers to this equation:

Planned end-of-month inventory	$15,000
+ Planned sales	+ 6,000
− Planned beginning-of-month inventory	− 18,000
− Orders in transit	− 2,000
	$ 1,000

The buyer should only spend $1,000 more (at retail) for merchandise this month. Naturally he or she will choose the most critical merchandise, those items on the Best Sellers list, and run out of the less important items. So then what about next month? Very similar:

Planned end-of-month inventory	$16,000
+ Planned sales	+ 8,000
− Actual beginning-of-month inventory	− 14,000
− Orders in transit	− 2,000
	$ 8,000

This month the buyer can spend up to $8,000 (at retail) for merchandise.

Month-by-month calculations can be confusing because the buyer may have placed orders three or four months ahead of time. And the system requires you to know inventory levels each month, meaning a P.O.S. register and inventory system or weekly tracking of book inventory levels manually. I strongly suspect most buyers at small and medium size museum stores, especially single location operations, would find the open-to-buy system a tedious exercise that only confirms what they already know: if actual sales are up, increase purchasing; if actual sales are down, cut back. When buyers are as close to the operation as they are in most small and medium size museum stores, they do not need to rely on a computer printout to tell what is in inventory—the inventory is stacked in front of their desk. For larger operations with multiple stores and warehouses, the open-to-buy can be a tremendous spending guide.

You can read more about open-to-buy in the winter 1987 issue of *Museum Store* magazine or in R. L. Allen's *Bottom Line Issues in Retailing* (Chilton Book Co.: 1984) if you think a more formal system is appropriate to your shop.

Reordering Merchandise

There are two reordering methods:

1. Probably the most common is the fixed reorder cycle method where an order is placed at specified intervals, say every month on the first working day of the month. If 14 coloring books are in stock and the pre-determined maximum stock level is 62 (based on estimated monthly sales of 40 and a delivery time, or "lead time", of 2 weeks) then 46 will need to be ordered.

Formula: (order cycle in weeks × average weekly sales) + (lead time in weeks × average weekly sales) + safety margin (if any) = maximum inventory

Example: (4 × 10) + (2 × 10) + 2 = maximum inventory of 62

An attractive price break may cause the buyer to override the formula. In this instance, suppose that there is a significant price break for orders in excess of 100; the buyer will probably choose to order 100.

2. The fixed reorder quantity method works best for some, where the order is placed at whatever time the stock on hand drops to a predetermined level, called the reorder point. In the example above, the buyer would reorder on whatever day that the inventory level for coloring books reached 22. How many to order is often a judgment call for the buyer. An estimated month's supply (40) might be reasonable, or if there was a price break for quantities over 100, then 100 (a two and a half month's supply) might be wiser. Naturally stock levels need continuous reevaluation as overall sales improve or decline, or as the coloring book's performance changes.

Notes

1. Aageson, p. 5.
2. Ibid., p. 13.

8

Merchandising

The art of selling merchandise by using attractive displays and product presentation is termed *visual merchandising*. Some of the best visual merchandisers come from art or theater backgrounds, not surprising when you consider their craft is to create a mood by setting a stage (your shop) with well-designed props (displays and merchandise) to enhance sales. Good visual merchandisers are jewels but few museum stores require a full-time person on their staff.

There are free-lance visual merchandisers who contract with stores to do displays and windows on a regular basis, often monthly. Your local retail merchants association or chamber of commerce might be able to refer names to you and the Yellow Pages listing "Display Designers and Producers" could point you toward a good person. The best referrals come from satisfied customers so ask at a few local shops where displays look especially appealing and find out who does their work. Explain your need to the manager at the nearest department store. Virtually all department stores have visual merchandisers on staff and the manager may give you the names of the employees who handle their display work and allow you to offer them occasional museum shop work on their own time.

Some shops are fortunate enough to have a sales person or volunteer with a flair for visual merchandising. Even so, having a professional come in occasionally to train that person, teaching your employee the tricks of the trade, working along with him or her a few times and offering constructive criticism can pay off handsomely.

Do you really need professional display work? Isn't that just fluff that museum stores can't really afford? After all, *anyone* can stack up some toys on a table with a bright red tablecloth, make it look nice, catch the customer's eye, and sell the product, right? That's what the late Sam Greenberg of the Smithsonian's museum shops thought when he first came to his job. He told a story at a seminar in 1986, describing his first plan to cut overhead by abolishing the small visual merchandising department. The doomed group convinced him to let them prove their worth, and within a few months had doubled and tripled sales wherever they worked their magic. Greenberg became a convert and instead of abolishing the department, authorized the addition of several new positions and watched his sales grow. The story may have stretched in the telling, but clearly here was a repentant skeptic who couldn't say enough in praise of his visual merchandising staff. The message was clear: money spent on visual merchandising will come back to the store many times over. It is anything but fluff.

Display

Many museum stores operate on a shoe string budget without enough money for a hot glue gun, let alone a professional visual merchandiser, so, until they grow enough to be able to afford regular assistance, here are some basics on the art of selling. Good display need not cost a fortune. The foundation of good display consists of:

Clean. Neatness counts a lot! Replace shopworn merchandise quickly, dust and straighten up often.

Full. Keep the display looking full at all times.

Variety. Change your displays and windows regularly, at least once a month.

When planning a display, professional visual merchandisers recommend first defining your market (parents on vacation with children, for example, or graduation gift shoppers) and then selecting the theme, whether seasonal (Christmas, Spring, Fourth of July) or topical (Ukrainians, quilts, insects, Abraham Lincoln, or organ music). Last, select merchandise to fit the market and the theme.

Ideally the merchandise you select should work together in color and in size. In practice this may be difficult but being aware of color and size relationships can only help the display's appearance. Where possible work in threes, selecting three colors (two warm and one cool, or vice versa) and three sizes (small, medium, and large) of related products.

Too many strong, bright colors only confuse and distract the eye. Watch out for clashing colors. Most people are familiar with color wheels. You can find one in an encyclopedia or art book at the library or buy one at an art supply store. It can be a useful tool for suggesting color combinations. Analogous colors (colors next to each other on the color wheel) and contrasting colors (colors directly opposite each other) are pleasing combinations. Sometimes the most attractive displays are those that use a one-color scheme, with varying shades of the same color such as navy blue, royal blue, and light blue, or several shades of purple and lavender.

Color Groupings

NEUTRAL TONES	WARM TONES	COOL TONES
Black	Yellow	Lavender
Gray	Gold	Purple
White	Peach	Lt. blue
Off white	Orange	Blue
Cream	Rust	Navy blue
Tan	Red	Lt. green
Lt. brown	Pink	Green
Brown		Forest green
Dark brown		Olive green

Before setting up a display, take time to clean everything. Then design a visual triangle with three points of interest for the eye to follow easily. Build the triangle with "build ups" or "risers" made of plexiglass,[1] wood, or wrapped boxes. Consider unusual risers like bricks, logs, books, wooden crates, bales of hay, or children's blocks. While creating displays, one visual merchandiser I know would chant, "Small in front down low, large or tall in back."

Two Ways to Display

1. *A static display.* The customer doesn't purchase the item off the display but picks it up from a nearby shelf. It is critical that the product be in close proximity to the display or the purchase impulse may be lost.
2. *A massed-out display.* This is a table or counter that holds dozens of the product and the customers help themselves from the display. It is particularly suitable for boxed merchandise and doesn't necessarily need to be on a table or counter. The Smithsonian's Museum of Arts and Industries shop once made an intriguing mass display by building a four-foot stack of a particular book by the register counter.

Something about that stack made people positively itch to take one and, no, the stack didn't fall—at least not while I was there.

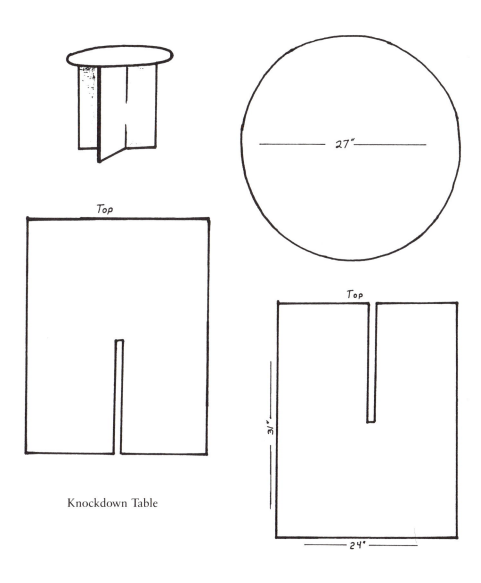

Knockdown Table

This simple display table is easy to make and store. Use ¹/₂" plywood and cut slots ¹/₄" wider than the thickness of your plywood. Select two tablecloths. The under cloth should be a neutral color such as white or off-white. It will be a 90" circle. Use alternating square top-cloths of 36" or more to allow for variety. *Drawing courtesy—Elizabeth A. Kane, Decoration et Art, Virginia Beach, Virginia.*

Accents can add visual appeal to a display but beware of overpowering your sales items with a more appealing accent. Good accents might include old furniture, plants (either very healthy live ones or good quality silks), baskets, or fresh flowers. Accents for display case merchandise, such as jewelry, can be very imaginative. Jewelry should never be displayed in its little box—that cheapens the piece. Instead arrange jewelry or other small display case merchandise on sand, seashells, driftwood, leaves, bricks, ornamental gravel, pine cones, tree bark, dominoes, marbles, genuine sponges, candles, a solid, dark fabric like velvet, or other pleasant but fairly neutral materials. Take care that your accents don't overwhelm your jewelry—a lovely rose may draw the customer's eye *away* from the necklace it is supposed to enhance. When completely out of ideas, visit a fine jewelry store in your city and examine their displays.

Some museum stores make effective use of "museum exhibit" display technique by designing their display along the lines of a typical exhibit. Especially good with one-of-a-kind, handcrafted or expensive items, this technique features the product enclosed in a display case accompanied by a descriptive label, the price marked discreetly in the lower corner. Some shops are permitted to incorporate antiques into their displays, a particularly valuable sales tool if the antique was reproduced or inspired a product and the two can be exhibited side by side safely under glass or lucite to advantage of both.

This clean, modern shop in the Smithsonian National Museum of Natural History uses the museum exhibit display technique, with displays and fixtures designed to evoke a mood that suggests quality and uniqueness. *Photos courtesy—Smithsonian Institution.*

Shops that are permitted to incorporate antiques into their displays are fortunate. Antiques can add immeasurably to a period store, as shown here in McKenzie's Apothecary in Williamsburg, or they can show off the qualities of a good reproduction with a side-by-side comparison display. *Photo courtesy—Colonial Williamsburg Foundation.*

When shops are housed in unusual spaces, such as outbuildings, stables, basements, or train stations, their architectural features may provide an unexpected bonus. Fireplaces, stairs, or ceiling beams can be used to show off merchandise. Look up—hang baskets from ropes, frame or tack prints, scarves, games, or kites high on the walls. Look down—strategically position large baskets, bins, crates, or barrels full of merchandise oriented toward children.

Countertop display cases are not the only way to show small items. Try a printer's drawer on the wall, buckets or baskets on the counter, or a large clear glass jar. Glass jars of the candy store sort are readily available, although you may find a handblown widemouth container with a leather or fabric top more in keeping with your shop's image.

Displaying posters, prints, and maps is a special concern. With abundant wall space you can hang framed samples and place a label and price in the corner of the frame or to the side. Few shops are blessed with enough wall space to display all their printed matter however. The best alternative, a print bin, is seldom seen in museum shops. This is puzzling because it is so cheap and easy to have one built to match the decor of the shop. A homemade print bin is essentially a box with slanted sides, raised from the floor about 12–18 inches. It can hold dozens of prints, maps, posters, and other graphics. Naturally there are commercial bins or racks available too. For under $200, Presentation Systems, Inc. (524 Geary Blvd. San Francisco, CA 94102; 415-885-2026) will sell you a simple tubular steel one that comes in two sizes. To prolong the longevity of floor samples, cover them with an acetate print sleeve, available from any art supply store in a variety of sizes, or dry mount them on foam board. Mounting the samples on a colored mat board to resemble a true mat gives the print more support and increases its visual appeal. Many art galleries find that customers appreciate it when they mat their prints and maps in a complimentary color because it helps the customers with framing the piece. It also makes the print look more expensive, thus justifying a higher retail. Fancier presentations that use a combination of two or three colored mats, that bevel the mat edge, or that color the beveled edge are popular these days.

Another display method, poster leaves, takes up more space than a bin but is efficient for large poster collections. Racks that flip like pages in a book hold a numbered sample of each poster; the stock bins below contain the posters already rolled up into tubes or plastic sleeves. Such racks are better purchased than made in house.

Present related merchandise together by using a theme: a stack of cookbooks with bunches of dried herbs, a group of toys or books on a particular topic, the same image in the form of a poster, a print, and notecards. Tie the display together with color using coordinated risers, fabrics, painted backgrounds, packaging, tissue paper, and so forth. Above all, experiment! Move things around. What works best in the front of the store may fail miserably in the back. An eye-catching display in the far corner may draw people in or help relieve a bottleneck. By the cash register the same display may bunch customers up and cause circulation problems. A terrifically successful display can be repeated periodically but don't allow it to become stale by leaving it up indefinitely.

Identify the best selling spaces in your store. These are likely to be any central free standing display tables visible from the doorway, any shelves at eye level and slightly below (adult eye level for adult items and children's eye level for juvenile products), and the counter or shelves nearest the cash register. Conversely, back corners, high shelves, and poorly lit sectors usually constitute dead spaces. The goal then becomes using the best areas for your top selling merchandise, or for your special promotions and seasonal products. Don't waste it on sale items or marginal sellers. Have floor-to-ceiling bookshelves? Use the two shelves at adult eye level (about four to six feet) for the top sellers and the one at about two to three feet for juvenile books. Place inexpensive impulse items near the cash register for people to pick up on the spur of the moment.

Achieving a full look is critical but it need not inflate your inventory. Fullness can be an illusion if your staff is vigilant about "facing" products to the front of the shelves. If an item can fit three deep on a shelf, two deep or even one faced to the front edge of the shelf will give the same impression. Grocery stores are famous for this. Use "dummies" in out-of-reach places. Empty boxes, boxes wrapped in the style of your historical period (brown paper or reproduction newspaper for example), or cheaply constructed wooden crates can fill those hard-to-reach top shelves without requiring supplemental inventory, all the while enhancing the store's atmosphere.

Achieving a full look need not add to your inventory. Here one or two rows of merchandise are faced to the front of deep shelves and dummy wooden crates, tied bundles, and empty boxes are arranged on top. *Photo courtesy—Colonial Williamsburg Foundation.*

Wherever and whenever you shop, look for ideas and encourage other store employees to do the same. Analyze good displays. What was it about that department store display that caught your eye? Its color, size, shape, juxtaposition of related objects? Why do those Ralph Lauren displays look so elegantly genteel? Steal ideas everywhere you go!

This display is the ultimate in flexibility! Arranged and rearranged almost daily—
sometimes by the staff and sometimes by visiting children—particle-board cubes in assorted sizes make shelves, tables, even seats for browsing customers. An easy-to-use,
inexpensive display idea that any museum store can adapt to its own needs. *Photo
courtesy—Smithsonian Institution.*

Packaging

The store packaging you select or develop can add a sophisticated,
coordinated look to your operation. Choose a color or design theme and
coordinate your product packaging with the store's bags and boxes.
If custom bags and boxes are too expensive or if minimum orders are
too high, create a bag design using logos or drawings of several local

Packages wrapped with plain brown paper or with reproduction eighteenth-century newspaper, tied with flax twine or closed with sealing wax are popular with visitors to Colonial Williamsburg's stores. Cloth bags or burlap wrapping add variety and interest as well as historical accuracy. All packaging forms used in the Historic Area stores are based on actual artifacts, original accounts and descriptions, or pictorial evidence. *Photos by author.*

museums. Split the upfront artwork expenses and the required minimum order among the group. If custom bags and boxes are *still* out of the question, buy stock bags and boxes in a solid color with a complimentary colored tissue paper and develop a coordinated ribbon or sticker imprinted or embossed with your museum name. Readily available and affordable, stickers (or seals) can transform stock packaging into something unique. Look into local suppliers or contact Susan Crane Inc. (8107 Chancellor Row, Dallas, TX 75247; 214-631-6490).

Is holiday gift wrapping a possibility for your shop? See what department stores in your region charge before deciding what you can charge for this service. If staff time is available, pre-wrap certain steady sellers at no charge to the customer and stack them out on display tables. Reproduction eighteenth- and nineteenth-century newspapers make an unusual and inexpensive wrapping paper for year-round use. Artifacts, Inc. (P.O. Box 3399, Palestine, TX 75802; 214-729-4178) carries nineteenth-century newspaper bags and wrapping paper; the Colonial Williamsburg Foundation (Wholesale Sales Dept., P.O. Box C, Williamsburg, VA 23187) sells eighteenth-century reproduction newsprint, specifically the *Virginia Gazette,* to be used for wrapping paper. If your museum has historic news-

Inexpensive custom bags are made by printing a design or logo in one color on stock paper bags, usually brown or white. Historic Charleston and the Preservation Society of Newport County, Rhode Island, each use a green-ink-on-white combination; Historic Savannah prints red-ink-on-brown bags; while the Smithsonian elaborates by adding a dash of red to its black design on white paper. *Photo by author.*

papers, a printer can copy one quite inexpensively and you'll have your own "exclusive" that is both interesting and educational.

Boxes and shopping bags with handles are too expensive to give away anymore. If you still do, start charging for them, at the very least when purchases fall under a set amount. You don't have to make a profit on these, although I recommend you try, but at least recoup your costs.

Unusual packaging adds to your store's unique atmosphere. Cloth bags for certain products could be fun. Millhiser Inc. (1125 Commerce Rd., Richmond, VA 23224; 804-233-9886) wholesales dozens of sizes and colors of cloth bags with drawstring closures, perfect for marbles, sets of children's items, candy, or other small items. Having something printed on the bags is especially nice, although naturally more expensive.

Mail Order Merchandising

The first mail order catalog in America was probably the list of several hundred books for sale mailed out in 1744 by that consummate hustler, Benjamin Franklin. The best known is most likely Montgomery Ward's, introduced in 1872. In 1989 an estimated 50 billion dollars were spent on mail order purchases—a staggering sum that is expected to increase significantly in years to come. It is not hard to fathom why museums are jumping onto the catalog bandwagon.

In spite of what you read about the boom in mail order shopping, beginning a full-fledged mail order program requires *a lot* of money to invest, a strong commitment to the idea, and five to seven years to wait for the profits. Many well-intentioned small and medium size museums have experimented with mail order and failed miserably. So have several large ones. In fact, some of the museum world's largest mail order programs have operated for years at a loss and continue to be subsidized by the museum for reasons unrelated to profit. A brief overview of catalog selling should illustrate its pitfalls and complexities.

There are four basic elements in any mail order program: the list, the products, the presentation (be it catalog, insert, flyer, or postcard), and fulfillment.

The List

How many names and addresses do you need? The industry considers a two percent response rate to a mail order offer good. That means you are doing well if 20 orders come from 1,000 catalogs mailed. Obviously you need tens of thousands of names and even then, there are no guarantees. One small New England science museum produced a classic mail order brochure for Christmas that was so well-executed it could have served as a model. They mailed what they thought was a large amount, 1,000. Their mailing list consisted solely of museum members, people who had an identifiable interest in the museum. A formula for certain success, right? They did not receive a single order. Determining why is speculation but it may have been because the mailing list comprised people who lived within a 45-minute drive of the museum and such people rarely order by mail. Their list was not large enough: 100,000 would have been a better size pool.

The Smithsonian's attractive catalog garners an impressive response rate of about 5% on well over 10 million catalogs mailed out annually (1986 figures). They began in 1975 and worked seven or eight years before they broke even. Now the catalog operation is very profitable, exceeding the annual revenues of all their museum stores, but it took a large investment in time and money to get there.

Where do you get a list? The phone book provides a free list, but using such a general roster is likely to result in a dismal response rate and a significant waste of money and effort. Your guest book at the museum's entrance and your membership roster are good starting points. They are not enough in themselves. You could try trading names with other museums or buying them from a publication whose readers might be interested in your products. A club or historical society might sell you their membership list. The idea is to identify probable customers from their organizational associations so that your response rate exceeds one or two percent. Buying lists from any source is not cheap and you are not really "buying," you are renting, which means you are only permitted to use the list once. Customers who respond to your initial mailing are then considered "yours" and those names can be added to your permanent list.

The Products

Select a mixture of proven sellers and new products that will photograph well. Try for at least a $10 price point or use a minimum order to keep order amounts from being so low that they actually *cost* you money to fill. Make certain the products are mailable, not too large or excessively fragile. Butter churns, straw hats, and glass hurricane shades have proven to be poor travelers.

Have the product on hand before you even contemplate including it in the catalog. The law requires shipment within 30 days of receipt of the order unless otherwise specified in the copy, or you must notify the customer, giving the anticipated shipping date and offering a refund. More rules kick in if you can't make *that* date and you soon find your time and profits going toward delay notices and follow-up record keeping.

When figuring catalog retails remember shipping, handling, wrapping, boxes, and insurance. Either add these costs to the regular retail or have the customer add them on the order blank. As you may have guessed by now, mail order merchandise needs a greater average markup than store items. Look for products that can carry better than a keystone markup—three times cost or more is best. Although the size of the Smithsonian catalog keeps it from being typical of museum store catalogs, it is interesting to note that its cost of sale goal for catalog merchandise is 40%.

The Presentation

There are professionals who design mail order pieces: designers who create the layouts, photographers who specialize in catalogs, copywriters who devise the selling message and product descriptions, printers who print, fold, and bind, and distributors (lettershops) who mail it out for you. All of these are expensive. So is postage. The 1991 hike in third class mail rates is so significant (it ranges from a 25% to 40% increase) that it is expected to put some mail order houses out of business.

One beginner's alternative might be to contact the art department at your local university. There may be art or design students and photographers willing to volunteer for the experience. This route is risky. Odds are you will get an amateurish, if imaginative, piece that flies in the face of standard catalog practice. To better your odds, study a copy of *How to Create Successful Catalogs* by the Maxwell Sroge Publishing Company, Inc. (Crain Books: 1985) which takes you step by step through the 21-week process (according to them) of producing a full-scale mail order catalog.

This book breaks down the catalog process and methodically covers the details of creating a catalog. It does not delve into list management, product selection or development, or fulfillment, each topic worthy of a "how to . . ." book in and of itself. *How to Create Successful Catalogs* is a workbook, designed to be used, not merely read. It provides a goldmine of ideas and information, good and bad examples, advantages and disadvantages to various approaches, all written in a friendly manner with plenty of good, sound advice from professionals.

Starting with a short history of catalogs, the book deals with the technicalities of planning and scheduling the 38 steps the authors identify that go into catalog production. Several chapters discuss different design approaches, various styles of page layouts, and how to present the visuals. Making decisions about the front cover, the back cover, and the "hot spots" inside are easier if you are aware of the issues involved. The intricacies of good page layout are explained, as is working within a grid and the many grid options. Ways to handle blank space or "air," how to avoid clutter, and how and when to separate the artwork from the descriptive copy are explained at length.

Your catalog can be illustrated with photographs or with artists' renderings, in black and white or in color. The selection depends largely upon your product and the budget. If photography is the chosen medium, finding the right photographer is critical. The relative merits of studio vs. location shooting and the potential for stock photography must be considered. Even the best, most experienced photographers and artists need direction from you or from the catalog designer. For instance, they need to know lighting preferences, background, picture size, product positioning, and whether any props are to be used.

Writing copy for your catalog is treated at length. In *How to Create Successful Catalogs* you will find the guidelines for writing front and back cover copy, inside references, headlines, and product copy, and for selecting the tone or style of the wording. The components of catalog credibility are discussed next: the guarantee you make to your prospective customers, the introductory letter, the company history, testimonials, and the importance of scrupulously honest copy without exaggerated claims or stretched truths. Following that are directions for selecting the typestyle and size for your publication and for dealing with the typesetter.

Composing the order form seems easier than it is. There is so much to forget and the result often defies the main rule: Keep It Simple! An entire chapter is devoted to the order form: its layout, its content, its position in the catalog. Even the envelope is a complex and important aspect of the whole.

Planning the production of the catalog comes next. This includes selecting a printer, choosing paper stock, dealing with color separators, choosing an address label method, finding a lettershop, and avoiding costly and time-consuming errors. Last are the legal issues, the responsibilities of mail order fulfillment: the FTC 30-day rule, Truth in Lending, guarantees, deceptive advertising, sales tax, Fair Credit Billing Act, merchandise substitution, and where to get copies of the pertinent regulations.

The Sroge *How to* book is not alone on the market; there are a host of others, some more specialized, to help you along. Write or call

Catalog Age Book Division, Box 4949, Stamford, CT 06907–0949, 203-358-9900 ext. 204 for a list of books and publications dealing with catalogs. They publish two magazines that you might find helpful, "Catalog Age" and "Catalog Product News." The mail order industry has its own trade show as well. Contact National Mail Order Merchandise Show, 47 Main Street, Clifton, NJ 07014 or call 201-661-9681 for more information about dates and locations.

Fulfillment

Fulfillment involves everything you must do to fill an order: determining adequate stock levels for each item so that you do not run out, having a warehouse for storage and a place to collect and pack the order, acquiring suitable packing materials, organizing shipment methods such as UPS pick ups or trips to the Post Office, having a good phone system and probably an 800 number, and of course, hiring and training employees to handle all the packing, filing, phone calls, and order processing. It would be hard to accomplish all this without a good computer system.

Alternatives

If this short treatment of mail order has dampened your enthusiasm for such projects, well and good. No museum shop should consider launching a full-fledged mail order program without having had years of proven success at more modest endeavors. There are several reasonable alternatives to big-time mail order for smaller institutions to consider.

1. Have a product and price list for customers to take home. Pile them by the cash register or stick one in every bag. This need not be a slick production: typed, sketched, and photocopied is fine for a start. Naturally, nicer is better. Try to feature merchandise that is exclusively yours, items with a strong educational relationship to the museum.
2. Run a page or a single item advertisement in a museum publication, either your own or that of another museum without its own mail order program.
3. Run an insert in the center of your museum's magazine. If your readership is primarily local, this will result in little mail order, but should bring you added walk-in business. If your readers live further than a 30 or 45-minute drive, you may collect some orders.

4. Put together a brochure of classroom teaching aids to send to schools and teachers in your region or state.
5. Print business cards with the store's name, address, and phone number to drop into every bag. Customers may want to reorder or purchase gifts that they remember seeing in your shop.

The Science Museum of Western Virginia is one establishment that has developed a successful, if modest, brochure. Their mailing list of 5,000 is composed of individual and corporate members, contributors, all the schools in their region, and all the newspapers. Theirs is not a full-fledged catalog, but more of an illustrated list with black and white photos. It has no order form at all because the museum's intent is not to get into the complexities of mail order in a big way, but rather to bring more people into the shop. To make a purchase, you either come into the shop to buy or call to order through the mail. There has been a noticeable increase in purchases at the shop since the brochures were mailed and the sales staff is able to handle the moderate number of mail requests each day. But one might well wonder, was all the expense worth the results? In this case, absolutely, because there was no expense. The store manager, Shirley Thompson, who is very involved in the community, asked for and received donations of paper and ink, a staff member volunteered to take the photos, the copy was typed rather than typeset, and the printing and postage was "free" since the brochure came out as part of a scheduled newsletter issue. Few shop managers are so active in their pursuit of outside help as this one, but she is not alone in asking for donations to benefit the museum's shop.

The Stonewall Jackson House in Lexington, VA created a very professional catalog consisting of a 17 x 11 inch sheet of paper folded in half. It featured their exclusive related items: a new cookbook that is both educational and related, historic posters and prints, mugs bearing famous Jackson quotations, and books. The response has transformed their traditionally slow winter period into what they term a busy season. This small shop plans to use the brochure to expand its customer base into the alumni groups of the town's two historic universities, Washington and Lee and Virginia Military Institute, where identification with the museum's main topics (Civil War, Jackson, Lee, and the town of Lexington) is strong.

List creators would profit from this example. There is usually a college or university nearby that may have a natural tie-in with your museum's focus. Universities seldom share their alumni lists, (ask anyway), but you might explore other options:

1. Place an advertisement in the alumni magazine or newsletter. Would they let you run a free ad in exchange for some merchandise? (Your overstocked maps or prints, for example.)
2. Buy a complete page in the alumni publication and fill it with photos and copy.
3. Offer to pay for postage of the alumni society's next newsletter mailing if they will include your brochure.
4. As a donation to your museum, would the school share its alumni list?
5. Can you set up a booth or distribute flyers or catalogs at the next homecoming, class reunion, or football game?

If a shop is tempted by mail order, the manager and the museum director should discuss how best to experiment. After all, your museum may have the potential to reach a full-fledged catalog program. You can find out without the risk of wasting large amounts of money and time if you start small and grow slowly.

Wholesale Operations

Wholesaling to gift shops and other museum stores is another of those endeavors that sounds great but needs to be approached with caution. As a sideline it may be an acceptable way to dispose of an inventory overstock, or to turn a little extra profit on a nice product, but as a full-scale business venture, wholesaling is not to be trifled with.

There is a good outlet for your merchandise through the Museum Store Association.[2] The MSA is a non-profit organization aimed directly at museum stores. Every museum store should join. Membership is not expensive—dues are based on the store's revenues—and you will receive a lot for the money.

Members can attend the annual trade show (one of the better ones) which is growing every year. Their magazine, *Museum Store,* carries good articles on retail management and deals with problems experienced by museum stores. Suppliers who cater to museum stores place ads in the magazine. The MSA brings members up to date on show schedules and tax information and it sponsors an annual convention where you can meet others in your field and expand your knowledge. MSA members can purchase the MSA membership list of history museums or of all museums for a nominal fee. The list is an excellent means of identifying potential wholesale customers. Also member shops can advertise at no charge the products they wish to wholesale in the "MSA Sales" section in the *Mu-*

seum Store magazine. If you wholesale several items, it may be worthwhile to exhibit at the Members Market, a special part of the annual trade show limited to museums that wholesale to one another.

The only products to wholesale are (1) those that will relate to other museums, (2) those that have enough mark up room to allow for wholesaling, and (3) those that are exclusively yours.

Publications, posters, and printed matter are at the top of the list for two reasons: they often deal with topics of broad applicability and the characteristics of printing (twice the quantity does not cost you twice the price) bring the cost of sale quite low on large runs. For example, if a box of notecards costs $2.00 to produce and your shop retails them for $4.00, they will make a poor wholesale product. To make a profit at wholesale you would need to charge around $2.50 to $3.00 for the box. The purchasing museum shop paying that would have to retail them for $5.00 to $6.00 at least. So what? Presumably they are not worth $6.00 (or *your* shop would be charging $6.00, right?), not to mention a $6.00 retail prices the purchaser way over the competition. Put yourself in the purchaser's place. That sort of deal wouldn't interest you, would it? There must be enough of a mark up to allow room for the purchaser to make at least a keystone mark up and still come equal to your retail. Printed matter (books, notecards, posters, maps, prints, brochures, and games) usually provides ample spread.

A better example is the box of notecards that cost you $2.00 which you retail for $6.00. The wholesale price of $3.00 permits the purchaser to mark it up to $6.00 and maintain a respectable profit margin. Wholesaling on this scale is manageable for most museum sales programs.

Notes

1. A good source for plexiglass risers is Roberts Colonial House, Inc., 570 GR West 167th Street, South Holland, IL 60473, with no minimums for prepaid orders. Call 708-331-6233 for catalog.
2. In 1955 representatives of 24 museums met in New York City and founded the Museum Store Association, Inc. According to its membership brochure, today's membership includes over 500 museum stores across the United States, with a few in Canada, Australia, the United Kingdom, and several other countries. The Association's purpose is "to promote the general welfare of the museum store industry by encouraging high standards of professional competence, conduct, and ethics in accordance with the association's code of ethics so that museum stores can professionally serve and profitably meet the needs of their museums and the public."

    The MSA acts as a clearinghouse for information that will help member museums improve their shops. To this end they sponsor an annual meeting full of practical workshops and seminars on topics from lighting to licensing, and a large trade show featuring several hundred vendors seeking to sell to museum stores. Science museums will find more vendors geared toward them than will history or art museums, but there is something for everyone. The Members Market allows member museum stores to wholesale products to one another, as does a regular section in the association's quarterly magazine, *Museum Store*. Thirteen regional chapters encompassing several states each meet once or twice a year.

The MSA began a major project in 1989 called "MSA Data Banque," which is intended to be a permanent, regularly updated data base of financial and statistical information on museum stores. The MSA compiled the information from questionnaires circulated to its member stores in 1988 (most of the information therefore was from 1987 figures) and summarized it in a book selling for $50.00. Unfortunately, the book did not appear until 1990, making most of the numbers obsolete. An update is not planned until 1995. The store managers I spoke with were disappointed with the first edition because it lacked any interpretation, explanation, or advice on how to improve or make changes. They and I preferred the format of the MSA's earlier publication, *Financial Analysis for Museum Stores,* finding it more useful in a constructive sense. If you want to examine the "Date Banque," call around town to other museum store managers and see if any of them have one to lend you. I do not recommend buying a copy until the numbers are updated, presumably in 1996.

Both museum stores and vendors can join the organization; only the former can vote. Dues are based on a shop's gross revenue and range from $35 for shops grossing less than $25,000 a year to a high of $150 for shops grossing in excess of one million dollars annually (1988 figures). Write for more information:

Museum Store Association, Inc.
501 South Cherry St., Suite 460
Denver, CO 80222
303-329-6968

9

Protecting Your Museum and Its Store

Theft: The Five-Fingered Discount

Far too many store managers and museum directors prefer to stick their heads in the sand and pretend that their store does not have a problem with theft. It is common to read that museum stores, due to their "better sort" of clientele, do not suffer from shoplifting to any degree worth bothering with; similarly one often hears that museum store employees, or especially volunteers, are simply not the sort of people who would steal. While this may have a kernel of truth to it, it is not a large enough kernel to allow store managers or museum directors to become complacent about this issue. *Every* store has a problem with theft; ignore it at your peril. Theft is not a pleasant issue to deal with. In order to deal with it as seldom as possible, take the necessary precautions.

First some sobering statistics: sticky-fingered employees and customers steal an estimated 9 BILLION dollars of merchandise a year from stores (1990 figures). Employee theft from all work places, offices, factories, and such, is thought to run ten times that amount. Losses due to employee theft account for the failure of six out of ten small businesses every year. To put this in a retail perspective, if a shop with a net profit of 9% loses a $100 item due to theft, it will take over $10,000 worth of sales to make up for that $91 of loss.

Basically there are two types of thieves: shoplifters and your own employees.

Shoplifters

Shoplifting has increased by 35 percent in the past four years, making it the fastest-growing larceny crime in the country. One depressing study figured that shoplifters get away with the crime 97% of the time. Christmas, the biggest season for retailers, is also the most active for shoplifters.

Stealing merchandise is harder in stores that were thoughtfully laid out during the initial design phase. Every part of the store should be visible from the cash register(s). There should be no hidden nooks, back rooms, or upstairs unless the area can be supervised by a salesperson. The cash register should be located fairly near the door and there should be only one door in regular use, not counting emergency doors. If your shop was not laid out by an interior designer or architect experienced in retail spaces, and most were not, try to move fixtures or re-work the space to make it more visible. Sales clerks must understand that they cannot ever leave the store or their section unattended, even for a moment. In many retail establishments, this alone is grounds for immediate dismissal. The manager should plan the merchandise arrangement so that the most expensive items are beyond easy reach on high shelves or locked in glass showcases.

Make sure that each store employee (salespersons, stockroom people, office clerical staff, etc.) is made aware of the hazards of shoplifting. Everyone can play an important role in preventing theft. Salespeople should acknowledge each customer who enters the store with a cheerful greeting and eye contact. They should avoid turning their backs to the customer and observe closely whenever certain types of people come into the shop.

Contrary to popular opinion, appearance is not generally a clue to identifying a shoplifter. Shoplifters can look rich or shabby, be male or female, black or white, young or old; they can come into your store carrying little babies or sitting in a wheelchair. It is usually by his or her *actions* that you become suspicious of someone. If you are uneasy, watch the person's hands closely. See whether he or she is constantly looking quickly around as if to check whether anyone is watching. The clumsy shopper who keeps dropping things on the floor, the person who studies tickets instead of merchandise, the customer who asks to see more items before the salesperson has been able to put some away, the absent-minded person who carries things about the shop before purchasing, the customer who hangs around the counters or display areas without wanting any assistance, and the hurried shopper who rushes in at the last minute as the sales clerks are closing out the registers, all need to be observed closely. Anyone who gets too near the door holding unpurchased merchandise should be approached and asked politely, "Can I ring that up for you now?" Watch particularly for:

1. Groups of juveniles who are unsupervised by teacher or adult.
2. People wearing large, loose coats or jackets, or heavy coats in warm weather.

3. People carrying large hand bags, shopping bags, umbrellas, strollers, baby carriers, back packs, or folded newspapers.

Amateur shoplifters, usually nervous and self-conscious, act on impulse and can be dissuaded if the situation looks too risky. Children and teen-agers may be responding to a dare, or may want the excitement of getting away with something. These sorts of shoplifters are generally easy to spot and easy to discourage with lots of pleasant attention from the salesperson. It is the professionals who are hardest to handle. I have seen films of some who are so smooth that, even though we were told who to watch, we were unable to catch him in the act. Most professionals are very cautious and will leave if they feel the salespeople are observing them. Often they operate in pairs, either entering the shop together like a couple or coming in separately so you don't realize they are "together." The idea is for one to monopolize the salesperson while the other steals. Crowds make it easier for thieves to steal. A shoplifter may manipulate legitimate crowds or he may have two or three friends provide a shield so that the salesperson cannot see what he is doing.

The Smithsonian Museum Shops put out a memorandum several years ago to their employees listing the most common methods of shoplifting.

1. *Palming*. The simplest way to steal small items.
2. *Handling*. Inspecting three or four items at the same time, constantly reaching between other customers to pick up articles, some returned, some stolen. Especially effective with jewelry.
3. *Ticket switching*. To buy something at a lower price, thieves will switch tickets or boxes. Experienced store employees who know the merchandise usually spot this, and no, you are not obligated to give the customer the incorrect price! Explain that "someone" has put an incorrect label on the item, apologize, and ask whether the customer (who may not be the guilty party, after all) still wants it at the correct price.
4. *Hiding objects*. Merchandise is hidden under coats, in pockets, up a sleeve, in purses, shopping bags, umbrellas, diaper bags, tote bags, briefcases, gym bags, or concealed in strollers or wheelchairs.
5. *Covering objects*. Laying a jacket, gloves, newspaper, or other item on the counter on top of a piece of merchandise and picking up the jacket and the merchandise together.

6. *"Hit and run."* The shoplifter comes into the shop, grabs something near the door, and leaves quickly. You see it all, but what can you do? Do not run after the person! Try to notice as much as you can about the thief: clothing, age, physical description, and which way he or she was heading. Call the museum's security or the police and let them handle it.

Salespeople should not accuse anyone of being a thief, nor should they touch, threaten, run after, or attempt to detain a suspected shoplifter. Store managers must have a clear policy on who to call (the manager or security officer usually) when the salesperson suspects someone of being a shoplifter. Luckily *the best deterrence against shoplifting is good retail manners: prompt and courteous service, pleasant acknowledgement of each customer, and lots of attention.*

Internal Theft

No one likes to acknowledge that their employees may be stealing from them. There are many reasons why employees steal. They often rationalize it as something the company owes them. "I deserve this, I'm so poorly paid," or "Everybody else does it," or "It'll serve them right for not letting me have Saturday off." These people know they are stealing but justify it as their due. "The company can afford it," they reason, "and I can't." They may feel no one will know, or worse, no one will care. These people steal merchandise or cash from the register.

Another group of employees steals without considering their actions "stealing." I have known people to sell something at 50% off as "damaged" to a friend who wanted it badly but couldn't afford it at full price, "just to help out." I've known people who extended their legitimate employee or museum member discount to an acquaintance, courteously getting them a discount they didn't deserve. I've known people who regularly "taste test" the edibles, and some who got in the habit of wearing the jewelry while at work because it helped sales (it really did) and then sort of adopting it permanently after a while. None of these people considered what they were doing as stealing, but it was. The best way to prevent this sort of theft is to acknowledge it. Let people know that buying something with their discount for someone else is STEALING and will be dealt with as such. Don't use sanitized words like "shrinkage" or "pilferage"—call it Stealing with a capital S. If you suspect this is a problem in your store, you might first give a generalized warning in the form of a clarification defining stealing, then take action against any violations.

Let employees know that if they are aware of someone stealing and do not report it, they could be considered an accessory and charged with a crime. No doubt your employees would quickly report it if they observed a customer or outsider stealing. The manager must impress upon them that it is no different when the thief works for the museum or for the shop itself.

Anyone with access to the store is a potential thief. No one is immune from temptation, including security officers, curators, trustees, and top administrators. Stores and stock rooms should be lockable and as few people as possible should have the key. Store employees need to ask polite questions whenever they see someone they do not recognize or someone who does not belong there in a stockroom or behind a counter. Non-employees like delivery people, sales reps, pest control people, or utility repairmen should always be escorted and accompanied when in sensitive areas. All of these precautions will have an added bonus: they will serve as evidence that the museum is serious about theft and can help discourage employees from stealing.

An experienced museum director due to open his museum's first store once asked me nervously what sort of controls he should establish prevent theft. His greatest concern, and I suspect the concern of many directors, was that he didn't know enough about retailing to recognize sophisticated theft, particularly if it originated with the manager. There is no easy answer; obviously the museum director can't oversee every detail or he may as well take the store manager job himself. The best policy is for the store manager and the director to work together as often as possible to establish procedures and regularly (weekly or at least monthly) review the books and the premises. Being alert to changes and asking questions about discrepancies sends a strong message to a potentially dishonest manager or assistant manager. Monitor the "shrinkage" levels closely, that's where theft usually shows up. Ask to have the shrinkage explained and documented. Pay particular attention if it goes above 2%. (There are valid reasons that shrinkage might be high or fluctuate wildly, just know what they are.) Set a policy as regards to damaged merchandise, for example, require the manager or another person to co-sign the damage sheet (a list of discarded merchandise) when something breaks so you aren't taking one person's word that the item was thrown out.

Never underestimate the power of setting an example. I once had a supervisor who would bend down and pick up trash as she walked the museum grounds. In no time, we were all imitating her behavior. If the director and the manager take pains to show their concern for honesty and theft prevention, it will filter down. Just knowing that your superiors care and pay close attention to details is often enough to discourage theft.

Another precaution to take involves background checks on prospective employees. It is shocking how few employers actually follow up on references. At the very minimum, call (don't write) the person's previous employer and speak with the supervisor, not the Personnel Department. Ask "We are considering Ms. Jones for a position involving cash handling. Did you ever have any reason to question her honesty when she worked for you?" Ask Ms. Jones and her previous employer why she left the job. Compare answers. Some companies, especially larger corporations, refuse to give out any information other than to confirm that the person worked there, when, and in what position, so you will not find out much from them. Keep going down the list of references until you reach someone who is able to help you. If you've exhausted the list, call Ms. Jones and ask for more work-related references. Be sure to exclude relatives or friends.

How do employees steal and what can be done to prevent it?

1. They can steal cash from the register in a number of ways: keep the receipt and ring up a return when the customer is gone; void a sale; write a fraudulent cash refund. The most common is probably accepting the cash from the customer and put it directly in their pocket without ringing up the sale at all. Insist every customer be given a receipt. (That's why in some retail shops the customer is offered a prize if the sales clerk fails to give them a receipt. You can do this too if you suspect this problem.) Have the manager or another employee co-sign all voided transactions, returns, and errors. Set aside a safe area for purses, if possible away from the register or the stockroom.

2. They can ring up their own sale for less than the correct amount. Never allow an employee to ring up his or her own sale.

3. They eat it, wear it out of the store, or give it to a friend. Require employees to keep sales receipts for the entire day if they purchase anything. Don't allow employees to wear anything they do not own, such as scarves, jewelry, or hats. If you find that wearing the items improves sales (and I believe you will), encourage employees to buy the items by offering a special discount in return for wearing the items at work. Just as employees do not ring up their own sales, they do not ring up sales to their friends or relatives. They can certainly wait on their friends and relatives, but should call for someone else to ring up the sale.

4. They conceal merchandise and carry it out of the store themselves; they can drop items out a window or carry them out
   to the trash bins to retrieve later. Packages leaving the store
   with employees should be inspected for a receipt. The manager and director should set an example by voluntarily opening any packages and showing the receipt to the clerk on
   duty when they leave the store. Be alert to any packages left
   where they shouldn't be, like near a trash bin or an exit.

If you suspect someone of stealing but cannot prove it, or if you think
something funny is going on but can't figure out who could be involved,
look into professional shopping services. These are little known outside
the retailing world, but they can be the answer to your dilemma. The
shopping service sends undercover "customers" to your store to make actual purchases, which are later returned. These "shoppers" are trained to
recognize suspicious cash handling procedures and they watch the salesperson closely, whereas a real customer seldom pays any attention to what
the salespeople are doing, as long as it's quick. These shopping services
aren't cheap, but then, neither is theft. Call your local Retail Merchants
Association for information; some offer such a service to members, others
will refer you to private firms. You can improvise if you have a friend
familiar with standard retailing practices and cash handling procedures,
who will not be recognized in your shop.

When an employee is caught stealing from the store, he or she should
be prosecuted. This is seldom done because the manager or director is
embarrassed by having been "taken" and the museum cringes at the
thought of the adverse publicity that might result from a trial. Nonetheless, an employee who is merely dismissed will be free to continue the
crime elsewhere and the museum will have failed miserably in showing its
commitment to honest business practices. Lenient treatment encourages
the belief that, yes, you *can* get away with it! If it is clear that guilty people
will not only lose their jobs, but suffer the shame of a trial and a police
record, temptations lessen.

Product Marking

Museums need to become more sensitive to the potential misuse of
the products they develop and sell. Curators in particular are extremely
concerned about the manufacture of what they consider "instant antiques," in part because most of them have been asked on more than one
occasion to examine or appraise an "antique" that turned out to be an

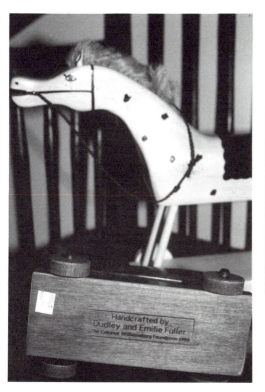

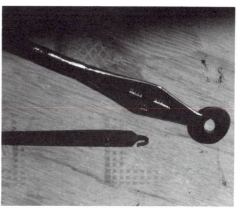

Relatively permanent product markings are not difficult to apply and go a long way toward addressing the concerns of those who worry about the unintentional creation of fakes. All products, whether reproductions or not, should be marked or identified in some fashion. *Photos by author.*

unmarked reproduction. Of course there will always be unscrupulous people who will try to pass off fakes as originals, but there is no need for the museum to contribute, albeit unwillingly, to the practice. A permanent mark on the product will go a long way toward preventing amateurs from being swindled or confused.

Reproductions that are made in precisely the same manner as the antiques differ so little from the original that, after only a few years of age, even the most knowledgeable curator or dealer is hard-pressed to make the distinction. The reproductions most susceptible to confusion are those made by craftsmen working with period tools in the period manner, notably handforged wrought iron, baskets, tinware, pottery (especially salt-glazed stoneware), and the like.

Relatively permanent marks are not difficult to apply. For wooden items, the date, logo, or name of the museum can be burned into the wood; for most metals, a stamp can be used to impress a mark; for ceramics, an impression stamped while the clay is still green or a painted mark applied underneath the glaze is sufficient. Some museums prefer to leave the original date off of a reproduction. For example, an antique earthenware dish marked with the date "1772" may be copied with the date omitted entirely or with the current year in its place.

Marks can consist of one or more of the following, the more the better:

- Date of manufacture.
- Museum's name.
- Museum's logo.
- Store's logo.
- Craftsperson's mark.
- Craftsperson's name or initials.

Not only do marks protect the product from being confused with an antique, they can also spread the museum's name and reputation and act as protection against cheaper imitations.

Product Liability Concerns

There is no way to prevent someone from filing a lawsuit against your museum should they choose to do so. An injured person, or one who believes or pretends to be injured, can sue the store, the museum, the distributor, and/or the manufacturer of a product for breach of express or implied warranty or for negligence.

Warranties are based on the Uniform Commercial Code which can be amended by state, so circumstances may differ depending upon your museum's location. Basically an express warranty is one that is explicitly stated, such as a five-year warranty on the parts of a television. An implied warranty is presumed; for instance, you presume that the ladder you buy can hold the weight of an average person. You can disallow implied warranties to some extent by labelling, thus limiting your liability. ("Caution: this ladder holds up to 250 pounds")

Negligence is a tort, a civil action as opposed to a criminal action. Negligence is a breach of duty of care, when your action or failure to act causes harm to others.

While you cannot completely eliminate the possibility of lawsuits, there are ways to discourage suits and certain precautions to take *now* that will improve your position should you ever find yourself in court. Print a warning on the package or product if the item is not intended for children. Of special concern are children under the age of three who put virtually everything into their mouths. At many children's or baby stores you can buy a simple device to test whether an item is of a size that would choke a toddler. Merely drop the item through the cylinder—if it fits into the tube (1 1/4 inch diameter), it is almost certain to be small enough to choke a young child. If you cannot locate one, send $1.00 to Toys To Grow On, Department Safe Toy, P.O. Box 17, Long Beach, CA 90801.

Consider the product's size, sharp edges, or poisonous content. Make certain all paints are non-toxic, particularly on goods imported from countries where laws against lead-based paints are weak or enforcement is lax. Lead glazes on ceramics are permitted in many countries, including the United States, but here such items must be marked "For Decorative Use Only" or "Not for Use with Food." Pewter is a similar case. Lead should not be part of its formula. Nor should lead solder be used to make tinwear if it is intended for use with food or beverages.

Instruct your sales staff to caution people who buy a product that is inappropriate for little children. "You realize, don't you, sir, that this is not intended for children under the age of three?"

If your store sells food products, follow all local Health Department regulations scrupulously and check that the companies with which you deal have adequate insurance. Ask that their insurer send you a statement confirming their liability policy and its amount and keep it on file. Verify annually.

Check with your museum's insurance carrier to ascertain whether or not your museum has product liability coverage and whether the amount is adequate. It may be included in the museum's "All Perils" coverage. You can buy specific product liability insurance or you can supplement existing coverage with an additional endorsement.

The best advice is: When in doubt, don't. If there is the slightest apprehension that those wonderful reproduction marbles that happen to resemble gumballs might break a tooth or get lodged in a toddler's throat, shelve the project. There are plenty of other ideas to pursue. No one needs those kinds of risks.

Copyrights

Copyright is a form of protection provided by the laws of the United States to authors and creators of *original* works. Many types of original works can be copyrighted. The two categories that are most likely to apply to museums are *literary works* and *pictorial, graphics, and sculptured works*. For a few institutions, *motion pictures and other audiovisual works* and *sound recordings* may be relevant.

Museum shops frequently copyright books, mail order brochures, stationery, posters, designs for bookmarks, tote bags, and so forth. Exact reproductions of two- or three-dimensional objects in the museum's collection cannot be copyrighted because they do not meet the criteria for originality.

Copyrighting provides the museum with an inexpensive form of protection for those designs and items that have commercial value. It prevents, or at least discourages, unscrupulous people from copying your successful creation and undercutting your price, your quality, and your good reputation. Copyrighting adds a little prestige to the object and professionalism to your museum by its implication that you are proud of the object and professional enough to recognize its value and commercial potential.

On January 1, 1978, a new copyright law took effect. As of that date, copyright is secured automatically upon the creation of an original work. In other words, the author of a book has the copyright to the work as soon as the book is completed. This is often misunderstood. Publication or registration is not required to secure copyright. However there are several advantages to registration and it is strongly advised.

Registration is a "legal formality intended to make public record of the basic facts of a particular copyright," says the government publication "Copyright Basics." It establishes proof of the date of your claim, thereby enabling you to protect your object from subsequent infringement. Should you need to take legal action against someone who has stolen your original design, registration is necessary before any suits can be filed in court and it will probably be your best evidence. Also, attorney's fees and statutory damages are available to the legitimate copyright owner if registration has occurred, otherwise only actual damages and profits can be awarded.

Registration is surprisingly simple. It involves sending three things together to the Library of Congress: a completed application, a $20 fee, and two copies of the actual work. Applications are short forms that come with detailed instructions. Form TX is used for non-dramatic literary works, form PA is for works of the performing arts such as audiovisual works, form SR is for sound recordings, and form VA is for the visual arts (two- and three-dimensional works of fine arts, graphic arts, applied arts, photographs, maps, charts, models, etc.). For an application form write:

Copyright Office
Library of Congress
Washington, DC 20559

or call 202-707-9100, a 24-hour line. Application forms are free.

Notice of copyright *should* appear somewhere on the item. Although it is no longer (March 1, 1989) required, it is still strongly recommended as it serves as a warning to potential infringers and adds that intangible touch of professionalism. Copyright notice consists of three elements: the symbol © or the word "Copyright," the year of first publication of the work, and the name of the copyright owner, in this case, your museum. The museum is copyrighting works made for hire by museum employees who prepared the work within the scope of their employment, or by non-employees commissioned and paid by the museum for their work. An example might look like this:

© 1991 Devonshire County Historical Society

The copyright for such "works made for hire" is thus secured for 75 years from publication or for 100 years from creation, whichever is *shorter*.

For details, write the Copyright Office (address above) and ask for their free circular R1 entitled "Copyright Basics." Special questions or problems not answered in that publication should be addressed to the Information and Publications Section, LM–455, at the same address.

Trademarks and Logos

A trademark can be defined as any word, name, symbol, or other device used by a merchant or manufacturer to identify and distinguish its products from those manufactured or sold by someone else. Its use is legally restricted to the owner.

Trademarks are not the same as trade names. COKE® is a registered trademark of the Coca-Cola Company (trade name). Trademarks are not the same as logos. A logo can become a trademark if it is used properly but, while many museums and museum shops have distinctive logos, few own trademarks.

Aside from distinguishing one manufacturer's goods from another's, a trademark guarantees a certain level of quality. Customers who choose to purchase a pair of LEVI® blue jeans or a box of CHEERIOS® cereal are indicating their preference for that quality level as opposed to another brand. Ideally a trademark creates and maintains a demand and helps establish a positive association between a museum and its goods.

Inspired by an important weather vane in the museum's collection, the rooster design is the registered trademark of the Abby Aldrich Rockefeller Folk Art Center (trade name). The Prentis mark, entwined initials of the four original partners who owned the Prentis Store in eighteenth-century Williamsburg, is the logo of the Historic Area Stores, the group of nine shops within Colonial Williamsburg's historic environs. Both marks are used the same way on products, tags, product literature, and paper bags, but one is protected and one is not.

For the greatest degree of protection under federal and state statutes, a trademark must be officially registered with the Department of Commerce. Trademark registration is considerably more expensive and complicated than copyright registration and would probably require an attorney's assistance. A mark must be registered for each and every category of goods for which protection is needed and the costs can run as high as $1,000 per category. At the time of registration, a thorough search must be carried out to insure that the proposed trademark is unique. If it is deemed too similar to one previously registered, the mark must be redesigned.

An encircled ™ can be used to indicate an unregistered "common law" trademark. The advantage of going this route is that you do not need to take any action with any government agency to have protection. A registered trademark is indicated by the encircled ®. Registration does provide certain benefits and protections, and deserves your consideration. The federal Lanham Act which establishes rules for registration was modified in 1988. One change makes it easier and less costly to register a mark since it permits you to apply for registration of a mark you *intend* to use instead of making you send examples of the mark already in use. The pitfall used to be that, after you had gone to the expense of putting your trademark on numerous items and literature, it was possible for the Commerce Department to find that your design conflicted with an existing registered mark and needed revision. By registering your trademark, you secure rights to that design that are superior to those of a prior, unregistered owner (with certain exceptions).

While the symbol ® indicates registration, registration in and of itself does not insure protection. You have probably heard the stories of lost trademarks: "aspirin" and "escalator," for example, and you probably see the advertisements certain trademark owners run urging you to use their trademark as an adjective instead of as a noun or verb. The Xerox Corporation, for example, is campaigning to get people to use the verb "to photocopy" instead of the verb "to xerox" and the Lego advertisements urge people to refer to their toys as "Lego blocks" rather than as "Legos." This is part of protecting their trademarks. Trademark rights come from continuous and proper use. They must receive special treatment—they must always be set apart from the surrounding copy with italics, capitals, or in the registered logo form. The trademark owner must act against all infringements. This can be as simple as a polite "cease and desist" letter or as complicated and costly as a lengthy legal battle.

It is not likely that a small or medium size museum would want to register a trademark, but look into the available information before making a decision. Write to:

U.S. Department of Commerce
Patent and Trademark Office
Washington, DC 20231

Ask for "General Information Concerning Trademarks." Museums interested in pursuing trademarks should ask their state bar association for recommendations for attorneys specializing in trademark law, or consult the Yellow Pages under "Patent and Trademark Attorneys." But for most museums and historical societies involved in product development, manufacture, and sales in a modest way, a simple logo or an unregistered trademark with the encircled ⓉⓂ is probably sufficient.

Tax Status and the IRS

An ancillary reason to restrict your museum shop to merchandise related to the museum's articulated purposes involves the Internal Revenue Service (IRS). The basic premise is that, by virtue of its educational character, your museum should qualify for nonprofit status. Therefore the revenue from the sales of items related to the museum's purposes is not taxable because it is viewed as a related activity within the scope of the museum's mission. The revenue from unrelated merchandise on the other hand is subject to tax, specifically the "unrelated business income tax," also known as UBIT. (Please note that we are not referring to sales tax, which your shop collects from the customer if required by your state.)

This is quite straightforward. The confusion and inevitable disputes arise over the term "related." Just how related is "related?" The IRS has put out little in the way of definitive guidelines. The only recourse is to read the laws, examine past Revenue Rulings, which *are* binding, and Technical Advice Memos, which are not, extrapolate the information onto your own circumstances, and hope for the best. It is plain to everyone that a book on Degas is related to the exempt purposes of an art museum with several of that artist's paintings displayed in its galleries, whereas a stuffed Santa doll is not. The going gets tougher when you start to slosh through the murky areas in between. Even the IRS admitted to its agents it its 1979 training manual, "There are many unresolved questions in this area." To say the least . . .

Complicating the problem is another variable, the IRS agent. Different agents may come to different conclusions about the same product and obviously you have no voice in which agent is assigned to your audit.

The two general categories of taxable items are items that are recognizably educational but not related to that particular museum's educational purposes (such as an astronomy game sold at a folk art museum) and items that have such a remote connection to the museum that their relationship to the institution's exempt purposes cannot be demonstrated (such as selling Perrier at an aquarium). In past audits, IRS agents have consistently cited specific products as unrelated: books and souvenirs relating to the city in which the museum is located, and T-shirts, caps, pennants, jewelry, ashtrays, tote bags, etc. bearing the museum's name or logo. "But those items spread our museum's name and give us good publicity, and that brings in more visitors. Surely that's educational, and it is part of the museum's purposes to attract more visitors to educate." Nice thought, and no doubt true, but not for tax purposes.

The fragmentation rule of 1969 allows the agent to sort through the products and demand taxes on those he or she deems unrelated. The task is then to come to some agreement with the agent on just what is unrelated and the amount of tax owed from past and current sales of the unrelated portion. Don't waste your breath arguing that all profits are used to further the museum's educational programs. The agents know that, and it hasn't mattered since Congress changed the tax laws in 1950. Prior to that year, interestingly enough, the *destination* of the funds was considered paramount; the 1950 laws changed that and now the *source* of the income is the determining factor.

You can have some effect on the outcome of an audit if you start preparing now. First, keep accurate records on sales—how many of what was sold each year. You can do this without point-of-sale registers if you keep copies of your orders or invoices. At least then you will know what you purchased each year and that should approximate what was sold fairly closely. Second, start now to rid your store of the merchandise that is obviously unrelated. Sell out and don't reorder, or reduce it to move it quickly. Third, begin using product information cards. Literature accompanying merchandise helps sustain your assertion that the item is related. This last point cannot be overemphasized.

All of this presumes that you *want* to maintain a nonprofit status. Contrary to what some believe, there is nothing illegal about selling unrelated merchandise, as long as you are paying federal tax on its income. If you are able to make significantly more money by selling unrelated products, should you? That fundamental decision is beyond the scope of the store manager. The museum's policymakers, presumably the Board of Trustees, must balance their need for revenue against their attitude toward the store. If the store is seen as an extension of the museum itself, its merchandise should be related for ethical reasons if no other. No doubt a circus would attract a larger crowd and more money than that exhibit on prehistoric pottery, but your museum doesn't entertain that idea. Why should the similar argument that selling Santa dolls is more profitable than books on Degas be given any more consideration at the store?

There is another way to attain a nonprofit classification: if "substantially all of the work is carried on by uncompensated volunteers." Many museums have stores staffed by volunteers. Those shops are automatically exempt whether their merchandise is related or not. However, ethically speaking, those shops should be just as motivated to sell related products as any shop with a paid staff. After all, *the purpose of carrying related goods is not to get out of paying taxes.* Related merchandise is the only sort that furthers the institution's educational purposes and, as an integral part of the museum, the store should be toeing the educational mark just like the exhibits, the living history program, the crafts, the lectures, and everything else the museum does.

It may not be realistic to expect that every single product in your shop can be related—at least not in the short run. Do limit the unrelated products, track their sales revenues, and pay tax on that portion of your income.

"But my shop is so small. It has gotten by forever without paying taxes and there has never been an audit. Should I really bother?" It is true that larger museums, like wealthy individuals, have a higher percentage of audits, but audits are initiated on museums of all sizes. With the phenomenal growth over the past decade of museum sales programs and the increasing controversy in the business world surrounding their nonprofit status, you can expect that *more* attention will be directed that way, not less.

Start paying UBIT on the items that are clearly unrelated. Start this year. Whether or not your sudden burst of taxes will wave a red flag and alert the IRS to your museum's past indiscretions no one can say but the IRS, and they won't. The question is really irrelevant. Ignoring the problem or delaying action will not make it go away. On the contrary, it will get worse. If you can show that you started to file as soon as you were made aware of the facts, you will at least demonstrate good faith and may be able to negotiate away the interest and penalties owed on back taxes.

Before you scare yourself silly with the implications here, ask your museum's tax attorney or accountant which statute of limitations (3 years, 6 years, or none) applies to your circumstances. Get a handle on the magnitude of the problem. Chances are it is a fairly minor one.

If you want to learn more about this issue, the IRS will send you its free Publication #598, "Tax on Unrelated Business Income of Exempt Organizations," explaining application of the law. The Published Resources section at the end recommends several excellent articles as well. You may like to look at the Internal Revenue Code yourself. Go to a law school library and ask for help in locating Sections 501, 511, 512 and 513. The Museum Store Association will send you a summary of recent Revenue Rulings pertaining to museum stores, or you can look these up yourself too. (Revenue Rulings 73–104 and 73–105.)

The Tax Reform Act of 1986 has little direct effect on museum stores. The indirect effect will probably become evident within a few years. If, as some tax experts predict, donations to museums in the form of both money and objects decline,[1] the pressure for increased income is likely to shift to the museum store. Throughout 1987, 1988, 1989, and 1990,

Congress considered, but did not act upon, revisions to the current tax exempt status of nonprofit sales programs. Some of the proposals would dramatically alter the tax status of museum stores and royalty programs but they were still being debated as of the spring of 1991.

Keep abreast of expected changes in the law through articles in the *Museum Store, History News,* and *Museum News.* Discuss changes with your accountant; if the laws change and your store is to pay tax on its profits, a revision of your bookkeeping procedures may be in order so that the actual expenses of running the store are accurately charged to the store. In most museums, the store is getting a free ride in many areas by not paying directly for its portion of legitimate business expenses such as security, electricity, heat and air conditioning, and other overhead, making the store's profits seem higher than they really are. You don't want to be taxes on unrealistically inflated profits.

Note

1. In a recent survey the Association of Art Museum Directors reported a 58% decline in the number of objects donated and a 16% decline in their value in 1987 as compared to 1986. The American Association of Museums reported a drop of 30.3% since 1987 in dollar value of donations to museums in general, not just art museums. The AAM estimates that, for all of its members (more than 2,200) 162,000 fewer objects were donated in 1987 over 1986. These figures would suggest that the doom-sayers' worst predictions are valid. The AAM is continuing to study the matter.

10

Planning for the Future

Be realistic. Changes, physical or attitudinal, cannot occur overnight. Before developing new products, packaging, training programs, and educational information, formalize a plan. Analyze your business. Where are the opportunities for greatest improvement? If your shop is not well positioned and easily accessible, that should be your first priority. If the store is being managed well and it has adequate support from the museum's hierarchy, then perhaps you can afford to turn to product improvement. Do not put the cart before the horse, for the best-selling, most educational and related merchandise in the world will go nowhere if the store is sloppily managed, the customers cannot find it, and the director actively opposes selling anything except books.

If one were to create a logical sequence of museum store action priorities, the list could look like this:

1. *The support and interest of the powers-that-be,* whether they are curators, directors, board members, or other significant staff; their willingness to commit time, thought, and money to the shop's improvement.
2. *Shop location, size, and accessibility.*
3. *Competent store management,* composed of a knowledgeable, dedicated shop manager not threatened by change, a well-trained and motivated sales staff or a strong volunteer corps working in the shop, and any necessary backup personnel such as stockroom help, buyers, product developers, secretaries, clerical staff, and interns.
4. *Merchandise improvement:* good inventory management, new product development, effective buying, realistic retail pricing, and related merchandise.
5. *Educational product interpretation,* written and oral.
6. *Other physical concerns* such as lighting, fixtures, visual merchandising, packaging, and background music.
7. *Advertising and promotion,* involvement in membership programs through discounts.

This should not be misconstrued as a list of relative merit, for it is not. In fact, one item low on the list, product interpretation, is one of the most important—after all, interpretation of educational products is what distinguishes the museum store from the corner gift shop. But it is a waste of time and money for a tiny store with poor accessibility, no support from above, and unrelated merchandise, run by a decrepit volunteer program to embark upon a product interpretation effort. It will quickly fail and for years to come people will shake their heads and say, "See? That educational stuff just doesn't work." Of course it didn't; the underpinnings weren't there. By working through this list or another approximating it, the shop will become incrementally stronger, able to support the next step.

Suppose that products is the area that offers the greatest potential for improvement for your store. Your schedule might begin like this:

Month I

Week 1. Talk to professional staff, set up advisory committee, garner support for plans to improve; exchange ideas for appropriate related merchandise.
Week 2. Identify overstocks and poor sellers; mark down.
Week 3. Identify unrelated merchandise and evaluate its financial contribution. Categorize it into three groups: (a) what to get rid of at once; (b) what to phase out gradually as new products can replace it; and (c) what, if anything, to keep.
Week 4. Begin action on category (a).

Month II

Target six new products to develop for your store within the next six months. Target twelve new products to buy. Identify appropriate shows or likely suppliers. Determine who is to do development and buying, how much money and time there is to spend. Recruit interns.

Month III

Discuss employee training. Set up plan and dates to begin. Start on employee reference book.

Month IV

Evaluate retails on all products; adjust where appropriate.

As you go, each month's goals should be broken down into easy-to-handle components that you schedule by the week or even by day. Remember that the process will probably take one to two years to produce significant results and it will never be completed. Every year will bring more opportunities for improvement. Just maintaining the existing level of accomplishment takes determined persistence.

For-profit businesses often develop a five-year plan in which the executives define their goals, where they expect the company to be five years from now, and what steps they believe will carry them there. It is usually a very specific document and one that is re-evaluated every six months or so to allow for unanticipated changes in the economy or in the marketplace. Museum store managers should run their business as carefully as if it were for profit, because it is. The time is past when excess money from the store was handed over to the financial officer at the end of the year to buy an extra "goodie" for the museum. Oh, there are still a few of those stores left that are run by an independent group of "friends" of the museum who keep their activities and financial information secret; then, when they are finished playing with the money, sponsoring picnics and supplying themselves with group T-shirts, turn over a couple thousand dollars to the museum in a sudden burst of generosity. I came across one such group this year but fortunately the museum's capable new director had already taken steps to divorce the "friends" from the store and put it on a closely-supervised and profitable basis for the first time. Stores cannot be the playthings of groups operating independently of the museum, they must be an integral part of the institution, managed with as close an eye to the bottom line as any for-profit store.

Each year the store manager should put together a brief report to his or her superiors, preferably the museum director and the Board of Trustees, outlining the store's achievements, financial and other. Such a report would include profits compared to previous years, of course, but also how many unrelated products discontinued, how many new related products developed or purchased, what percentage of revenue the new merchandise generated, staff training efforts and results, product information achievements, publicity generated, etc. Praise yourself and your store when it is appropriate.

Do not presume (or lead your superiors to assume) that improvements will immediately cause a great leap in revenue or profits. It costs money and persistence to effect many of these changes and the pay off may not occur overnight.

It will pay off in the long run. A genuine museum store that contributes significantly to the museum's educational purposes with related merchandise and that functions with professionalism and efficiency will persuade almost any opposition within the museum community that the store can be an integral part of the museum, deserving their support and praise. A true museum store fosters a sense of pride and accomplishment where once, perhaps, only apologies and embarrassment prevailed. Most successful managers will attest to the fact that, despite initial skepticism, their shops made bigger profits as they became more related and more closely tied to the museum's overall operational stream. Thus the true museum store as defined in chapter 1 serves two masters, Mammon and the Muses, and serves them equally well. Who says you can't have your cake and eat it too?

Published Resources

Some attention has been paid to the effective retail management of museum stores but little to their unique problems and opportunities. Virtually nothing is available on the educational aspect of the shop or the interpretive potential of related museum products.

The most relevant single publication for museum stores is *Museum Store* (formerly titled *MUST*), the quarterly magazine of the Museum Store Association. Every issue contains good articles, many of them written by museum store managers. Most contributors have retail backgrounds only so the treatment leans heavily toward retail store management aspects. Other museum publications, notably *History News* and *Museum News,* offer pertinent articles on occasion.

The Museum Store Association's *Financial Analysis for Museum Stores* (1986) by T. H. Aageson of Mystic Seaport's museum stores allows amateurs and experienced store managers alike to conduct a financial analysis of their shop, to compare their figures to those of other shops, and to spot weaknesses and plan improvements. Unfortunately this excellent publication is out of print and, even worse, the MSA shows no interest in reprinting or updating it. To see if any extra copies are available, write to Tom Aageson at Mystic Seaport Museum Stores, Mystic, CT 06355. Even though the numbers are out-of-date, it will still prove a valuable resource.

For a philosophical look at museum stores and their purposes, D. H. Krahel's "Why A Museum Store?" in *Curator,* 14 (1971) presents a good perspective on the goals of a museum store. T. Truco's article in *Art News* (Oct. 1977) entitled "The Shopping Boom at your Local Museum" deals with the ethical aspects of museum shop sales. British author D. Sekers discussed what he calls the propaganda value of a shop and the importance of integrating the shop into the museum through educational and curatorial oversight and assistance in *Museums Journal,* 76 (Mar. 1977). T. Kramer and E. Lang co-authored "Starting a Museum Shop" in *Museum News,* 63 (June 1985) with some good advice for those who may be looking in that direction.

Critical treatments of museum shops and sales programs abound and no wonder—there are still many deplorable ones around to give the whole genre a bad reputation! The negative point of view is important to read because such sentiments are frequently encountered within one's own organization by museum store "stepchildren." It is best to understand what you're up against. One of the most articulate is W. Hunt's "Comment: Museums, Profits, and Reproductions" in *Ceramics Monthly,* 34 (Apr. 1986). The author in a scathing assessment of museum reproductions, ceramics in particular, seems most offended by the distinction museum people make in reproducing "crafts" versus "art." Part of this stems from lingering dissatisfaction with society's estimation of craftspeople as inferior to artists and part stems from the author's well-presented personal skepticism about the underlying philosophy of museum reproduction. Thought provoking. S. E. Lee's article in *Art Journal* (Summer 1978) entitled "Life, Liberty and the Pursuit of . . . What?" is philosophical and wordy, however as it is written by a prominent museum professional opposed to sales programs, you might want to labor through it. Then read R. Zurofsky's "Sharp Shop Talk" in *Museum News* (July/Aug. 1989) for some responses to the most common accusations against stores.

Those institutions considering licensing programs would be well advised to read H. R. Alber's "And Visions of Royalties Danced in their Heads" in *Museum News,* 52 (Sept. 1973), R. Faul's "Licensing Programs: A Second Life for Museum Collections" in the Nov./Dec. 1975 issue of that magazine, and especially S. Hodes and K. Gross's "Museums in the Commercial Marketplace: the Need for Licensing Agreements." The latter can be found at any law school library in the *Connecticut Law Review,* 10, No. 3 (Spring 1978). It offers a sample draft of a licensing agreement, which is reprinted in the appendix here with the authors' permission, that could be indispensable to a museum considering a licensing program.

Museums toying with the idea of a mail-order program would do well to read M. Hebner's "Profits and Pitfalls in Mail-Order Merchandising" in *History News,* 35 (Nov. 1980) for the basics; also G. G. Murrey's "Catalog Sales: Mail Order Merchandising Makes Money for Museums" in the Feb. 1983 issue of that publication, and E. Sohn's "Almost All About Catalogs" in *MUST* (Winter 1985). Another informative piece is J. Kaminsky's "The Mail Mystique" in *GR: Gift Reporter* (July 1988), a gift store industry publication. *How To Create Successful Catalogs* (1985) by Maxwell Sroge Publishing Inc. is indispensable.

Those small museums naive enough to contemplate printing a dated product such as a calendar should look at A. Symons' "Entering the Calendar Race" in *MUST* (Winter 1985).

The best articles on the IRS and UBIT are S. D. Murphey's "Minding the Store: New Pronouncements from the IRS" in *Museum News,* 62 (Oct. 1983) and more recently A. Worley's "The Unrelated Business Debate: Wait Until Next Year," in *History News,* 43 (Nov./Dec. 1988). Also, M. Brown, a former IRS agent, wrote "Keeping an Eye on Each Other: the IRS and the Museum Store" for *Museum News,* 61 (Sept./Oct. 1982) with good advice on handling an audit. One museum director whose store has been audited twice was interviewed by B. D. Elder in *History News,* 35 (Nov. 1985) in a piece entitled "What to Expect if the Auditor Comes." An attorney, J. N. Gilbert, wrote "Coming to Terms with the Tax Man" for *Museum News,* 61 (Sept./Oct. 1982), defining and giving examples of unrelated business income. She also discussed other sorts of questionable income: parking lots, cafeterias, travel programs, licensing programs, etc. "Audit" in *History News,* 35 (Aug. 1980) is another good one. Don't let the title of K. H. Liles and S. E. Roth's articles mislead you—*all* types of museums could benefit from reading "The Unrelated Business Income Problems of Art Museums" with its in-depth discussion of UBIT and its definitions of the terminology in the Internal Revenue Code. Clearly written, it is easy to locate in any law school library in the *Connecticut Law Review,* 10, No. 3 (Spring 1978). A general piece by P. Gill appears in *Museum News* (Jan./Feb. 1988) titled "Relating the Shop to the Gallery." I am guessing that the reason there have been so few recent articles written on this topic is due to the tax law revisions Congress continues to flirt with. People keep expecting something to happen momentarily. As soon as it does (and it may never), you will see a flurry of articles in all the museum magazines explaining the changes and evaluating their impact.

Changes in the copyright laws resulting from U.S. participation in the Berne Convention copyright treaties, effective March 1, 1989, are discussed in *History News,* 44 (March/April 1989). "For the Administrator," by L. D. DuBoff and S. H. Caplan. To learn more about trademarks, consult L. D. DuBoff's "Trademark Law for Museums and Historical Organizations" in *History News,* 43 (Nov./Dec. 1988) and then read "Use Trademarks to Protect Your Most Precious Possession," in *Museum News,* (July/Aug. 1989), by authors B. M. Wolff and L. G. Grant for an update on the 1988 revisions to the Lanham Act.

Appendixes

Appendix A

Formulating a Visitor Survey

When conducting your visitor survey be certain to select people at random in order to avoid prejudicing your results. One method is to choose every third person, or every third adult if you want to exclude schoolchildren, who walks out of the store. Always introduce yourself, explain what you are doing, and ask whether the person has five minutes to complete the survey. Most people are flattered to be asked their opinion. You can hand them a pencil and ask them to fill in their answers or you can read the questions and note their responses yourself. The second method usually gives you more feedback and is preferable. The following examples may help you in formulating your questionnaire.

Visitor Survey

Personal Information

Residence: You could ask for state or for city and state. Some ask local visitors for their zip codes.

Age (give a range): 18–25
26–45
46–65
65+

Educational Level: Have not finished high school
Finished high school
Some college
Finished college
Graduate degree

Employment Information

Employment Status: Child
Homemaker
Employed full time outside the home

201

                            Employed part time outside the home
                            Unemployed
                            Retired

Occupation: _____

Income (give a range): Under $15,000
                         $15,001–25,000
                         $25,001–50,000
                         $50,000+
                         Not salaried (This would include home-makers, children, students, unemployed, volunteers, retired people, etc.)

Visit Information

How many times have you visited our shop? First time _____
                                            2–3 times _____
                                            4–5 times _____
                                            Many times ____
Would you recommend our shop to others? _____

Purchase Information

Are you just browsing or seriously shopping?
Did you make a purchase?
If so, what did you purchase?
    What was the dollar value of the purchase?
    Who is the purchase for? Yourself _____
                            Spouse _____
                            Child _____
                                What age? _____
                            Other _____
If you did not make a purchase, why not? _____

Now add questions that focus on your shop's particular "unknowns" or areas where you suspect a problem. For instance—

For product ideas and areas of product weaknesses—
    Were you looking for something in particular? If so, what?
    Did you find it?
    What would you have liked to see for sale that you did not?
    Where does the shop need improvements in its product line?

For information on salespeople—
> Was your transaction handled accurately and efficiently?
> Were the salespeople courteous and helpful?
> Did you have to wait for help? How long?
> Were your questions answered?

For information on product interpretation—
> Did the salesperson tell you anything about the item you purchased?
> Did you notice any product information on any of the products? (Be prepared to define "product interpretation.")

If you have concerns about physical aspects of the shop—
> Was the shop too crowded?
> (Note day and time if affirmative.)
> Was the lighting adequate?
> Did you have any difficulty locating our shop?

Always ask an open-ended question or two at the end to catch comments that would not have surfaced otherwise. Examples—
> What, in your opinion, could be done to improve our shop?
> Are there any other observations you would like to share with us?

Appendix B

Licensed Manufacturers

In 1987 and 1988 I surveyed the major history and art museums in the United States, asking them to share the names of the companies with which they had a licensing agreement. Not all responded and a few politely declined. This is a summary of the information received. It is only a partial list.

The companies on this list are or have been licensed by one or more American museums to produce and sell products based on objects in their collections and to pay royalties on these sales. The advantages and disadvantages of using a company already licensed by another museum are discussed in "Licensing Programs" in chapter 3.

The addresses were provided by the museums and may not correspond to the company's main offices. Some are showroom addresses or the address of the office nearest the museum, not the headquarters. When contacting any of these companies, it would be prudent to ask first for the name and address of the appropriate person and direct your inquiry accordingly. In large companies, the title of the person who handles royalty agreements is often director or vice president of marketing; in smaller companies it is generally the president or owner.

Architectural Features
Focal Point, Inc.
P.O. Box 93327
2005 Marietta Rd., NW
Atlanta, GA 30318

Morgan Products, Ltd.
P.O. Box 2466
Oshkosh, WI 54903

Beverage Mixes
The Added Touch
1678 Brandon Ave.
Petersburg, VA 23805

Candles
Yankee Candle Co.
Route 5 & 10
S. Deerfield, MA 01373

Ceramics
Avon Products, Inc.
9 W. 57th St.
New York, NY 10019

Faience d'Hiereville
Design Center—HIG, Concourse 22
300 D St. SW
Washington, DC 20024

Ceramics—*Continued*
Foreign Advisory Service Corp.
Princess Anne, MD 21853

Jacques Jugeat
225 5th Ave.
New York, NY 10010

Lenox China and Crystal
Pomona, NJ 08240

Lenox Collections
One Lenox Center
P.O. Box 519
Langhorne, PA 19047

Mottahedeh and Co.
225 5th Ave.
New York, NY 10010

Rowe Pottery Works, Inc.
404 England St.
Drawer L
Cambridge, WI 53523

Charles Sadek Import Co.
35 Winthrop Ave.
New Rochelle, NY 10802

Turtle Creek Potters
3600 Shawhan Rd.
Morrow, OH 45152

Waterford/Wedgwood
P.O. Box 1451
Wall, NJ 07719

Williamsburg Pottery Factory
Rt. 3, Box 148
Lightfoot, VA 23090

Bill Yee Associates Inc.
140 Woodland Ave.
Rochelle Park, NJ 07662

Clocks
Hamilton Clock Co.
1817 William Penn Way
P.O. Box 3008
Lancaster, PA 17604

Clothing
Harlequin "Nature Graphics"
16145 Old U.S. 41 Rd.
Ft. Myers, FL 33912

Schreter Neckwear
600 South Pulaski St.
Baltimore, MD 21223

Decorative Objects
Kurt Adler Inc.
1107 Broadway
New York, NY 10010

David Pine
Rt. 1, Box 93X
Mt. Crawford, VA 22841

Port Royal
226 Linwood Rd.
Gastonia, NC 28052

V.B.I.
185 Berry St., #265
San Francisco, CA 94107

Dried Flowers and Herbs
The New Englander
231 Washington St.
Weymouth, MA 02188

Woodbine Herb Co.
100 Court Square Terrace
Suite F
Charlottesville, VA 22901

Enameled Boxes
Crummles and Co.
Albion Close
Poole Dorset, BH12 3LL
England

Halcyon Days
14 Brook St.
London, W1Y 1AA
England

Fabrics and Wallpapers

Bradbury & Bradbury Wallpapers
P.O. Box 155
Benicia, CA 94510

Brunschwig & Fils
410 E. 62nd St.
New York, NY 10021

Galacar & Co.
444 Natoma St.
San Francisco, CA 94103

S. M. Hexter Co.
2800 Superior Ave.
Cleveland, OH 44114

Lee Jofa, Inc.
800 Central Blvd.
Carlstadt, NJ 07072

Katzenbach & Warren
200 Garden City Plaza
Garden City, NY 11530

Kravet Fabrics, Inc.
225 Central Ave., S.
Bethpage, NY 11714

Scalamandre
37–24 24th St.
Long Island City, NY 11101

F. Schumacher Co.
79 Madison Ave.
New York, NY 10016

Stroheim & Romann
31–11 Thomson Ave.
Long Island City, NY 11101

Albert Van Luit & Co.
200 Garden City Plaza
Garden City, NY 11530

Waverly Fabrics
7 Hoosac St.
Adams, MA 01220

Furniture

Baker Furniture
1661 Monroe Ave., NW
Grand Rapids, MI 49505

Brown Jordan Co.
9860 Gidley St.
P.O. Box 5688
EMonte, CA 91734

Century Furniture Co.
P.O. Box 608
Hickory, NC 28603

Cohasset Colonials
Cohasset, MA 02025

W. Cushing & Co.
P.O. Box 351
North St.
Kennebunkport, ME 04046

Freeman and Co.
416 Julian Ave.
Thomasville, NC 27360

Henkel-Harris Co., Inc.
P.O. Box 2170
Winchester, VA 22601

Kindel Furniture Co.
100 Garden St., SE
Grand Rapids, MI 49507

Sarreid, Ltd.
P.O. Box 3548
Wilson, NC 27895

Southwood Reproductions
P.O. Box 2245
Hickory, NC 28306

Eldred Wheeler
60 Sharp St.
Hingham, MA 02043

Garden Accessories

Garden Source Furnishings
45 Bennett St.
Atlanta, GA 30309

Garden Accessories—Continued
Dan Wilson & Co., Inc.
P.O. Box 566
Fuquay-Varina, NC 27526

**Gift Publications, Calendars, Art
  Books, Publications**
Harry N. Abrams, Inc,
100 5th Ave.
New York, NY 10011

Bandelier
P.O. Box 9656
Sante Fe, NM 87501

Design Look Inc.
P.O. Box 8724
Calabasas, CA 91302

Globe Pequot Press, Inc.
Old Chester Rd., Box Q
Chester, CT 06412

GMG Publishing
25 W. 43rd St.
New York, NY 10036

Pomegranate Artbooks
503 Tamal Plaza
Corte Madera, CA 94925

Pomegranate Publications
Box 808022
Petaluma, CA 94975

Potpurri Press
P.O. Box 19566
Greensboro, NC 27419

Random House, Inc.
201 East 50th St.
New York, NY 10022

Thomasson-Grant
505 Faulconer Dr.
Suite 1C
Charlottesville, VA 22901

Universe Books
381 Park Ave., S.
New York, NY 10016

House Plans
Russell Oatman
Merick Rd.
Princetown, MA 01541

Jewelry
DVB, Inc./Alva Museum Replica
  Jewelry
611 Broadway, Ste. 622
New York, NY 10012

Hand & Hammer
2610 Morse Ln.
Woodbridge, VA 22192

Liberty Workshop
Box 1171 Old Village Station
Great Neck, NY 11023

Museum Reproductions
62 Harvard St.
Brookline, MA 02146

Procreations
133 East Main St.
Marlborough, MA 01752

Lamps
As You Like It
P.O. Box 1270
536 Townsend Ave.
High Point, NC 27261–1270

Paul Hanson Co.
610 Commercial Ave.
Carlstadt, NJ 07072

Norman Perry/Chartwell Group
501 W. Green Dr.
High Point, NC 27260

Lt. Moses Willard & Co.
1156 U.S. 50
Cincinnati, OH 45150

Leather Upholstery
Lackawanna Leather Co.
P.O. Box 939
Conover, NC 28613

Middletown Leather Co.
200 Valentine St.
P.O. Box 30
Hacketttstown, NJ 07840

Linens: Kitchen, Bed, and Dining
Bates Fabrics, Inc.
P.O. Box 591
Lewistown, ME 04240

Kay Dee Co.
P.O. Box 448
Skunk Hill Road
Hope Valley, RI 02832

Fallani & Cohn, Inc.
295 5th Ave., Ste. 319
New York, NY 10016

Palais Royal
923 D Preston Ave.
Charlottesville, VA 22901

Stevens Linen Associates, Inc.
P.O. Box 220
Webster, MA 01570

Wamsutta Mills
111 W. 40th St.
New York, NY 10018

Metals
Baldwin Brass Corp.
841 Wyomissing Blvd.
Box 15048
Reading, PA 19612–5048

Cazenovia Abroad
67 Albany St.
Cazenovia, NY 13035

Mottahedeh & Co.
225 5th Ave.
New York, NY 10010

Port Royal
226 Linwood Rd.
Gastonia, NC 28052

Reed & Barton Silversmiths
144 W. Britannia St.
Taunton, MA 02780

Kirk Stieff Co.
800 Wyman Park Dr.
Baltimore, MD 21211–0821

Virginia Metalcrafters, Inc.
P.O. Box 1068
Waynesboro, VA 22980

Dave Webber, Village Pewter
320 W. Washington St.
Medina, OH 44256

Woodbury Pewterers
Woodbury, CT 06798

John Wright Co.
N. Front St.
Wrightsville, PA 17368

Miniatures
C J Originals
P.O. Box 538
Bridgeville, PA 15017

Craftmark, Inc.
147 Lake St.
Delaware, OH 43015

Gerald Crawford
51 Remuda Rd.
Sedona, AZ 86336

Hurley Porcelain
Rt. 7, Box 44D
Kingston, NY 12401

Mini Graphics
11322 Southland Rd.
Cincinnati, OH 45240

Mudlen Originals
P.O. Box 909
Temecula, CA 92390

Miniatures—*Continued*
Plaid Enterprises, Inc.
P.O. Drawer E
Norcross, GA 30091

Johanna Welty
61 Crest Ave.
Walnut Creek, CA 94595

Mirrors
Friedman Brothers Decorative Arts
9015 N.W. 105 Way
Medley, FL 33178

Mirror Fair
1495 3rd Ave.
New York, NY 10028

Needlework
Designs by Jerry and Jane
P.O. Box 7916
Paducah, KY 42001

The Examplarery
22731 Beech St.
Dearborn, MI 48124

Johnson Creative Arts
445 Main St.
W. Townsend, MA 01474

Scarlet Letter
P.O. Box 397
Sullivan, WI 53178

Traditionals by Tricia
3591 Forest Haven Ln.
Chesapeake, VA 23321

Notecards and Stationery
Allison Greetings, Inc.
770 Broadway, 3rd Fl.
New York, NY 10003

H. George Caspari
41 Madison Ave., Rm. 15C
New York, NY 10010

Creative Card Co.
1500 W. Monroe St.
Chicago, IL 60607

Evergreen Press, Inc.
P.O. Box 4971
Walnut Creek, CA 94596

C. R. Gibson Co.
32 Knight St.
Norwalk, CT 06856

GMG Publishing
25 W. 43rd St.
New York, NY 10036

Hallmark Cards
2440 Pershing Rd.
P.O. Box 580
Kansas City, MO 64108

Kedron Design
35 Farm Rd.
Sherborn, MA 01770

Overly Publishing, Inc.
P.O. Box 177
Harvard, MA 01451

Prima Designs
P.O. Box 325
Mirror Lake, NH 03863

Starwood Publishing
P.O. Box 40503
Washington, DC 20016

Winslow Papers
22 Alexander St.
Princeton, NJ 08540

Paint
Pratt & Lambert
Box 22
Buffalo, NY 14240

Martin Senour Co.
101 Prospect Ave.
Cleveland, OH 44113

Stulb Company
P.O. Box 297
Norristown, PA 19404

Paper Products (Plates, Napkins, Bags)
C. R. Gibson Co.
32 Knight St.
Norwalk, CT 06856

Haut Papier
P.O. Box 1465
E. Hampton, NY 11937

Placemats and Coasters
Pimpernel, Inc.
P.O. Box 6 Consett
Co. Durham, DH8 8LY
England

Polymer Scrimshaw
Artek, Inc.
Route 9
Antrim, NH 03440

Prints, Framing, and Posters
Artizans Hall
135 S. Hamilton St.
P.O. Box 2476
High Point, NC 27261

Chelsea House
226 Linwood Rd.
Gastonia, NC 28052

Dawber & Co., Inc.
26711 Northwestern Hwy.
Suite 204
Southfield, MI 48034

The Dietz Press, Inc.
109 East Cary St.
Richmond, VA 23219

Graphique de France
46 Waltham St.
Boston, MA 02118

Greenwich Workshop
30 Lindeman Dr.
Trumbull, CT 06611

Hedgerow House
230 5th Ave.
New York, NY 10001

Highland House Publishers
500 N. Henry St.
Alexandria, VA 22314

Kedron Design
35 Farm Rd.
P.O. Box 126
Sherborn, MA 01770

J. J. Korman & Son, Inc.
P.O. Box 5232
Roanoke, VA 24012

Mersky Etchings, Inc.
70 Bernard Circle
Centerville, MA 02632

Military Gallery
821A East Ojai Ave.
Ojai, CA 93023

New York Graphic Society, Ltd.
35 River Rd.
Cos Cob, CT 06807

Waterline Publications, Inc.
60 K St.
Boston, MA 02127

Records
Folkway Records
180 Alexander St., Box 2072
Princeton, NJ 08540

Mark 56 Records
P.O. Box 1
Anaheim, CA 92805

Rugs and Floor Coverings
W. Cushing & Co.
North St.
Kennebunkport, ME 04046

Fritz & LaRue Co.
295 5th Ave.
New York, NY 10016

Karastan Rug Mills
P.O. Box 3089
Greenville, SC 29602

Mountain Rug Mills, Inc.
P.O. Box 188
Fletcher, NC 28732–0188

Tianjin-Philadelphia Carpet Co.
7700 Germantown Ave.
Philadelphia, PA 19118

Thos. K. Woodard
835 Madison Ave.
New York, NY 10021

Sculpture
Aus Ben
P.O. Drawer 1670
Boone, NC 28607

Decoy Shop
P.O. Box 270
Bowdoinham, ME 04008

Southern Statuary & Stone Co.
3401 5th Ave., S.
Birmingham, AL 35222

Stencils and Theorems
American Traditional Stencils
Rt. 1, Box 281
Northwood, NH 03261

Jane Barton Theorems
4170 Orchard Way
Birmingham, MI 48010

Toiletries and Colognes
Caswell-Massey Co., Ltd.
111 8th Ave.
New York, NY 10011

Tote Bags
Prima Designs
P.O. Box 325
Mirror Lake, NH 03863

Toys and Games
Cooperman Fife and Drum Co.
P.O. Box 242
Centerbrook, CT 06409

Keypunch Software Inc.
1221 Pioneer Bldg.
St. Paul, MN 55101

Putnam-Berkely Group
200 Madison Ave.
New York, NY 10016

Revell, Inc.
363 N. 3rd Ave.
Des Plaines, IL 60016

Safari Limited
Box 630685
Ojus, FL 33163

B. Shackman & Co.
85 5th Ave.
New York, NY 10003

Trudy Corp.
35 Lois St.
Norwalk, CT 06856

V.B.I. Inc.
185 Berry St., #265
San Francisco, CA 94107

Waco Products Corp.
51 Kulick Rd.
Fairfield, NJ 07006

Weapons
Navy Arms Co.
689 Bergen Blvd.
Ridgefield, NJ 07657

Appendix C

Model Museum
Licensing Agreement

This model licensing agreement is intended to serve as a starting point and should be adapted to meet the particular needs of each museum and licensing situation. If museums intend to license the use of their name in connection with the reproduction of works from their collections, they should take every possible step to ensure that they protect the rights that they consider important. Because a formal licensing agreement sets forth the rights and responsibilities of both the museum and the licensee, it is the best method of maintaining control over those elements the parties consider central to a harmonious and profitable relationship. It is our hope that the Model Agreement contained herein will provide museums with some practical insight as to how best to proceed in achieving this end.*

MODEL MUSEUM LICENSING AGREEMENT

This Agreement made the _____ day of _____,
19_____, by and between _____NAME_____,
_____ADDRESS_____ ("Museum"), and _____NAME_____, a
_____STATE_____ corporation, _____ADDRESS_____, ("Licensee").

WITNESSETH:

WHEREAS, Licensee is engaged in the making of reproductions and adaptations of museum originals and in the distribution and sale of such reproductions and adaptations; and

WHEREAS, Licensee wishes to reproduce or adapt for reproduction and sale certain works in the collection of the Museum; and

WHEREAS, Licensee wishes to utilize the Museum's name on the repro-

---

*Reprinted with permission of the authors. Scott Hodes and Karen Gross, "Museums in the Commercial Marketplace: The Need for Licensing Agreement," *Connecticut Law Review,* 10, No. 3 (Spring 1978), pp. 620–637.

while in the possession or control of or resulting from but not limited to the copying, reproduction, photographing or other use of the Permitted Works by Licensee. All liability of Licensee, if any, as provided for in subparagraphs (c) and (d) shall be covered by insurance in form, type, amount and by a carrier Museum in connection therewith, upon the terms and conditions hereinafter set forth;

NOW, THEREFORE, It Is Mutually Agreed As Follows:

NON-EXCLUSIVE AND EXCLUSIVE RIGHTS

1. (a) Subject to the conditions set forth herein, the Museum grants to Licensee the non-exclusive, personal, and nonassignable right for the term of this Agreement to use the Museum's name on the reproductions or adaptations as well as in labeling, advertising, and promoting the sale of the reproductions and adaptations of the following works from the Museum's collections:

(1)
(2)
(3)

and on such other and additional works, if any, as the parties hereto from time to time agree upon in writing, (the "Permitted Works").

(b) The Museum grants to Licensee the exclusive right during the term of this Agreement to make or cause to be made and sold throughout the United States of America reproductions or adaptations of the Permitted Works in the following medium(s):

(1)
(2)
(3)

MANNER OF REPRODUCTION

2. (a) The Museum shall provide Licensee with photographs, dimensions, weight, if applicable, and reasonable access to the Permitted Works, subject to the Museum's conservation and security requirements, and shall permit Licensee to make molds, casts, photographs, negatives, and drawings and to utilize other reasonable methods to reproduce or adapt the Permitted Works either in the Museum's workrooms or at such other place or places as may be agreed upon by the parties hereto.

(b) Licensee shall pay all costs of making any molds, casts, photographs, negatives, drawings, or utilizing any other method of reproducing or adapting any Permitted Work, including but not limited to the cost of all materials, machinery, equipment, labor, including employees of the Museum if needed and used, services, insurance and other expenses.

(c) Licensee will use due care in reproducing and adapting any Permitted Works to protect and safeguard such works from damage, defacement, destruction, or any acts of its employees or agents.

(d) Licensee shall indemnify the Museum and hold it harmless from and against all loss of and damage to the Permitted Works suffered or incurred ductions and adaptations as well as in labeling, advertising, and promoting the sale of such reproductions and adaptations; and

WHEREAS, the Museum is willing to cooperate in the reproduction or adaptation of such works and to grant Licensee the right to use the name of the approved by the Museum. Said policy of insurance shall be delivered to the Museum before the possession of any Permitted Works is delivered to Licensee and before the commencement of any copying, reproduction, photographing or other use of any Permitted Work by Licensee. The entire cost of such insurance shall be paid by Licensee.

(e) In the event that one or more of the Permitted Works shall be removed from the Museum by Licensee to a place or places agreed upon by the parties, all expenses of transporting, packing, mailing and insuring each such object shall be paid by Licensee. Licensee further agrees to reimburse the Museum in full for the additional insurance premium required to insure each such object against theft, loss, damage or destruction for the period commencing with its removal from the Museum and ending with its return to the Museum, the form and type of insurance, amount of coverage and the insurance carrier to be selected by the Museum in its sole discretion.

QUALITY CONTROL

3. (a) A prototype of each reproduction or adaptation shall be submitted to the Museum for its written approval prior to its manufacture or sale. The Museum may, in its sole discretion, refuse to approve any prototype, in which event Licensee shall neither manufacture nor sell such reproduction or adaptation, and shall cancel or destroy the same in a manner satisfactory to the Museum, but in no event shall the Museum approve any prototype which is not of a different weight from the Permitted Work, if applicable.

(b) If the Museum approves a prototype in writing, Licensee shall use its best efforts to assure that all reproductions and adaptations conform to the approved prototype. The Museum and its agents or employees shall be permitted at any time or times during the normal business hours to examine production-line reproductions and adaptations, and if the Museum determines in its sole discretion that any reproduction or adaptation does not conform with its approved prototype, at the request of the Museum, Licensees shall refrain from manufacturing or selling such reproduction or adaptation and shall cancel or destroy the same in a manner satisfactory to the Museum.

(c) Licensee shall submit to the Museum by registered mail, return receipt requested, all advertising copy, promotional material and packaging to be used in connection with the sale or offering for sale of any reproduction or adaptation, and shall not use any such copy, material or packaging unless and until approved in writing by the Museum.

(d) Licensee shall have the obligation and responsibility of prominently displaying on all reproductions and adaptations made by it as well as on any advertisement, labeling or other promotional material that said reproductions and adaptations are derived or copied from original works owned by the

Museum. All such notifications of origin shall be of a type and in form and content approved in writing by the Museum and whenever possible shall be made by means of a permanent impressed or incised mark on the reproduction or adaptation.

(e) At the discretion of the Museum, all reproductions and adaptations shall be accompanied by a brief description and history of the original work, including, if applicable, a reference to its original weight. Such copy shall either be provided or approved in writing by the Museum.

(f) Licensee shall provide the Museum with _____ copy(ies) of each reproduction and adaptation of each Permitted Work without charge.

(g) Licensee shall inform the Museum in writing of the initial production quantity of each reproduction and adaptation and of all subsequent quantities.

(h) During the term of this Agreement, any copyrights of said reproductions or adaptations shall be the sole property of Licensee, and the Museum shall lend to Licensee such cooperation as shall be necessary to enable Licensee to obtain copyrights thereto. Upon termination of this Agreement, all copyrights obtained of said reproductions or adaptations shall be assigned to the Museum at no cost and free and clear of any lien or encumbrance.

ROYALTIES

4. (a) Initially, for the sale of the first _____ reproductions, Licensee shall pay the Museum a royalty of _____% of Licensee's gross receipts from the sale of reproductions and adaptations, including sales to the Museum or the Museum Store. Thereafter, Licensee shall pay the Museum a royalty of _____% of Licensee's gross receipts from the sale of reproductions and adaptations, including sales to the Museum or the Museum Store.

If the payment of royalties based on said gross receipts falls below $_____ for any calendar year, the Museum may terminate this Agreement in its sole discretion, and the parties will be subject to the termination provisions set forth herein in Paragraphs 5(b) and 5(c).

(b) Gross receipts shall exclude sales and use taxes, shipping charges and costs of frames or mountings used in conjunction with reproductions or adaptations, if separately stated.

(c) Licensee shall pay said royalties to the Museum three times annually on April 15th, August 15th and December 15th of each year for the four calendar monthly periods ending on the preceding April 1st, August 1st and December 1st, respectively.

(d) In addition to the above stated royalty, Licensee shall pay to the living artist of any original work selected for reproduction or adaptation by the Museum and Licensee a royalty of _____%, in accordance with the above described manner of payment. Payment of this royalty is not intended to and shall not be construed as making said artist a party to this Agreement except as a third party beneficiary of the royalty described herein, and the payment of any such royalty to any living artist shall not inure to the benefit of his/her estate, heirs, legatees or assignees.

(e) Licensee shall keep accurate records of its sales of each reproduction and adaptation and shall submit a periodic statement of production and sales with each royalty payment. Said statement shall be signed and sworn to by the chief accounting officer of Licensee. The Museum and its designated officers, accountants, attorneys and agents shall have the right at any time or times and from time to time during the normal business hours, to inspect and copy Licensee's books and records pertaining to its production and sale of reproductions and adaptations of the Permitted Works for the purpose of verifying the correctness of statement and royalty payments received. Once each calendar year, Licensee shall employ, at its own expense, an independent firm of certified public accountants acceptable to the Museum to audit Licensee's books and records relating to the production and sales of reproductions and adaptations of the Permitted Works and to deliver to the Museum a certified audit of said reproduced or adapted works, sales and royalty payments. Any living artist entitled to a royalty pursuant to subsection (d) herein may request a copy of the certified audit for the purpose of verifying the correctness of the royalty payments received.

TERMINATION

5. (a) This Agreement shall be binding upon the parties hereto for a period of three (3) years from the date first written above and shall be renewed automatically for successive terms of one (1) year each thereafter unless at least three (3) months prior to the end of the original termination of this Agreement or prior to the end of any said one (1) year renewal period, either party shall have notified the other in writing of its intention to terminate this Agreement at the end of the then current year.

(b) Upon termination of this Agreement, all molds, casts, photographs, drawings, negatives and other methods developed or used by Licensee to make said reproductions or adaptations of any Permitted Works shall be destroyed in a manner satisfactory to the Museum.

(c) Upon termination of this Agreement, Licensee shall use all reasonable efforts to avoid having on hand on the termination date an excessive inventory of reproductions, adaptations, and/or work in progress. Any work in progress on such termination may be completed and sold by Licensee, provided this is done within _____ months after said termination date. All reproductions and adaptations on hand as of the termination date shall first be offered to the Musuem or the Museum store at prices and discounts applicable to sales to the Museum and the Museum store. Any such reproductions and adaptations not purchased by the Museum or the Museum store within sixty (60) days after such offer may be sold by Licensee through its regular channels at such prices as it may deem necessary to effect prompt sales, subject to the payment of the established royalties and reporting requirements as set forth herein.

(d) In the event that the Museum or Licensee breaches any material terms or conditions of this Agreement and fails to cure said breach within fourteen (14) days after written notice of such breach from the other party hereto, this Agreement may be cancelled by any party not in breach hereof. In the event of such cancellation, the parties shall have no further obligations under this Agreement other than those, if any, which have accrued as of the termination date. Licensee shall have no further right to manufacture or sell reproductions or adaptations of the Permitted Works or to use the Museum's name, except as specifically provided herein.

(e) Notwithstanding any of the foregoing, in the event Licensee files a petition under any federal or state bankruptcy or insolvency law seeking reorganization, arrangement or any relief thereunder, or a petition is filed against Licensee under any federal or state bankruptcy law and such petition is not dismissed within thirty (30) days after the filing thereof, or Licensee makes an assignment for the benefit of creditors or seeks or consents to the appointment of a receiver, or a receiver is appointed for Licensee or its property and such appointment is not vacated within (30) days after such appointment, or Licensee sells or otherwise transfers all or substantially all of its assets or business, or merges or consolidates with any other corporation or other entity or the management control of Licensee is changed by whatever means, then this Agreement shall terminate automatically, and Licensee shall return to the Museum all casts, molds, negatives, drawings, photographs and other methods of reproducing or adapting any Permitted Work and shall offer to the Museum or the Museum store all inventory of reproductions adaptations of the Permitted Works then on hand at a price equal to Licensee's out of pocket costs incurred in connection with the production thereof. No trustee, receiver, assignee, transferee or successor of Licensee shall have any rights under this Agreement.

ARBITRATION

6. (a) All claims, demands, disputes, suits and causes of action of every kind and nature or breaches arising out of or in any manner related to or connected with this Agreement shall be resolved by arbitration in the city in which the Museum is located, and the parties agree, to the extent allowed by law, that arbitration shall be the sole and exclusive method of resolving said claims, demands, disputes, suits, causes of action or breaches. Arbitration shall be invoked by written notice thereof from one party to the other, stating the nature of the dispute and the claim(s) of the party invoking arbitration.

(b) In the event of arbitration, the parties shall mutually select one (1) arbitrator. In the event that they are unable to agree mutually upon or either party refuses to participate in the selection of an arbitrator within thirty (30) days after the sending of the notice invoking arbitration, either party may submit the matter to the American Arbitration Association for the appointment of an arbitrator, in which event such arbitrator shall be selected by the American Arbitration Association in accordance with its commercial arbitration rules then in force and effect. The fees and expenses of the arbitrator shall be paid one half by the Museum and one half by Licensee. The commerical arbitration rules of the American Arbitration Association shall govern said arbitration.

(c) The arbitrator shall be limited to the terms of this Agreement but shall have the right to invoke and order, to the extent allowed by law, all remedies at law or in equity including but not limited to damages and injunctive relief.

(d) Upon motion by either party, to the extent allowed by law, any court of competent jurisdiction shall have the power to order the parties to arbitrate all claims, demands, disputes and suits, or causes of action in law or equity or breaches arising out of or in any manner related to or in connection with this Agreement in accordance with the foregoing provisions, and to enforce, upon motion by either party, the decision of the arbitrator.

LIABILITY

7. (a) Licensee shall defend and indemnify the Museum against, and hold the Museum harmless from and against all manner of claims, demands, disputes, suits, causes of action, damages, obligations and liabilities, including but not limited to product liability, Federal Trade Commission and other governmental compliance, retailer's liability and copyright infringement with respect to the reproduction, adaptation, labeling, advertising and promoting of the reproductions or adaptations authorized hereunder.

(b) Nothing in this Agreement is intended to or shall be deemed to constitute a partnership or joint venture between the parties. This Agreement shall not constitute Licensee as agent of the Museum for any purpose whatsoever, and Licensee shall have no right or authority to assume, create or impose any obligation, liability or responsibility, express or implied, on or in behalf of, or in the name of the Museum.

NOTICE

8. Any notice or demand pursuant to this Agreement shall be made in writing and delivered by registered mail, return receipt requested, or delivered or telegraphed and confirmed in writing to the parties at their respective addresses as specified herein unless such address has been changed by notice to the other party hereto in writing.

ASSIGNMENT

9. This Agreement is personal to Licensee and may not be assigned or otherwise transferred in any manner by operation or law or otherwise without the prior written consent of the Museum, which consent may be granted or withheld in the sole discretion of the Museum.

MODIFICATION

10. This Agreement may not be modified or altered except by a writing signed by both parties, and this Agreement shall be construed in accordance with the laws of the State of _____.

PAROL EVIDENCE

11. This instrument contains the entire Agreement between the parties and no statement, negotiations, promises or inducements made by either party or any agent of either party that is not contained in this Agreement shall be valid or binding.

12. Wherever possible each provision of this Agreement shall be interpreted in such manner as to be effective and valid under applicable law, but if any provision(s) of this Agreement shall be prohibited by or invalid under applicable law, such provision(s) shall be ineffective to the extent of such prohibition or invalidity without invalidating the remaining provisions of this Agreement.

IN WITNESS WHEREOF, the parties hereto have executed this Agreement on the day and year first written above.

        _____ MUSEUM

By _____

        _____ LICENSEE

By _____

Gift and Trade Shows

Gift Show Management

Contact some of the following management companies and ask them to place you on their mailing lists. You will be deluged with information about gift shows.

ACC Craft Fair
P.O. Box 10
New Paltz, NY 12561
914-366-0039

AMC Trade Shows
905 Mission St.
South Pasadena, CA 91030
213-747-3488

American Booksellers Association
137 W. 25th St.
New York, NY 10001
212-463-8450

Americana Sampler
P.O. Box 8222
Nashville, TN 37207
615-865-1962

Amigo Gift Association
6800 W. 115 St.
Overland Park, KS 66211
913-491-6688

Association of Crafts and Creative Industries; Gift Retailer, Manufacturers & Reps Assoc.; Miniatures Industry Assoc. of America; Southwest Craft & Hobby Assoc. all can be reached at:
P.O. Box 2188
Zanesville, OH 43702
614-452-4541

Atlanta Market Center
240 Peachtree St.
Atlanta, GA 30043
404-688-8994

Beckman's Gift Show
P.O. Box 27337
Los Angeles, CA 90027
213-962-5424

Chicago Merchandise Mart
Suite 470
Chicago, IL 60654
312-527-7600

Dallas Market Center
2100 Stemmons Freeway
Dallas, TX 75207
214-655-6100

Denver Merchandise Mart
451 E. 58th Ave.
Denver, CO 80216
303-292-MART

Exhibition Management Co.
6143 S. Willow Dr., Ste. 100
Englewood, CO 80111
303-850-9119

George Little Management
2 Park Ave., Ste. 1100
New York, NY 10016
212-686-6070
    and
577 Airport Blvd., 4th Floor
Burlingame, CA 94010
415-344-5171

Indian Arts and Crafts Assoc.
4215 Lead Ave., SE
Albuquerque, MN 87108
505-265-9149

L.A. Mart
1933 S. Broadway
Los Angeles, CA 90007
213-749-7911

Mahone Associates
Charlotte Merchandise Mart
2500 E. Independence Blvd., D–328
Charlotte, NC 28205
704-377-5881

Miami International Merchandise
    Mart
777 NW 72nd Ave.
Miami, FL 33126
305-261-2900

Mid-Atlantic Gift & Deocrative
    Accessories Assoc.
12260 Sunrise Valley Dr.
Reston, VA 22091
703-620-5640

Museum Store Association
One Cherry Center
501 S. Cherry St., Ste. 460
Denver, CO 80222
303-329-6968

New York Merchandise Mart
41 Madison Ave.
New York, NY 10010
212-686-1203

Organization of Associated
    Salespeople in the Southwest
1130 E. Missouri, Ste. 750
Phoenix, AZ 85014
602-230-1237

Rosen Agency
Ste. 300 Mill Centre
3000 Chestnut Ave.
Baltimore, MD 21211
301-889-2933

San Francisco Gift Center
888 Brannan Street
San Francisco, CA 94103
415-861-7733

Seattle Market Center
5601 6th Ave. S.
Seattle, WA 98108
206-762-2700

225 5th Ave.
New York, NY 10010
212-684-3200

Upper Midwest Allied Gifts Assoc.
10301 Bren Rd. W.
Minneapolis, MN 55343
612-932-7200

Western Exhibitors
2181 Greenwich St.
San Francisco, CA 94123
415-346-0168

Regularly Scheduled Gift Shows

The following is a list of regularly scheduled gift/craft shows of possible interest to museum stores. It divides into two geographic sections for quick reference. A phone number is provided so you can contact the ones in your region for dates and registration information. Show locations and dates change frequently and some have been cancelled recently when attendance and sales were poor.

This is not a complete list. It would be impossible to include every show in the country as there are hundreds—thousands if you count the smaller local events. It is meant to acquaint you with the larger shows in your area with the hope that there will be at least one close enough so that even managers with *no* travel budget can attend!

East of the Mississippi River

American International Toy Fair
New York, NY
212-675-1141

Atlantic City Gift Show
Atlantic City, NJ
212-686-6070

Bedford Gift Show
Bedford, MA
617-275-2775

Boston Gift Show
Boston, MA
212-686-6070

Charlotte Gift Shows
Charlotte, NC
704-377-5881

Chicago Craft and Creative
  Industries Show
Chicago, IL
614-452-4541

Chicago Gift and Accessories Market
Chicago, IL
312-527-7600

Chicago Gift Show
Chicago, IL
212-686-6070

China, Glass, Gifts and Gourmet
  Market
New York, NY
212-684-3200

Creative Gift and Souvenir Show
Traverse City, MI
313-791-4650

Columbus Gift Mart Shows
Columbus, OH
614-876-2719

Daytona Beach Gift Show
Daytona Beach, FL
305-261-1213

Early Bird Gift Market
Chicago, Il
312-527-7600

Florida International Gift Show
Orlando, FL
303-850-9119

Indianapolis Gift Shows
Indianapolis, IN
317-546-0719

International Jewelry Fair
New Orleans, LA
312-922-0966

Kentucky Gift Show
Louisville, KY
614-452-4541

MAGDAA Shows
Reston, VA
703-620-5640

MAGS Gift Shows
Northville, MI
313-348-7890

Memphis Gift and Jewelry Show
Memphis, TN
312-922-0966

Miami Mart Gift Association Show
Miami, FL
305-261-2900

Museum Source Show
(part of New York International Gift
 Fair)
New York, NY
212-686-6070

Nashville Gift Show
Nashville, TN
704-377-5881

National Gift and Decorative
 Accessories Market
Atlanta, GA
404-688-8994

National Jewelry Show
1271 Avenue of the Americas
New York, NY 10020

National Merchandise Show
New York, NY
516-627-4000

National Stationery Show
New York, NY
212-686-6070

New Orleans Gift and Jewelry Show
New Orleans, LA
312-922-0966

New York Gift Show
New York, NY
212-686-1203

New York Gourmet Food and
 Beverage Show
New York, NY
212-686-6070

New York International Gift Fair
New York, NY
212-686-6070

New York Tabletop and Accessories
 Show
New York, NY
201-779-4997

Ocean City Gift Show
Ocean City, MD
301-655-3828

Ohio State Gift and Decor Show
Columbus, OH
614-452-4541

Orlando Craft and Creative
 Industries Show
Orlando, FL
614-452-4541

Philadelphia Gift Show
King of Prussia, PA
312-922-0966

Pittsburgh Gift Show
Pittsburgh, PA
716-254-2580

South Carolina Gift Show
Myrtle Beach, SC
305-261-1213

Southern Furniture Market
P.O. Box 5687
High Point, NC 27262–5687

Sun Coast Gift Show
Tampa, FL
305-261-1213

SunState International Gift Show
Tampa, FL
404-688-8994

Tennessee Gift Show
Gatlinburg, TN
305-261-1213

Washington Gift Show
Washington, DC
212-686-6070

Western New York Gift Show
Rochester, NY
716-254-2580

Wisconsin Gift Show
Oconomowoc, WI
614-452-4541

World Souvenir and Gift Show
Orlando, FL
305-261-1213

West of the Mississippi River

Amigo K.C. Country Gift Show
Overland Park, KS
913-491-6688

Beckman's Gift Shows of Los
  Angeles
Los Angeles, CA
213-962-5424

Calgary International Gift Show
Calgary, Alberta, Canada
303-850-9119

California Gift Show
Los Angeles, CA
213-747-3488

Dallas Gift Show
Dallas, TX
800-634-2630

Dallas Market Center's Americana
  Gift Show
Dallas, TX
214-655-6100

Dallas Toy Show
Dallas, TX
800-634-2630

Denver Merchandise Mart Shows
Denver, CO
303-292-MART

Early Bird Show and other Gift
  Shows
Seattle, WA
800-433-1014

Hawaii Gift Show
Honolulu, HI
213-747-3488

Houston Gift and Jewelry Show
Houston, TX
312-922-0966

Houston Wholesale Jewelry and Gift
  Shows
Houston, TX
512-261-4223

Indian Arts and Crafts Association
  Shows
Denver, CO and Phoenix, AZ
505-265-9149

Juvenile Products Manufacturers
  Association Show
Dallas, TX
609-234-9155

L.A. Giftware and Home
  Furnishings Show
Los Angeles, CA
213-749-7911

OASIS Gift Shows
Phoenix, AZ
602-230-1237

Oregon Gift Show
Portland, OR
503-228-PARK

Phoenix Gift Show
Phoenix, AZ
213-747-3488

Portland, Gift Show
Portland, OR
415-346-0168

St. Louis Missouri Gift Show
St. Louis, MO
614-452-4541

San Diego Stationery and Gift Show
San Diego, CA
415-344-5171

San Francisco Gift Market Shows
San Francisco, CA
415-346-0168

San Francisco Gourmet Show
San Francisco, CA
415-344-5171

Seattle Gift Show
Seattle, WA
415-346-0168

Seattle Trade Center's Toy Fair
Seattle, WA
206-441-1881

San Antonio Jewelry and Gift Show
San Antonio, TX
512-261-4223

Southwest Craft and Hobby
    Association Show
Dallas, TX
614-452-4541

Tucson Mineral and Gem Show
P.O. Box 42543
Tucson, AZ 85733

UMAGA Gift Association Shows
Minneapolis, MN
612-932-7200

Shows Where Location Varies Each Year

American Booksellers Association
    Show
212-463-8450

Fancy Food and Confection Show
800-255-2502

Hobby Industries of America
201-794-1133

Miniatures Industry Association of
    America Show
614-452-4541

Museum Store Association Trade
    Show
303-329-6968

Craft Shows

Americana Sampler, Inc.
P.O. Box 8222
Nashville, TN 37202
615-865-1962
Annual folk art and country craft fairs in Boston [June], Kansas City [June], Valley Forge (PA) [February], Nashville [August, November, February].

American Craft Enterprise, Inc. of the American Craft Council
P.O. Box 10
New Paltz, NY 12561
914-255-0039
Annual craft fairs in Baltimore, San Francisco, West Springfield (MA), and St. Paul (MN).

American CraftFocus
415-346-0168
Held in Seattle and San Francisco each February and August.

American Crafts Festival
32 Union Sq., Ste. 418
New York, NY 10003
201-746-0091
Twice a year in New York.

American Craft Showroom
Rosen Agency
Ste. 300 Mill Centre
3000 Chestnut Ave.
Baltimore, MD 21211
301-889-2933
Every April and October at the Design Center, as part of the High Point (NC) Furniture Show.

Buyers Market of American Crafts
301-889-2933
Annually in Boston, Anaheim (CA), Atlantic City (NJ), and Miami (FL).

Country Heritage Wholesale Market of Traditional Crafts and Folk Art
717-249-9404
King of Prussia (PA) and other locations.

Indian Arts and Crafts Association
4215 Lead Ave., SE
Albuquerque, NM 87106
505-265-9149
Denver in the spring; Arizona in the fall.

Kentucky Crafts Market
502-564-8076
Annual craft fair in late winter.

New York International Gift Fair
Section on American and International Crafts.
212-686-6070

Appendix E

Cost Codes

Using a cost code on the price tag may speed the inventory process along by giving you cost information without the extra step of looking it up in the books. It is more appropriate for larger operations with extensive inventories. There are many methods, among them:

1. Develop a ten-letter word or phrase with no two letters alike, or just use part of the alphabet. Translate the numerical cost to letters:

$$\begin{array}{cccccccccc} D & E & F & G & H & I & J & K & L & M \\ 1 & 2 & 3 & 4 & 5 & 6 & 7 & 8 & 9 & 0 \end{array} \quad \$2.50 = EHM$$

or

$$\begin{array}{cccccccccc} P & A & R & K & I & N & G & L & O & T \\ 1 & 2 & 3 & 4 & 5 & 6 & 7 & 8 & 9 & 0 \end{array} \quad \$2.50 = AIT$$

2. A bit easier, though less "secret," is to mix the cost with other numbers. Our $2.50 item could look like this:

   92509

   if we decided to put a nine on either end of the cost, or like this:

   89250

   if we decided to prefix each cost with the numerals 8 and 9.
3. Similar to no. 2 but use the surrounding numbers to mean the product's date of receipt. This enables you to tell at a glance when that item was placed in your inventory. For a product that arrived at the store in September of 1988 you could write:

   988250

   or

   925088

   or

   250988

4. Another way is called 5/10. You add 5 to the dollars and 10 to the cents and separate with a slash instead of a decimal point. This code is used frequently in the home-furnishings industry. A cost price of $2.50 would look like 7/60 on the ticket. Subtract in your head and you know the cost.

Of course, you can create your own shop's cost code by using any other combination of numbers. Whatever you develop will obviate the need to look up cost prices for everything and if that would be a benefit to you, you need to give cost codes a try.